ECOLOGICAL ECONOMICS

The Science and Management of Sustainability

ECOLOGICAL ECONOMICS

The Science and Management of Sustainability

Mahesh Chandra Prasad

MADHAV BOOKS
GURGAON (HARYANA)

First Published – 2011

ISBN: 978-93-80615-06-6

Published by

MADHAV BOOKS
F-2562, Palam Vihar
Gurgaon-122 017 (Haryana)
Phone : 0124-2365193, 9810373248

Contents

Preface

The balancing of economic, environmental and social issues, i.e. sustainability, has received significant attention and caused additional pressures–competitive, regulatory or otherwise- on industrial manufacturers throughout the world. Organizational environmental sustainability has been the mantra of many management theorists and forward thinking practitioners throughout the early part of the 1990s and continues even today. It is unlikely that this shift in thought and philosophy will return to the classical economic perspective of the firm as a single-minded profit-seeking entity. As progress continues and industrial society continues to mature, the pressures that have been felt for an increased focus on the natural environment will not cease. The role of the manufacturing firm with respect to environmental practice and strategies has evolved over a period of time. In the early 1970s, organizations were under a command-and-control mentality that required them to comply with regulations and legislation. More recently, firms and government agencies, in the US and internationally, have sought a compromise situation that could best be termed collaborative. Regulatory pressures still exist, but organizations have taken on a more enlightened and strategic viewpoint that there may exist competitive advantages from appropriate environmental strategies. Some of these advantages may arise from reactive measures, such as responses to regulatory policy. These advantages may also arise from such more proactive measures as green marketing, technology development reduction in wastes, and product stewardship. These win/win situations (where improved environmental and financial performance of organizations correlate positively) many times do exist.

This book is not intended to be a stand-alone ecological economics text book, nor is it a comprehensive treatment of the wide range of activities currently going on in the trans-disciplinary field of ecological economics. Rather, it is an introduction to the field from a particular perspective.

When a person is convinced that his basic relationship behind all other worldly, physical or work relationship are that of 'spiritual brothers' because all are children of God, then one's angle of vision changes. It widens one's concern from what has made a man look towards a small family or a small circle of friends to the whole family of mankind as 'Vasudhaiva Kutumbkam' or 'Global Village'. One's love is no longer directed towards a few but to all. This awakens in man the attitudes or qualities of sympathy, service and fellow-feeling and puts his behavior on a new and a higher pedestal.

The book is structured in four chapters. We begin with a description of some of the current problems of society and their underlying causes. We trace the causes to problems in the conventional way in which the world, and the individual's role in it, is viewed. Environmental economics is essentially a rethinking of this fundamental relationship and a working out of the implications of a new way of thinking for how we manage our lives and our planet. In chapter II we present a historical narrative of how worldviews have evolved. This emphasizes how much worldviews do evolve and change. We outline what we think the next step in this evolution will be (or should be). We present various ideas and models in their proper historical context and as a living narrative, rather than as a list of sterile abstractions. The third chapter is a distillation of what we view as the fundamental principles of ecological economics that are the result of this evolutionary process. The fourth chapter is a set of policies that follow from the principles and a set of instruments that could be used to implement the policies. It lays out the process of shared envisioning as an essential element to achieving sustainability. A brief conclusion summarizes and gives prospects for the future.

In writing this book I benefited immensely from the studies of a number of scholars spread over various books, journals and magazines. I am grateful to all of them.

The book has been written in the memory of my youngest brother *Anil Kumar* who left this world at the age of twenty one.

I express my deep sense of gratitude to Dr. Tapan Kumar Shandilya, Pro Vice-chancellor VKS University, Arah for rendering assistance in various forms in preparing the manuscript of this book. I would like to thank Professor (Dr.) Pulin B. Nayak, Delhi School of Economics, Delhi University, Dr. M. M. Kothari, Executive Editor, *The Economic Challenger*, and Professor (Dr.) P. C. Verma, Patna College, Patna University for supporting my collaborative work. I convey my gratefulness to Professor (Dr.) Asha Singh, Head, Department of Economics, Magadh Mahila College, Patna University, Patna for her constant encouragement and favorable guidance from time to time.

I am extremely thankful to Professor (Dr). H. K. Singh, BHU, Varanasi, and Professor (Dr) K. K. Agrawal, MGKV, Varanasi for his constant help and encouragement in my academic pursuits. I have also benefited from helpful discussions with Dr. Bipin Kumar, R.R.S. College, Mokama. I am deeply indebted to the publisher Sri S. K. Jha, M/S Madhav Books, Gurgaon (Haryana), for bringing out this book in a record time.

I am most grateful to Dr. Ratri Roy, Retired Professor in English, Patna University, Patna for motherly love and English word, sentences and grammar correction. I also appreciate the support of my wife, Rekha Rani and son, Shikhar Sinha for my strenuous work.

Above all the academic atmosphere at Patna University has been quite favorable to me in the accomplishment of this academic work.

Mahesh Chandra Prasad
Patna University, Patna.

1

Development of Economics and Environment

Economics is the social science that studies the allocation of scarce resources to satisfy unlimited wants. This involves analyzing the production, distribution, trade and consumption of goods and services. Economics is said to be positive when it attempts to explain the consequences of different choices given a set of assumptions or a set of observations, and normative when it prescribes that a certain action should be taken. It is concerned with environmental issues. Environmental science is the science of the interactions between the physical, chemical and biological components of the environment, including their effects on all types of organisms but more often refers to human impact on the environment. As recently as three hundred years ago, philosophers built systemic, logical arguments with respect to the nature of the cosmos, social order, and moral duty. Empiricism was largely associated with the description of broad geographical differences between regions and cultures. The sciences as we now know them arose with the joining of systemic thinking and empirical analyses of different aspects of the natural world. Francis Bacon (1561–1626) argued for joining logic and empiricism. Galileo Galilei (1564–1642) provided evidence in support of the sun-centered systemic theory of Nicolaus Copernicus (1473–1543) with telescopic observations. Discrepancies between Copernicus' theory and astronomical observations were resolved by Isaac Newton (1642–1727) through his theoretical advances with respect to gravity and the mechanics of motion. Thereafter, scientific disciplines began to arise, defined by the subject matter to which logical thinking was applied rather than by the patterns of logic used.[1] Nevertheless, for several centuries scholars continued to work across broad areas of knowledge. Newton wrote about religion and morals as well as physics. John Locke (1632–1704) contributed to medical knowledge and the revival of the idea of atoms even while his most important contributions were to social philosophy. This scholarly tradition of contributing across disciplines lasted through the 19th century. Well into the 20th century, many scholars maintained an awareness of developments beyond their speciality. Frank Knight (1895–1973), for example, expounded at some length on recent developments in physics and their implications for economic theory and methodology.[2] By the latter half of the 20th century, however, transdisciplinary scholarship was extremely rare.

Economics arose in the midst of the transdisciplinary tradition. During the second half of the 18th century, at a time of great social change and scientific promise, the formal field of economics emerged from moral philosophy.[3] Long-standing moral questions with respect to the obligation of individuals to larger social goals were being challenged by the development of markets and scientific advances, both of which brought new opportunities for personal material improvement and fueled great hopes for a plentiful future. Then, in the second half of the 18th century, as today, people were concerned that following one's own interests might hurt society as a whole. Economists began to argue, as they continue to do, that markets guided individual behavior, as if by an "invisible hand," to the common good.

About a century later, the formal field of ecology arose from biology and natural history. Like economics, it too was concerned with how systems as a whole could work for the common good of the species that composed them. The two disciplines share some theoretical features and at various times each have drawn on advances in the other. How two conceptually complementary fields have become associated with such opposing prescriptions for how people should interact with their environment is a fascinating story.[4]

And it is a story that must be understood for ecological economics to emerge from the separate disciplines. The sections in this chapter briefly document some of the historical development of the two disciplines, showing how they have learned from each other and explaining how they have evolved such different environmental prescriptions from shared conceptual bases. The two disciplines differ markedly in that economics, especially in India and as practiced through the international agencies, is conceptually monolithic, while ecology consists of many competing and complementary conceptual frameworks. Similarly, environmental economics (a sub-discipline of economics concerned with environmental problems) today presents itself as a single, grandly conceived coherent theory. The following sections explain how today's environmental economics was constructed from earlier economic theories while the assumptions that drive the theories to policy conclusions are rooted in popular beliefs about nature and technical progress. The earlier theories which were once very influential within economics are central to environmental understanding today. Ecology, in addition to maintaining its diverse theoretical roots, also contrasts with economics in that it has combined with quite a different, yet still popular, set of beliefs about both nature and technology.

A few of these popular beliefs have long histories. Until 300 years ago, material security was thought to be one of the rewards of moral conduct. Increasingly after the Renaissance, however, it was argued that material security was needed to establish the conditions for moral progress. Scarcity caused greed and even war; scarcity forced people to work so hard that they did not have time to contemplate the scriptures and live morally. Material progress, in short, was necessary to establish the conditions for moral progress. Thus, as economics emerged two centuries ago, the individual pursuit of materialism was justified on the presumption that once the basic material needs of food, shelter, and clothing were met, people would have the time and conditions to pursue their individual moral and collective social improvement. Today, these earlier concerns with moral and social progress have largely been forgotten while individual materialism for many people has become an end in itself.

Two centuries ago, as now, technological optimists were convinced that the essentials of life would eventually be assured through the advance of human knowledge leading to a mastery of underlying natural laws. The presumption has been that such laws are relatively few in number and that their mastery would make superfluous our dependence on the particular ways that nature and people's place therein, evolved. To those only concerned with material well-being, the expectation of such mastery meant that people did not have to be concerned with long-term scarcities or how their activities otherwise might affect the future.[5] Over the past two centuries, scientists have touted the eventual mastering of nature and have justified research on this basis. The idea that scientific progress will inevitably lead to the control of nature and material plenty is still popularly held and frequently invoked, even by scientists, to support further population increases, technological change, and economic development along their historic, environmentally destructive, unsustainable paths.

Economic thought evolved in the context of these dominant moral, material, and scientific beliefs. Reality, however, does not always unfold as expected; the social and environmental

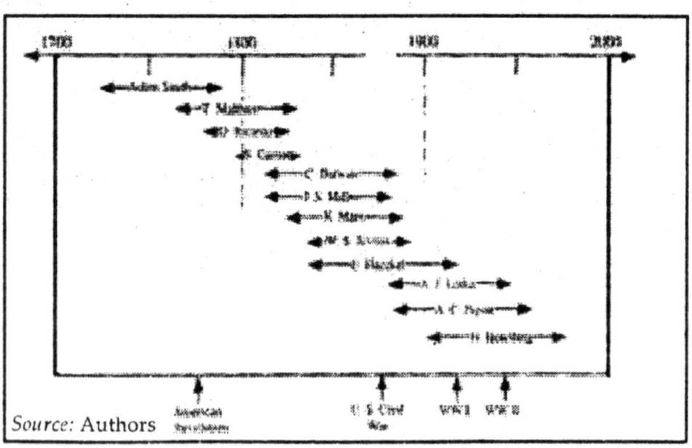

Source: Authors

Figure 1: Life Spans of the Individuals Mentioned in the Text

problems associated with economic growth have dampened earlier dominant beliefs and empowered other interpretations. Natural historians and then ecologists have long harbored concerns about the wisdom of human transformation of natural environments. Most scientists no longer think of the world as a system that will soon be understood and brought under control. Rather, the world is an evolving, complex, and uncertain system. With less confidence in their ability to predict and prescribe, scientists tend to be more humble and take a precautionary approach. The most notable among them are environmental scientists, ecologists, and conservation biologists who argue that we need to direct the best of our scientific expertise and far more of our educational effort at learning how to work with nature[6]. Similarly, environmental ethicists are challenging the vacuity of individual material progress for its own sake. While economic thought is also beginning to evolve in the context of these newer understandings, the historical beliefs remain dominant within the profession as a whole and still influence environmental economics.

As the following sections highlight, throughout most of their historical development economics and the natural sciences interacted extensively. Of course, there were fewer scientists then and the specialization and fragmentation that characterize modern academia had not yet occurred to the degree it has today. Ecological economics represents an attempt to recapture the spirit of integrated, interactive analysis of problems that characterized the early history of science. It is only through this reintegrated analysis that we can hope to comprehend and solve our most pressing and complex social problems.

The sections that follow give a brief overview of the historical development of both economics and the natural sciences, especially ecology. Each section is structured around a prominent individual who began a line of inquiry that has been continued and elaborated by subsequent scholars to this day. These lines have tangled over the years and ecological economics attempts to reorganize them into a coherent whole.

Figure 1 shows the life spans of the various individuals we mention on a time line.

Co-development of Economics and Natural Science

There has been no revolution in economic science, and [there] is not likely to be any. The question we have really to determine is how we can make the best use of the accumulated knowledge of past generations, and to do that we must look more closely into the economic science of the 19th century. – William A. S. Hewins, 1911, p.905. Among the natural sciences, ecology was a "late bloomer." People interested in biology described natural environments and contemplated how biological systems developed historically, but such empirical descriptions were not combined with systemic thinking until the second half of the 19th century. Thus our story starts with economics.

The "physiocrats," a group of French social philosophers writing in the mid 18th century, were the first school of economics. They believed that the universal laws of physics (hence the school's name) extended their grand rule in some yet to be identified way to create a natural social order. This social order was made up of people with sovereign rights entitled to the produce of their labor. According to the physiocrats, real economic activity consisted in working the land. Food wholesalers, processors, and retailers were simply living off the fruits of others and their take should be minimized. The belief that natural law determines social order has taken many forms since the physiocrats and inevitably generates controversy. The physiocrats never identified how the laws of physics applied to economic systems, but their insistence on treating individuals as sovereign entities, like atoms, in the tradition of key liberal social philosophers such as Hobbes and Locke who assumed that society is merely the sum of its individuals, has stayed with mainstream economics ever since. While subsequent economists never discovered how the laws of physics ruled economies, they did duplicate the pattern of thinking of mechanics in their conception of market interactions. Adam Smith initiated this pattern of reasoning.

Adam Smith and the Invisible Hand

Adam Smith (1723–1790), widely recognized as the founder of modern economics, was a moral philosopher. While economics since Smith has assumed a heavy scientific gloss, critical ethical issues have always been embedded in its theory. And the key ethical issue has always been whether the pursuit of individual greed can be in the interest of society as a whole. Smith reasoned that if two people who are fully informed of the consequences of their decision choose to enter into an exchange, it is because the exchange makes each of them better off. Appealing to Judeo-Christian images of God, Smith invented the metaphor of the "invisible hand," arguing that markets induce people to behave for the common good *as if* they were guided by a higher authority.

Modern economics typically continues to assume that society is simply the sum of its individuals, the social good is the sum of individual wants, and markets automatically guide individual behavior to the common good. By the end of the 19th century, the market model had been formalized mathematically and it turned out to be the same mathematics as used by Newton for mechanical systems. This atomistic view of individuals and mechanistic view of a social system contrasts sharply with the more organic, or ecological, view that community relations define who people are, affect what they want, facilitate collective action, and have a historical continuity of their own. While Adam Smith was a moral philosopher, his economics made morality less important. For most of human history, people's sense of identity has come through living within a community and its moral precepts. Today, this is increasingly less important among either the materially wealthy or aspirants to material wealth (and may indeed account for their frequent visits to the psychiatrist). Among the multiplicative factors affecting environmental degradation, the role of materialism and its relation to moral behavior is rarely discussed and is in need of broader, more serious scientific and public discourse. We discuss these points in later sections.

The growth of individualism and materialism associated with modernity and the consequent decline in community and concern with moral conduct are not Adam Smith's fault, but he played a decisive role in setting up the reasoning that justified individual greed[7]. In an age when Europeans and North Americans were rebelling against the tyranny of church and state and social philosophers were building theories from the individual up to the society rather than from society down to the individual, Adam Smith argued that markets link individual greed to the common good without coercive social institutions. And ever since Smith, the critical question, if too rarely discussed, has been whether markets really do this as well as he believed. One glaring contradiction is that the economic model of society argues that individual behavior supports the common good while simultaneously arguing that communities are not needed because markets will provide for the common good. The issues of market and community are being addressed at the end of the twentieth century by a variety of scholars who argue that communities are necessary at different geographic scales to define the social good, adapt the social order, and manage environmental systems[8].

Thomas Malthus and Population Growth

The cleric-turned-economist Thomas R. Malthus (1766–1834) explained the prevalence of war and disease as secular, material phenomena rather than as acts of God. He argued

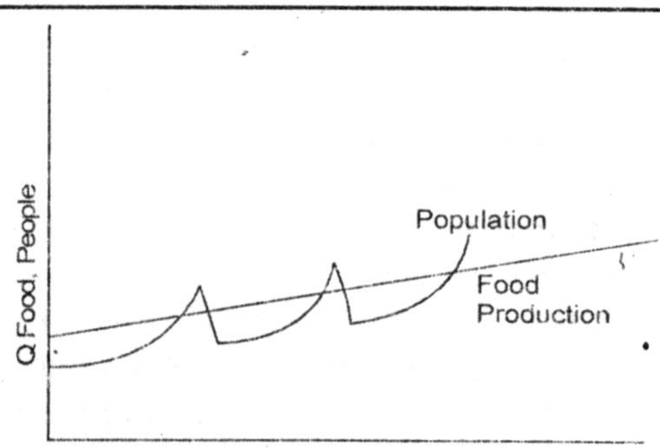

Source: Authors

Figure 2: Thomas Malthus' Model of Population Growth and Collapse

that human populations were capable of increasing exponentially and would do so as long as sufficient food and other essentials of life were available[9]. He further hypothesized that people could expand their food supply arithmetically through new technologies and expansion into new habitats. Given the potential for geometric increases in population and only arithmetic increases in food supply, population periodically surpasses food supply (Figure 2). At these times, Malthus argued, people would ravage the land, go to war over food, and succumb to disease and starvation. Human numbers would consequently drop to sustainable levels whence the process would repeat. This basic model from economics is still widely used today by biological scientists.

Malthus' model is beguilingly simple and consequently demographic history never quite supports it precisely. Yet periodically in specific places, Malthus' model has been confirmed, and history may yet confirm it globally. Few question whether population must ultimately be stabilized in order to sustain human well-being at a reasonable level. The expansion of human populations into previously unpopulated or lightly populated regions, the intensity with which firewood is collected, and the push to increase food production through modern agrochemical, mono-cultural techniques, so harmful to biodiversity, are driven over the long run by population increase. The continued rapid rate of population growth in the poorest nations threatens to keep them poor while diminishing the possibilities that the people of these nations will ever be able to consume at levels comparable to people in the rich nations using current modern technologies without vastly accelerating environmental degradation.

Malthus' model has become a part of human consciousness, making it difficult to contemplate, let alone discuss, the issues of population and its effects on the environment without his framing becoming central to the discussion. The success of Malthus' model stems from its simplicity, but the dynamics of population growth and how people depend on the environment are much more complex than the model suggests. Thus, while Malthus provided us with a powerful model, its simplicity restricts its usefulness for policy making beyond the obvious prescription, that fewer people would probably be better for sustainability than more people.

In addition to his influence on economic and demographic thought, Malthus had an enormous influence on other key intellectual figures. Both Charles Darwin and Alfred Russell Wallace credited Malthus with providing them the key insight that led them to the theory of natural selection. Marx developed many of his views in opposition to Malthus. Even John Maynard Keynes (1883–1946) was influenced by Malthus' theory and incorporated it in a theory of under consumption, inventory buildups, and the business cycle.

David Ricardo and the Geographic Pattern of Economic Activity

David Ricardo (1772–1823) introduced a second model of how economic activity relates to the environment, not because he was concerned with environmental degradation or human survival, but rather because he wished to justify why landlords received a rent from land ownership[10]. Ricardo argued that people would initially farm the land that produced the most food for the least work (labor per unit of food, the y-axis of Figure 3). As population increased, farming would extend to less fertile soils requiring more labor (the extensive margin). Food prices would have to rise to cover the cost of the extra labor on the less fertile land. This means that the initial land

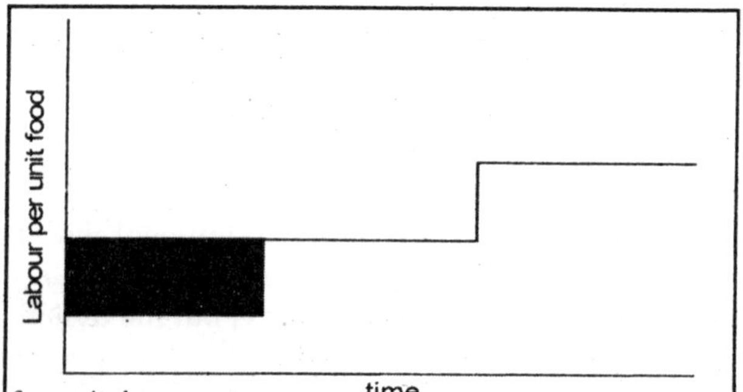

Source: Authors

Figure 3: Ricardo's Explanation of Rent, Represented by the Shaded Area

would earn a rent, a return above production cost, indicated by the shaded area in Figure 3. Higher food prices, in turn, would also induce a more *intensive* use of labor on the better land (the intensive margin). This model indicates how increasing population drives people to farm in previously undisturbed areas and how higher food prices lead to the intensification and, in modern agriculture, to the greater use of fertilizers and pesticides on prime agricultural lands. This model also gives us insights into how fluctuations in food prices can result in the periodic entry and exit of farmers on the extensive margin and in shifts in farming practices on the intensive margin. Ricardo's model of how agricultural activities are patterned on the land in response to population growth and changes in food prices is critical to our understanding of the complex interrelations between human survival and ecological life-support systems.

Ricardo's model of resource use patterns is similar to how those in the earth sciences think about the use of mineral resources. Petroleum geologists and mineralogists often presume, just as Ricardo did, that the best quality resources are used first even though history shows that a significant portion of the best quality resources are frequently not discovered until poorer quality resources have already been used.

The models of Malthus and Ricardo led to classical economics being called the "dismal science." The carrying capacity limits of Malthus' model and the lower quality of the next available resources in the model of Ricardo conflicted with the beliefs in progress which were so prevalent during the 19th century. The Ricardian theory of differential rent also had dismal distributive consequences since an increasing share of the total product of the land went to landlords.

These models are now touted by environmental scientists concerned about population growth, excessive consumption, and environmental degradation, and argued against by mainstream economists. During most of the twentieth century, economists built new models with different assumptions in combinations that support beliefs in unlimited material progress.

Sadi Carnot, Rudolf Clausius and Thermodynamics

Sadi Carnot (1796–1832) founded thermodynamics with his classic 1824 study of the efficiency of steam engines, *Reflections on the Motive Power of Fire*. Carnot was the first to recognize that the amount of work that could be extracted depended on the temperature gradient between the source and sink. He effectively identified what were to become formalized as the laws of thermodynamics by Rudolf Clausius (1822–1888) a quarter century after Carnot's death. The first law of thermodynamics states that energy can neither be created nor destroyed. The second law, also known as the entropy law, states that the amount of energy available for work in a closed system only decreases with use. The laws of thermodynamics are frequently invoked in the construction of models of ecosystems and have been extended to models of human-environment interactions as well[11].

The second law effectively makes physics the dismal science for it states that the total useful energy in the universe, the amount of work remaining that can be done is constantly declining. Since any action requires energy, any activity today is at the expense of potential activity in the future. What hope is there for progress in a constantly degrading universe? This question has been pursued again and again for well over a century. Whether and how it is resolved depends on how fast the entropy of the universe is increasing and just how far into the future we are concerned[12].

An important point to remember, however, is that the Earth is an "open" system, and even if the entropy of the universe is increasing, the entropy of Earth may be declining (by a smaller amount, of course). The study of the thermodynamics of open, non-equilibrium systems came much later and we discuss it further in Section.

Charles Darwin and the Evolutionary Paradigm

Charles Darwin (1809–1882) was influenced by the economic arguments of Malthus as he began thinking about the question: why are there so many different types of plants and animals? After years of observing the natural and human-dominated ecosystems of his time (most notably as a naturalist aboard the H.M.S. Beagle on its voyage around the world in 1831–1836) and thinking about this question, he arrived at what, to him, seemed the only possible explanation. His answer, which has come to be a cornerstone of modern biology and ecology, was that species evolve by the processes of adaptation and natural selection. Population pressure, associated with the ability of species to expand their numbers to the carrying capacity of their environment, favored the survival of those individuals with the particular characteristics that made them more effective at reproducing themselves.

Darwin waited until late in his professional career to publish his findings. His *On the Origin of Species by Natural Selection* was first published in 1859 when the author was 50 (the same year, by the way, as Karl Marx's *Critique of Political Economy*). Darwin was immediately attacked by those holding what was then the mainstream view of "divine creation." The evolutionary paradigm continues to be attacked to this day by those espousing "creationism," but, in spite of its gaps, no other theory possesses anything approaching the explanatory power of evolution.

Since Darwin's day, the paradigm of evolution has been tested and broadly applied to both ecological and economic systems[13] as a way of formalizing our understanding of adaptation and learning behaviors in non equilibrium dynamic systems. The general evolutionary paradigm posits a mechanism for adaptation and learning in complex systems at any scale using three basic interacting processes: 1) information storage and transmission; 2) generation of new alternatives; and 3) selection of superior alternatives according to some performance criteria.

The evolutionary paradigm is different from the conventional mechanical paradigm of economics in at least four important respects[14]: 1) evolution is path dependent, meaning that the detailed history and dynamics of the system are important; 2) evolution can achieve multiple equilibrium; 3) there is no guarantee that optimal efficiency or any other optimal performance will be achieved due in part to path dependence and sensitivity to perturbations; and 4) "lock-in" (survival of the first rather than survival of the fittest) is possible under conditions of increasing returns. While, as Arthur notes, "conventional economic theory is built largely on the assumption of diminishing returns on the margin (local negative feedbacks)," life itself can be characterized as a positive feedback, self-reinforcing, autocatalytic process[15] and we should expect increasing returns, lock-in, path dependence, multiple equilibrium, and suboptimal efficiency to be the rule rather than the exception in economic and ecological systems.

In biological evolution, the information storage medium is the genes, the generation of new alternatives is by sexual recombination or genetic mutation, and selection is performed by nature according to a criterion of "fitness" based on reproductive success. The same process of change occurs in other ecological, economic, and cultural systems, but the elements on which the process works are different. For example, in cultural evolution the storage medium is the culture (the oral tradition, books, film, or other storage medium for passing on behavioral norms), the generation of new alternatives is through innovation by individual members or groups in the culture, and selection is again based on the reproductive success of the alternatives generated, but reproduction is carried out by the spread and copying of the behavior through the culture rather than biological reproduction. One may also talk of "economic" evolution, a subset of cultural evolution dealing with the generation, storage, and selection of alternative ways of producing things and allocating that which is produced. Evolutionary theories in economics have already been successfully applied to problems of technical change, to the development of new institutions, and to the evolution of means of payment[16].

For large, slow-growing animals like humans, genetic evolution has a built-in bias toward the long run. Changing the genetic structure of a species requires that characteristics (phenotypes) be selected and accumulated by differential reproductive success. Behaviours learned or acquired during the lifetime of an individual cannot be passed on genetically.

Genetic evolution is therefore usually a relatively slow process requiring many generations to significantly alter a species' physical and biological characteristics.

Cultural evolution is potentially much faster. Technical change is perhaps the most important and fastest evolving cultural process. Learned behaviours that are successful at least in the short term, can be almost immediately spread to other members of the culture and passed on in the oral, written, or video record. The increased speed of adaptation that this process allows has been largely responsible for *Homo sapiens'* amazing success at appropriating the resources of the planet. As already mentioned, humans now directly control from 25 to 40% of the total primary production of the planet's biosphere[17] and this is beginning to have significant effects on the biosphere, including changes in global climate and in the planet's protective ozone shield.

Thus the costs of this rapid cultural evolution are potentially significant. Like a car that has increased speed, humans are in more danger of running off the road or over a cliff. Cultural evolution lacks the built-in long-run bias of genetic evolution and is susceptible to being led by its hyper-efficient short-run adaptability over a cliff into the abyss.

Another major difference between cultural and genetic evolution may serve as a countervailing bias, however. As Arrow[18] has pointed out, cultural and economic evolution, unlike genetic evolution, can at least to some extent employ foresight. If society can see the cliff, perhaps it can be avoided.

While market forces drive adaptive processes[19], the systems that evolve are not necessarily optimal, so the question remains: what external influences are needed and when should they be applied in order to improve an economic system via evolutionary adaptation? The challenge faced by ecological economic systems modelers is first to apply the models to gain foresight, and then respond to and manage the system feedbacks in a way that helps avoid any foreseen cliffs[20]. Devising policy instruments and identifying incentives that can translate this foresight into effective modifications of the short-run evolutionary dynamics is the challenge[21].

John Stuart Mill and the Steady-State

John Stuart Mill (1806–1873) was the son of social philosopher James Mill (1773–1836), who also wrote on economics. Mill is important for having expanded on the linkages between individual behavior and the common good suggested by Adam Smith, arguing that competitive economies had to be based on rules of property use and a sense of social responsibility that favored the common good. At the same time, he argued that competitive markets were essential to freedom. As a social philosopher seriously concerned with liberty, Mill also wrote on the immorality and waste of human productive talent that resulted from the subjugation of women by men. While his concern with subjugation of women was perhaps too instrumentally based, he neither saw material prosperity as an end in itself nor foresaw that continuous growth in material well-being was possible. Mill was one of the first economists to plead for conservation of biodiversity, or against the conversion of all natural capital into man-made capital. Mill envisioned economies becoming mature and reaching a steady-state in which people would be able to enjoy the fruits of their earlier savings, or material abstinence, which had been necessary for the accumulation of industrial capital. The idea that economies would reach a steady-state was both consistent with the Newtonian view of systems so dominant at the time and consistent with natural phenomena. Unceasing growth is not observed in nature, and relatively steady-states rather than random change are perceived as "natural." Herman Daly builds on Mill and argues for a steady-state economy where flows of resources into production and of pollutants back to the environment are kept at a steady level. The steady-state metaphor has become critical to finding common ground for achieving sustainable development[22].

Karl Marx and the Ownership of Resources

Karl Marx (1818–1883) addressed, among his multiple critiques of capitalism, how the concentration of land and capital among a small portion of society affected how economies worked. There is an extensive collection of literature written by scholars influenced by Marx. Some of this literature addresses the sustainability of development and how the ownership of resources affects the path of development[23]. Neoclassical models also readily show how resource ownership affects resource use[24]. However, for a variety of political reasons, this facet of the neoclassical model was ignored in the West during the Cold War. Indeed, in the United States, economists who were concerned with the distribution of ownership of resources were politically disempowered through their association with a central concern of Marx. Western neoclassical economists, including resource and environmental economists, addressed questions of the efficient allocation of resources, leaving the initial distribution of resources among people as a given, not to be questioned. We now recognize that the initial distribution of rights to resources and to the services of the environment is critically important to resource and environmental conservation and the prospects for sustainability[25].

It has long been known that how economies allocate resources to different ends depends on how resources are distributed among people, that is, whether they are owned by or otherwise under the control of different people. Peasants or others who work land and interact with biological resources owned by someone else have little incentive to protect them. Landlords can only counteract this lack of incentive by diverting their own labor or that of managers under them from other productive activities and employing it to monitor and enforce their interests in protection. This diversion of human potential would not be necessary with a more equal distribution of control. Furthermore, especially wealthy landlords may have little interest in protecting any particular land or biological resource for their descendants when they hold land in such abundance that their foreseeable descendants are certain to have an adequate share.

To illustrate why distribution is important, imagine two countries with identical populations and identical resources allocated by perfect markets. In the first country, rights to resources are distributed between people approximately equally, people have similar incomes, and they consume similar products, perhaps corn, chicken, and cotton clothing. In the second country, rights are concentrated among a few people who can afford luxury goods such as beef, wine, caviar, fine clothes, and tourism, while those who have few rights to resources, living nearly on their labor alone, consume only the most basic of goods like rice and beans. In each country, markets efficiently allocate resources to the production of products, but how land is used, the types of products produced, and who consumes them depend on how rights to resources are distributed. For different distributions of rights, the efficient use of resources is different.

Within the 20th-century global discourse on development policy, many have argued that economic injustices within nations as well as between nations have limited the development options of poor nations and thereby, in the long run, those of the rich as well. Similarly in the late 20th century global environmental discourse, many argued that environmental injustices and the international ecological order limit the possibilities for conservation. The vast majority of the people on the globe still consume very little. The poor are poor for two reasons. First, they do not have sufficient long-term access to resources to meet their ongoing material needs. Second, they are well aware that others consume far more than they do, that their poverty is relative, and rightfully strive to improve their own relative condition. Striving to meet their material needs and aspirations without long-term secure access to adequate resources, the poor have little choice but to use the few resources at their disposal in an unsustainable manner. The poor, excluded from the productivity of the fertile valleys or fossil hydrocarbon resources controlled by the rich are forced to work land previously left idle because of its fragility and low agricultural productivity: the tropical forests, the steep hillsides, and arid regions.

An environmental justice movement addresses why the poor and people of color bear a heavy share of the environmental costs of development. The poor and people of color are more likely to live near waste disposal sites and more likely to work in polluted environments. This movement also speaks to the excessive material and energy consumption of the wealthy 20–30% of the world's population made up of the middle classes and rich in the northern, industrialized nations as well as the elite in middle income nations and in some poorer ones. The rich consume the bulk of the resources and account for many of our environmental problems. The global access to resources' by the rich means that many of the environmental impacts of their consumption decisions occur at a great distance, beyond their view, beyond their perceived responsibility, and beyond their effective control. The relationships between unequal access to resources, the un-sustainability of development generally, and the loss of biodiversity in particular were major themes of the United Nations Conference on Environment and Development held in Rio de Janeiro in June 1992. Rich peoples and political leaders of northern industrialized countries generally have understandably had some difficulty participating in this discourse and even greater difficulty participating in the design of new global institutions to address the role of inequity in environmental degradation.

Our understanding of the environmental consequences of concentrated ownership and control are rooted in economic thinking, especially that of Karl Marx. Questions of equity are extremely important to the process of environmental degradation and to the possibilities for sustainable development. The occupation and ecological transformation of the Amazon have been partly driven by the concentration of the ownership of land in the more productive regions of Amazonian nations and partly driven by the economic power and hence political influence of the rich that has enabled them to obtain subsidies to engage in large-scale land speculation or cattle ranching. The ongoing efforts to establish international agreements on the management of biodiversity and climate change have been repeatedly forestalled by debates over the ownership and control of resources. But it is not simply a debate over fairness. The structure of the global economy and how specific economies interact with nature in the future will depend on which nations—the nations of origin or of the

Northern commercial interests, the likely discoverers of new uses for heretofore unused species—receive the "rent" from resources.

Marx and his followers in communist countries have made a negative contribution to the allocative efficiency problem, even while highlighting issues of just distribution. Their ideological rejection of rent and interest as necessary prices, and their insistence on a labor theory of value that neglected nature's contribution were responsible for much of the environmental destruction in communist countries.

W. Stanley Jevons and the Scarcity of Stock Resources

W. Stanley Jevons (1835–1882) contributed initially to metrology, logic, induction, and statistics while also making contributions to economics. He was one of the pioneers of the marginal utility theory of value. However, of more interest to ecological economics is his recognition of the critical importance of energy, which in his day meant coal. It was his argument that the British economy and the success of the empire were dependent on coal, a rapidly dwindling resource (*The Coal Question*, 1865) that brought him notoriety as an economist and a chair in political economy. He subsequently contributed to the mathematical formalization of economics (The *Theory of Political Economy*, 1871), continued to write on the philosophy of science (*The Principles of Science*, 1874), and speculated on the relationship of sunspots and financial crises (published in *Investigations in Currency and Finance*, 1884).

Ernst Haeckel and the Beginnings of Ecology

While ecology has been said to have its roots in the Greek science of Hippocrates, Aristotle, and Theophrastus, or in the 18th-century natural history of Linnaeus and Buffon, or in Darwin and Wallace's evolutionary biology, ecology as a named science did not emerge as a "self-conscious" discipline with its own name until Ernst Heinrich Haeckel (1834–1919) first used the word ecologies in 1866. Practitioners began to use this term in the last decade of the 19th century[26], Eugenius Warming (1841–1924) published the first ecology text in 1895[27], and the first formal ecological societies formed during the second decade of the 20th century. Thus, as a practical and practiced science, ecology is a 20th-century phenomenon.

In 1870 Haeckel produced the first full-fledged definition of ecology:

> By ecology we mean the body of knowledge concerning the economy of nature—the investigation of the total relations of the animal both to its inorganic and to its organic environment including above all, its friendly and inimical relations with those animals and plants with which it comes directly or indirectly into contact—in a word, ecology is the study of all those complex interrelations referred to by Darwin as the conditions of the struggle for existence[28].

Thus, even in this initial definition of the field, a deep conceptual relationship with economics is evident. Ecology was, in Haeckel's words, the study of the economy of nature. Economics, conversely, can be thought of as the ecology of humans. But historically the science of ecology evolved out of biology and etiology (the science of animal behavior) and thus had very different intellectual roots than economics. In practical terms, ecology became the study of the economy of that part of nature that does not include humans.

Since Haeckel's early definition, many other interpretations of the definition of ecology proliferated based on changing areas of interest and emphasis. When there was a focus on animal populations, ecology was "the study of the distribution and abundance of animals"[29]. Later, when ecosystems became a major focus, ecology was: "the study of the structure and function of ecosystems"[30]. But what has remained at the core is the relationship of organisms to their environment. As the dominant species of animal on the planet, *Homo sapiens* and its relationship to its environment are obviously central to the scope of ecology by any of its various definitions.

Thus, from the very beginning of ecology as a science, there have been continuing attempts to incorporate humans and the social sciences. Most of these attempts, unfortunately, did not get very far. The tendency in the social sciences was to consider humans somehow outside the laws and constraints that applied to other animals and ecologists were not persistent or effective enough in their attempts to extend ecological thinking to *Homo sapiens*.

As McIntosh points out:

> If human factors are beyond ecological consideration, what then is human ecology? It is not clear whether ecology will expand to encompass the social sciences and develop as a meta-science of ecology. The alternative is a more effective interdisciplinary relationship between ecology and the several social sciences[31].

Ecological economics can be seen as an attempt to build this more effective interdisciplinary relationship as a bridge to a truly comprehensive science of humans as a component of nature that will fulfill the early goals of ecology. This reintegration of ecology and economics (and the other social sciences) is explored in the last section in this chapter.

Alfred J. Lotka and Systems Thinking

Alfred J. Lotka (1880–1949), was trained as a physical chemist, but his broad interests in chemistry, physics, biology, and economics led to a far-reaching synthesis of these fields together with thermodynamics in his 1925 book, *Elements of Physical Biology*[32]. Lotka was the first to attempt an integration of ecological and economic systems in quantitative and mathematical terms. He viewed the whole world of interacting biotic and a biotic components as a system, where everything was linked to everything else and nothing could be understood without an understanding of the whole system. He also stressed the importance of looking at systems from an energetic point of view.

Lotka's work was grand in scope and, although recognition was slow in coming, it eventually influenced both noted ecologists (like E. P. Odum and H. T. Odum) and economists (like Paul Samuelson, Henry Schultz, and Herbert Simon)[33]. Lotka's work was clearly in the synthetic, trans-disciplinary spirit of the 19th century, but was coming at a time when the disciplines had already started to fragment. Lotka was not a professional scholar until late in his career, and his isolation from the pressures of the academic disciplines probably allowed him to more easily achieve and maintain his broad perspective.

While *Lotka* is, probably best known for his equations, describing two-species population dynamics (which were simultaneously discovered by Vito Volterra and have come to be known as the Lotka-Volterra equations), and these equations occupied only two pages of his 1925 book. His more important contributions from the perspective of ecological economics were his attempts to treat ecology and economics as an integrated whole, exhibiting nonlinear dynamics and constrained and structured by flows of energy. He attempted to model quite explicitly the economy of nature, and developed a general evolutionary approach to this problem. But since he was interested in systems, not just species and populations, he developed systems criteria to drive evolution. What has come to be known as "Lotka's energy principle" or "Lotka's power principle" posited that systems survive by maximizing their energy flow, defined as the rate of effectively using energy, or power. In single species populations this reduced to the usual criterion of reproductive success, but his formulation allowed the generalization to all systems, from simple chemical systems to biological, ecological, and economic systems. These ideas presaged the development of general systems theory (discussed later) and were very influential on later attempts to reintegrate ecology and economics.

A. C. Pigou and Market Failure

Arthur C. Pigou (1877–1959) formally elaborated how costs and benefits that are not included in market prices affect how people interrelate with their environment. An *externality* is a phenomenon that is external to markets and hence does not affect how markets operate when in fact it should. Consider, for example, pesticide use in agriculture and the associated loss of biodiversity. In Figure 4 below, S_0 illustrates the willingness of farmers to *supply* food at different prices. As the price of food increases (the y-axis), the quantity of food (the x-axis) that farmers are willing to supply increases. D is the demand curve illustrating the willingness of people to purchase greater quantities of food at lower prices. The market clears, in the sense that the quantity supplied equals the quantity demanded, at the price P_0 and quantity Q_0.

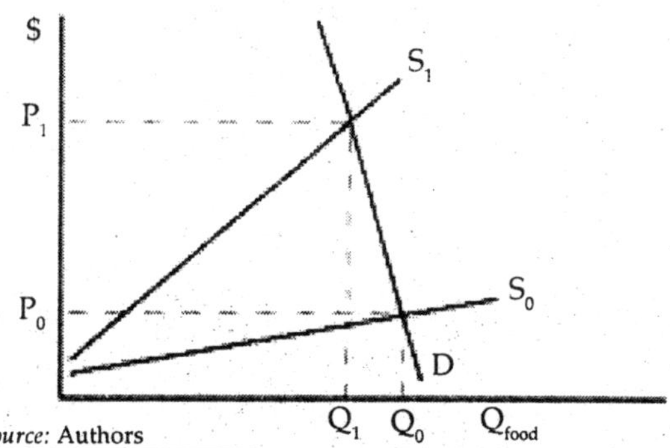

Source: Authors

Figure 4: Market Distortion Due to an External Cost

Now imagine that we could measure, for example, the value of biodiversity lost through pesticide use and add this to the cost of pesticides. The higher cost of pesticides would reduce the quantity of food that farmers could produce at any given price, shifting the supply curve to S_1, the price of food to P_1, and the quantity of food supplied and demanded to Q_1. By internalizing the cost of lost biodiversity through farmers' decision to use pesticides, we internalize a cost that was previously external to the market and thus affect how the market operates. Following the logic of Pigou and numerous environmental economists since, biodiversity is not protected adequately because its value is not included in the market signals that guide the economic decisions of producers and consumers and thereby the overall operation of the economic system. The logic of market failure has led economists, and increasingly biologists as well, to argue that the critical environmental resources need to be incorporated into the market system[34].

One way of doing this is to grant to private individuals the sole rights to use particular environmental resources. This individual then both reaps the economic benefits from using the resource now but also may benefit through conserving the resource for use at a later date. This means consumers will pay a higher price, reflecting the costs of managing the species in a more sustainable manner. It is important to keep in mind, however, that incorporating species into the market system may not result in their conservation and indeed could even accelerate their extinction. Species within the market system, for example, will not be conserved if their value is expected to grow at less than the rate of interest unless other controls are also put on their harvest.

The processes of biodiversity loss also interact with each other in a larger, reinforcing process of positive feedbacks. The degradation of any particular area increases the economic pressure on other areas. The loss of woody species through climate change reduces the possibilities for carbon fixation and reduces the opportunities to ameliorate further climate change. To bring a system into equilibrium, negative feedbacks are needed. Economics helps us see how biodiversity is decreasing because so few genetic traits, species, or ecosystems have market prices, the negative feedback signals that equilibrate market economies. In market systems, prices increase to reduce the quantity demanded when supplies are low and prices drop to increase the quantity demanded when supplies are high, keeping demand and supply in equilibrium. The problem, economists argue, is that most genetic traits, species, and ecosystems are being lost because they do not have prices acting as a negative feedback system to keep use in equilibrium with availability. When individuals of the species become fewer, there is no increase in price to decrease the quantity used. By putting economic values on species and through various ways including them in market signals, biodiversity loss would be reduced. Furthermore, the economic explanation and solution is systemic. Unlike bio reserves, which reduce human pressures on species within the protected area but typically increase them beyond it, including the value of biodiversity in the price system would beneficially affect decisions in every sector of the economy.

Biologists also find the idea that we need to know the economic values of species compatible with their own understanding that if the true value of species to society were understood, more species would be conserved. Clearly, if we knew the value of biological resources, we would be in a better position to manage them more effectively. And, to the extent these values could be included in the market system; markets themselves could assist in the conservation of biodiversity. The situation can frequently be improved through amending market signals. At the same time, it is important to remember that market values only exist within a larger system of values, which for many people include the preservation of nature for ethical or religious reasons[35].

Even when species cannot be better conserved through the market, knowing their economic value can help convince people and their political representatives that the species deserves protection. Environmental valuation can also improve how we analyze the benefits and costs of development projects that affect biodiversity. Techniques for valuation include determining people's willingness to pay to maintain diversity through questionnaires and through analyses of their expenditures to observe interesting environments and particular species[36].

While several techniques for estimating the value of the environment are proving interesting, valuation is by no means an easy task and estimates should be used cautiously. A major difficulty is related to the systemic nature of economics, ecosystems, and the process of environmental degradation. Market systems relate everything to everything else. When the price of oil changes, for example, the price of gasoline changes, the demand and hence the price of products that use gasoline such as automobiles changes, the demand for and hence the price of coal changes, and so on. Prices bring markets to equilibrium and their flexibility is essential to this task. Similarly, the "right" price for a given species or ecosystem will depend on the availability of a host of other species or ecosystems with which they are interdependent as well as with other species and ecosystems that may be substitutes or complements in use. To think that a species or ecosystem has a single value is to deny both ecosystem and economic system interconnections. Nevertheless, environmental valuation can assist us in understanding at least the minimal importance of ecological services and conveying this understanding to the public to improve the political process of finding common ground.

Harold Hotelling and the Efficient Use of Resources over Time

Harold Hotelling (1895–1973) developed a model of efficient resource use over time that helps us understand how resources are exploited over time and the conditions under which conservation or depletion occur[37]. Hotelling reasoned that the owner of mineral resources had two options: that of extracting the resource and putting the profits in the bank where they would earn interest, and that of leaving the resource in the ground to appreciate in value. The owner would choose the first option unless the potential profits that could be earned from mining the resource in the future were increasing in value at a rate faster than the rate of interest. If this were the case, then it made sense to leave the resource in the ground. He then reasoned that, under particular conditions, a mining industry consisting of competitive resource owners would behave such that resources in the ground would increase in value at the rate of interest, for this would be the condition under which resource owners would be indifferent between mining and not mining a little more. If this condition were not met, they would all mine more if they could earn more by putting their revenues in the bank, or mine less if they could earn more by leaving the resource in the ground. Expectations about the future are critical in Hotelling's model, and are embodied in the expected interest rate and expected future price of the resource.

Clearly the level of the interest rate affects how biological resources are managed and hence the rate and direction of ecosystem transformation and species extinction. Any species or ecosystem that cannot be managed at a level such that it is generating a flow of services at a rate greater than the rate of interest "should" be depleted (see Figure 5). Since even many economists find exploitation to extinction rather crass, there has been considerable interest in whether the interest rate produced by private capital markets reflects the social interest and whether, when these interests are factored in, a social rate

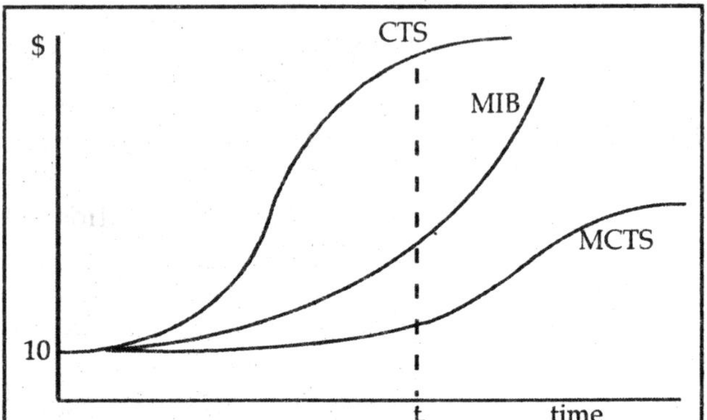

Source: Authors

Figure 5: Commercial and Noncommercial Tree Growth and Harvest Time

of interest would not be significantly lower than the private interest rate. Might private capital markets work imperfectly, generating rates of interest that are too high and hence leading to excessive biodiversity loss[38]? There are good reasons to expect that lower interest rates would favor the conservation of biodiversity, though there are situations when this would not be the case. Low interest rates allocate investments from the fastest growing projects, but increase the total number of projects that are worth investing in. Thus, low interest rates favor conservation in terms of their effects on allocation, but in terms of their scale-increasing effect they work against conservation. This has not been simply an academic argument. The World Bank now realizes how its own evaluation policies have hastened biodiversity loss and, in part for this reason, has a policy of not financing the transformation of natural forest habitat.

Economics and Environment Specialize and Separate

By the end of the 19th century the trend to increasing specialization and professionalization in science was well under way, and economics as a profession became more and more popular[39]. What has come to be called the "reductionist" paradigm was beginning to hold sway. This paradigm assumes that the world is separable into relatively isolated units that can be studied and understood on their own, and then reassembled to give a picture of the whole. As the complexity of science increased, this was a very useful idea, since it allowed dividing up the problem into smaller, more manageable pieces that could be attacked intensively. Chemists could study chemistry without being distracted by other aspects of the systems they were studying. Also, the rapid increase in the sheer number of scientists that were actively working made it necessary to organize the work in some way, and the disciplinary structure seemed a logical and useful way to do this. But once university departments were set up in the various disciplines, internal reinforcement systems came to reward only work in the discipline. This rapidly led to a reduction in communication across disciplines and a tendency for the disciplines to develop their own unique languages, cultures, and ways of looking at the world.

In economics, this led to a growing isolation from the natural resource (or land) component of the classical triad of land, labor, and capital, and with it a growing isolation from the natural sciences. Economics departments began to reward theory more highly than applications and the discipline as a whole attempted to pattern itself on physics, which was probably the most successful example of the advantages of the disciplinary model of organization.

This trend continued in the early through mid-20th century and, by the time of the renewed environmental awareness of the 1970s, economics had become highly specialized and abstracted away from its earlier connections with the natural environment. Textbooks at the time barely mentioned the environment and concentrated instead on the microeconomics of supply, demand, and price formation and the macroeconomics of growth in manufactured capital and GNP.

At the same time, economics was becoming absorbed with professionalization. As A. W. Coats noted:

> At least since the marginal revolution of the 1870s, mainstream economists have sought to enhance their intellectual authority and autonomy by excluding certain questions which were either sensitive (such as the distribution of income and wealth, and the role of economic power in society) or incapable of being handled by their preferred methods and techniques, or both. These are precisely the questions which are emphasized by their professional and lay critics and, more recently, by many economists who cannot be dismissed by their professional colleagues as either ignorant or incompetent[40].

The story in ecology is somewhat different. As we have previously noted, ecology is a much younger science, and it has always been more explicitly pluralistic and interdisciplinary. But its roots were in biology and the trend in biology was much the same as in other areas of science. The initial split into botany and zoology was followed by further specialization into biochemistry, biophysics, molecular biology, and so on. In ecology itself there was something of a split between the population ecologists (e.g., Robert MacArthur), who concentrated on individual populations of organisms, and systems ecologists (e.g., E. P. and H. T. Odum), who focused on whole ecosystems. But this split never got to the point of separation into distinct departments and disciplines, although many academic programs took on a decided flavor in one direction or the other.

Through all of this, ecologists, more so than any other discipline, have maintained communication across most of the natural sciences. To study ecosystems, one has to integrate hydrology, soil science, geology, climatology, chemistry, botany, zoology, genetics, and many other disciplines. The dividing line for ecologists has been at a particular species: *Homo sapiens*. Even though Haeckel's original definition explicitly included humans, and many ecologists have argued and worked to operationalize this integration, for the vast majority of active ecologists, the study of humans is outside their discipline, left to the social sciences. Indeed, most ecologists looked for field sites as remote from human activities as possible to conduct their research. Ecological economics is an attempt to help rectify this tendency to ignore humans in ecology, while at the same time rectifying the parallel tendency to ignore the natural world in the social sciences.

Environmental Economics: Path of Development

Environment and economics have been pursued as separate disciplines through most of the 20th century. While each has certainly borrowed theoretical concepts from the other and shared patterns of thinking from physics and other sciences, each has addressed separate issues, utilized different assumptions to reach answers, and supported different interests in the policy process. To be sure, individual scholars kept trying to introduce the issues addressed by natural science into economics, but they were systematically rejected by economists as a group[41]. Indeed, in their popular manifestations as environmentalism and economism, these disciplines became juxtaposed secular religions, preventing the collective interpretation and resolution of the numerous problems at the intersection of human and natural systems.

Environmental economics arose during the 1980s among a group of scholars who realized that improvements in environmental policy and management and protecting the well-being of future generations were dependent on bringing these domains of thought together. Numerous experiments with joint meetings between economists and ecologists were held, particularly in Sweden and the United States, to explore the possibilities of working together[42]. Meanwhile, there was also growing discontent with the deficiencies in the system of national accounts that generates measures of economic activity such as gross domestic product, while ignoring the depletion of natural capital through the mining of resources such as petroleum and through environmental degradation[43]. Economists and ecologists joined to encourage the major international agencies to develop accounting systems that included the environment[44]. Buoyed by such initial efforts, the International Society for Ecological Economics (ISEE) was formed during a workshop of ecologists and economists held in Barcelona in late 1987, and the journal, *Ecological Economics*, was initiated in 1989. Major international conferences of ecologists and economists have been held since then, many ecological economic institutes have been formed around the world, and a significant number of books have appeared with the term ecological economics in their titles[45].

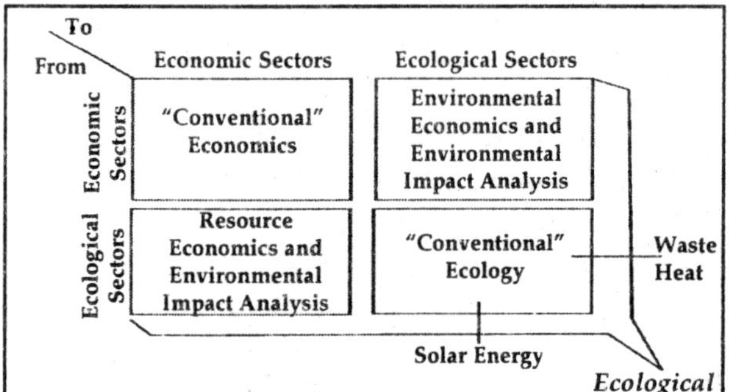

Source: Costanza, Daly, and Bartholomew 1991[1]

Figure 6: Relationship of Domains of Ecological Economics and Conventional Economics and Ecology, Resource and Environmental Economics, and Environmental Impact Analysis

Ecological economics is not a single new paradigm based in shared assumptions and theory. It represents a commitment among economists, ecologists, and others, both as academics and as practitioners, to learn from each other, to explore new patterns of thinking together, and to facilitate the derivation and implementation of new economic and environmental policies. To date, ecological economics has been deliberately conceptually pluralistic even while particular members may prefer one paradigm over another[46]. One way of looking at it is to view ecological economics as encompassing economics and ecology and their existing links in the form of resource and environmental economics and environmental impact analysis as shown in Figure 6. Ecological economists are rethinking both ecology and economics by, for example, extending the materials balance and energetic paradigm of ecology to economic questions[47], applying concepts from economics to better understand the nature of biodiversity[48], and arguing from biological theory how natural and social systems have coevolved together such that neither can be understood apart from the other[49].

Today's ecological economists are indebted to particular scholars who, though they have been predominantly ecologists or economists themselves, have maintained and demonstrated the advantages of a trans-disciplinary approach. We highlight the new patterns of thinking introduced by many of these scholars in the next sections while acknowledging that there are many more who have contributed to the founding of ecological economics in diverse ways.

General System Theory

Systems analysis is the study of systems that can be thought of as groups of interacting, interdependent parts linked together by complex exchanges of energy, matter, and information. There is a key distinction between "classical" science and system science. Classical science is based on the resolution, or reduction, of phenomena into isolatable causal trains and the search for basic, "atomic" units or parts of the system. Reductionist approaches are appropriate if the interaction between the parts is nonexistent, weak, or essentially linear so that they can be added up to describe the behavior of the whole. While these conditions are met in some physical and simple chemical systems, they are almost never met in more complex living systems. A "living system" is characterized by strong, usually nonlinear, interactions between the parts. Such complex feedbacks make resolution into isolatable causal trains difficult or impossible and also mean that small-scale behavior cannot simply be "added up" to arrive at large-scale results. Of course, this has not prevented scientists from assuming that living systems can be reduced to causal trains and isolatable parts, but this also explains why disciplinary environmental science and economics has produced inappropriate policies and management schemes.

As we noted earlier in our discussion of A. J. Lotka, some scientists have long addressed the difficulties of working with complex systems. Ludwig von Bertalanffy, however, is especially credited with advancing the formal study of systems through a paper he wrote in 1950. This paper drew the attention of others who then chose to explore the field together. In *General System Theory* (1968), von Bertalanffy and his cohorts argued that similar patterns of interaction could be found in quite different systems and ventured the argument that once these basic patterns were understood, all systems could be understood. While this has not proved to be the case, one participant of the general system theory group, Kenneth Boulding, produced a series of books drawing parallels between economic and ecological systems, inspired other potential ecological economists in their formative years, and then helped in the founding of ecological economics as a formal effort[50].

Ecological and economic systems obviously exhibit the characteristics of living systems, and hence are not well understood using the methods of classical, reductionist science. While almost any subdivision of the universe can be thought of as a "system," systems analysts look for boundaries that minimize the interaction between the system under study and the rest of the universe in order to make their job easier. Some systems theorists claim that nature "herself" presents a convenient hierarchy of scales rooted in these interaction-saving boundaries, ranging from atoms to molecules to cells to organs to organisms to populations to communities to ecosystems—including economic, or human-dominated ecosystems—to bioregions to the global system and beyond[51]. By studying the similarities and differences between different kinds of systems at different scales and resolutions, one can develop hypotheses and test them against other systems to explore their degree of generality and predictability.

One might define systems analysis as the scientific method applied both across and within disciplines, scales, resolutions, and system types. In other words, it is an integrative manifestation of the scientific method, while most of the traditional or classical scientific disciplines tend to dissect their subjects into smaller and smaller parts hoping to reduce the problem to its essential elements. Thus, systems analysis forms a more natural scientific base and worldview for the inherently integrative trans-discipline of ecological economics than classical, reductionist science.

Beyond this distinction between synthesis and reduction, systems analysis usually applies mathematical modeling to these integrative problems. While this is neither a necessary nor a sufficient condition for systems analysis, it is a common characteristic, if for no other reason than that systems tend to be complex and mathematical modeling, especially on computers, is often necessary to handle that complexity. According to von Bertalanffy[52] "the system problem is essentially the problem of the limitations of analytical procedures in science." Recent years have seen an explosion in our ability to overcome these limitations and to actually model the complex, nonlinear, scale-dependent behavior of systems; hence the history of systems analysis is now understood to be tightly linked with the history of the computer. While computers first appeared in the 1950s, their widespread use did not commence until the 1960s and 1970s, and did not become common until the 1980s. With the increasing availability, power, and "user-friendliness" of computers has come an increasing feasibility of systems analysis. Today, many people can buy a personal computer and relevant software and begin to do practical systems analysis. Now the limitation is clearly the availability of appropriate data.

The possibility for this sort of analysis was recognized early and practical applications were developed more or less independently by modelers in economics, ecology, industrial management, and what was then called cybernetics[53]. Early "systems analysts" in economics include Wassily Leontief[54] and John Von Neumann and Oscar Morgenstern[55] who mainly focused on static input–output networks and games. Jay Forrester of MIT began modeling complex industrial systems in the early 1960s[56] and has spawned one of the most prolific schools of systems analysis. In ecology, H. T. Odum[57], B. C. Patten[58], and Bruce Hannon[59] were among the early practitioners of both dynamic computer simulation and static network analysis. The International Biosphere Program (IBP) was an early large-scale attempt to perform ecological systems analysis for a range of ecosystems[60]. Students of Jay Forrester developed the world systems model reported in *The Limits to Growth*[61] which launched an impressive debate[62] as well as expansions in their analysis[63].

Open-Access Resource

When nature can be divided into separate properties that are individually owned, the owners have an incentive to use the property carefully so that they can continue to use it in the future. When nature cannot be so divided and many people use the resource together, problems can arise. Resources used by multiple users without rules governing their use will be overexploited. Both traditional and modern societies typically develop rules for the use of resources held in common. The important point is that nature rarely can truly be divided into separate parts, the very premise of systems theory discussed in the previous section, so the problems raised by collective use of resources must always be addressed. Indeed, as population and material consumption increase, the contradictions between the indivisibility of nature and the use of private property for environmental management become ever more critical.

A. C. Pigou addressed the problem of collective resource use in the 1920s and subsequent economists have developed formal models. The phenomenon did not become widely understood, however, until it was popularized in an article in *Science* magazine written by Garret Hardin, titled "The Tragedy of the Commons"[64]. The problem Hardin addressed is more accurately referred to as "open access" resources rather than "common property." Common ownership is not in itself a tragedy since many resources have been successfully managed as commons.

Open access can develop through the destruction of common institutions regulating the use of resources used jointly by people, leading to tragic consequences. Societies in transition between traditional and modern form frequently experience the tragedy of over use when neither traditional nor modern forms of common control prevail. Similarly, resources for which access is difficult to restrict, such as on frontiers beyond the control of governments, in the open sea, and wildlife that crosses national boundaries, are frequently overexploited[65]. The absence or destruction of institutions regulating commons has led to the extinction of diverse species and the genetic impoverishment of many.

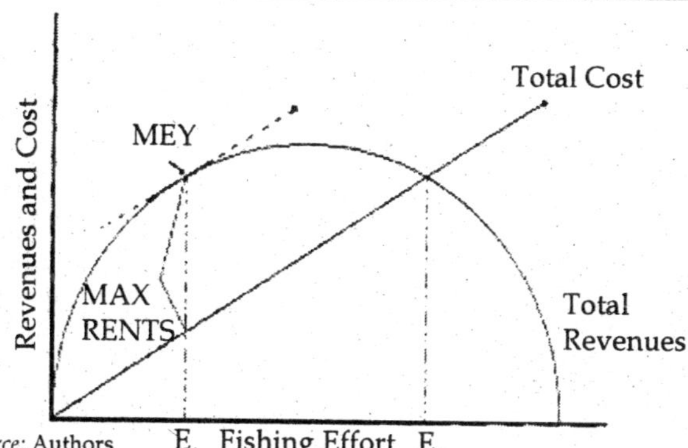

Source: Authors

Figure 7: Excessive Fishing Effort occurs in an Open-access Fishery because Existing Fishermen Expand their Effort and New Fishermen Enter the Fishery beyond Level E_1, the Point of Maximum Profit. Each Fisherman Continues to Make a Profit by Increased Fishing Up to Level E_2, where the Total Revenues Equal Total Costs. Further Fishing Beyond this Point is Economically Counterproductive because Costs Exceed Revenues

H. Scott Gordon[66] formulated the problem of open-access resources as shown in Figure 1.7. Imagine an open-access fishery with total costs and total revenues from fishing effort as shown. Profits or rents from the fishery are maximized at level of effort E_1 but with unrestricted access, people would put more effort into fishing until the level E_2 was reached where no rent would be earned from fishing and no one would consider additional fishing worth the effort since costs would now be greater than revenues. Since more fish are caught at greater levels of effort, overfishing is more likely to occur in an open-access fishery than in a fishery managed as a commons.

To the extent that biodiversity is manifested as different genetic traits, species, and ecosystems that cannot be owned by individuals and incorporated in market systems, we need common management institutions to conserve biodiversity for our descendants. At the end of the 20th century, international biodiversity agreements began to be formulated and implemented. In some cases, traditional common property institutions for the protection of biodiversity can be maintained in the face of modernization. In other cases, new institutions will be needed. Common property institutions may be communal, regional, national, or global. The health of institutions at all of these levels will be critical to conserving biological diversity and ecosystem integrity. For this reason, commons institutions are central to the work of many ecological economists[67]. Similarly, it is now well understood that the global climate–regulating system is a common resource in need of common management institutions. For centuries, industrializing nations have dumped carbon dioxide, a by-product of fossil fuel combustion, and other greenhouse gases into the atmosphere without regard for their impacts on the climate system as a whole. Commons institutions for the management of the global climate system are in the process of being agreed to and implemented.

While Garret Hardin as a biologist "discovered" a phenomenon long understood by economists, Hardin was able to convey the larger meaning of the phenomenon to a broad audience and awake natural scientists to the importance of institutions for environmental management. His article is still one of the most frequently found among the readings for environmental courses. Hardin, by crossing disciplines and demonstrating the significance to policy of economics and ecology used together, contributed to the rise of ecological economics.

Energetic and Systems

In the year 1971 two influential books were published by two authors who did not yet know of each other, one a noted ecologist and one a noted economist. The books were very different in style and in many other ways, but both books were about energy, entropy, power, systems, and society and both can be said to have made a major contribution to setting the stage for ecological economics. One was Howard T. Odum's *Environment, Power, and Society* and the other was Nicholas Georgescu-Roegen's *The Entropy Law and the Economic Process*.

At the time, relatively few people were interested in the overall importance of energy to people in modern economies. But the public's attention was soon galvanized in late 1973 by the Arab oil embargo and the agreement by the Organization of Petroleum Exporting Countries to significantly increase the price of oil. Subsequent further energy price increases during the Iran–Iraq War in the late 1970s and then a rapid decrease in the price of oil in the mid-1980s seriously perturbed both industrial and developing economies. In the process, the role of energy became a central theme in our understanding of economic systems and how we relate to the environment[68].

Nicholas Georgescu-Roegen (1906–1994) was born in Romania, trained in mathematical statistics in France, assumed academic and government positions in his native country, and fled to the United States after World War II to become an economist, working with Professor Joseph Schumpeter at Harvard. His contributions to the further mathematical refinement of standard neoclassical economics in the areas of utility and consumer choice, production theory, input–output analysis, and development economics were honored by his being designated a Distinguished Fellow of the American Economic Association. He is most noted, however, for his contributions in the area of entropy and economics, which still stir considerable controversial discussion among economists.

Georgescu-Roegen argued that all economic processes entail the use of energy and that the second law of thermodynamics, the entropy law, clearly indicates that the available energy in a closed system can only decline. Like others before him, he also noted the parallel between the degradation of the availability of energy and the degradation of the order of materials. Economic processes entail using relatively concentrated iron resources, for example, which are then further concentrated through the use of energy, but ultimately end up being dispersed as rust and waste, less concentrated than the original iron ore. Biodiversity degradation can also be thought of as a parallel problem. New technologies do not "create" new resources; they simply allow us to degrade energy, material order, and biological richness more rapidly.

Critics have argued that the entropy law is not important because the earth is not a closed system. It receives sunlight daily and is expected to continue to do so for another several billion years. Yet modern industrial economies are fueled by fossil hydrocarbons, accumulations of past solar energy which are clearly limited, and while current solar energy is of limited flow and of relatively low concentration.

Georgescu-Roegen's message is controversial, in part, because it conflicts with beliefs in progress that are still strongly held by economists. The message is also difficult to interpret because it does not inform us how quickly we need to make the transition from stock energy resources to flow energy resources. In this sense, we simply need to look at resource constraints as well as the ability of the global system to absorb carbon dioxide and other greenhouse gases; the entropy law itself does not provide additional information. The entropy law, however, does provide a strong bass beat to the sirens being sounded by scientists studying climate change, biodiversity loss, and soil degradation.

Nicholas Georgescu-Roegen not only motivated one of his students, Herman Daly, to address the long-term human predicament (discussed later), but also inspired many others to ponder the various ways the entropy law helps us understand irreversibility, systems and organization, and our options for the future[69].

The hourglass analogy can be extended by considering the sand in the upper chamber to be the stock of energy in the sun. Solar energy arrives to earth as a flow whose amount is governed by the constricted middle of the hourglass that limits the rate at which sand falls. Suppose that in ancient geologic ages some of the falling sand had gotten stuck against the inner surface of the bottom chamber, but at the top of the bottom chamber, before it had fallen all the way. This becomes a terrestrial dowry of low entropy, a stock that we can use up at a rate of our own choosing. We use it by drilling holes in it through which the trapped sand can fall to the bottom of the lower chamber. This terrestrial source of low entropy can be used at a rate of our own choosing, unlike the sun whose energy arrives at a fixed flow rate—we cannot "mine" the sun to use tomorrow's sunlight today, but we can mine terrestrial deposits and in a sense use up tomorrow's petroleum today.

There is thus an important asymmetry between our two sources of low entropy. The solar source is stock abundant, but flow limited. The terrestrial source is stock limited, but flow abundant (temporarily). Peasant societies lived off the solar flow; industrial societies have come to depend on enormous supplements from the unsustainable terrestrial stocks.

Reversing this dependence will be an enormous evolutionary shift. *Georgescu-Roegen* argued that evolution has in the past consisted of slow adaptations of our end somatic organs (heart, lungs, etc.), which run on solar energy. Now evolution has shifted to rapid adaptations of our exosomatic organs (cars, airplanes, etc.) that depend on terrestrial low entropy. The uneven ownership of exosomatic organs and the terrestrial low entropy from which they are made, compared to the egalitarian distribution of ownership of end somatic capital, was for Georgescu-Roegen the root of social conflict in industrial societies.

Howard T. Odum was born in Durham, North Carolina in 1924, the son of Howard W. Odum, a noted sociologist. H.T. Odum was a meteorologist in the American tropics during World War II, received an A.B. in Zoology from the University of North Carolina in 1947, and a Ph.D. from Yale University in 1951, under ecologist G. Evelyn Hutchinson. He has been concerned with material cycles and energy flow in ecosystems and he produced one of the first energy flow descriptions of a complete ecosystem in his famous study of Silver Springs, Florida[70]. He also contributed heavily to his brother Eugene P. Odum's influential textbook, *Fundamentals of Ecology*, first published in 1953[71]. This textbook was the standard in ecology for several decades and helped to establish several important ecological concepts, both in the profession and in the public consciousness. In particular, the concept of the ecosystem was fully developed and was quantified using units of energy and material flows.

In addition to his father and Hutchinson, H. T. Odum was influenced in his thinking by *Lotka* and *von Bertalanffy*, and he was concerned with many of the same problems as *Georgescu-Roegen*. His approach was broader than Georgescu-Roegen's, however, and went beyond economics and thermodynamics to include systems in general, from simple physical and chemical systems to biological and ecological systems to economic and social systems. In *Environment, Power, and Society* he laid out a comprehensive integration of systems with energy flow used as the integrating factor. He even developed his own symbolic language (similar in intent and use to Forrester's systems dynamics symbols) to help describe and model the common features of systems. This language was both an indispensable aid to the initiated practitioner in helping to understand systems concepts and a barrier to outsiders gaining access to these same concepts.

Odum's work on energy flow through systems and dynamic modeling of systems spawned, or at least paralleled and encouraged, an immense amount of work by his students and others ranging from input-output studies of energy and material flow in ecological and economic systems[72] to dynamic simulation models of whole ecosystems and integrated ecological economic systems[73]. Probably the most concise and complete treatment of the application of many of H. T. Odum's ideas to ecological economics is the 1986 book by C. A. S. Hall,

C. Cleveland, and R. Kaufmann titled *Energy and Resource Quality: The Ecology of the Economic Process.*

Both E. P. and H. T. Odum's work has inspired a whole generation of ecologists to study ecology as a systems science and to link it with economics and other disciplines. While many (if not most) of H. T. Odum's ideas were controversial, they have spawned discussion of what we think are the right questions: How do systems work? How do they evolve and change? How do human systems and ecosystems interact over time? How can we develop an interdisciplinary understanding of systems? What patterns of human development are sustainable? All of these questions were being asked by H. T. and E. P. Odum in the 1950s, 1960s, and 1970s and are among the core questions of ecological economics today.

Spaceship Earth and Steady-State Economics

Kenneth Boulding's classic "The Economics of the Coming Spaceship Earth"[74] set the stage for ecological economics with its description of the transition from the "frontier economics" of the past, where growth in human welfare implied growth in material consumption, to the "spaceship economics" of the future, where growth in welfare can no longer be fueled by growth in material consumption. This fundamental difference in vision and worldview was elaborated further by Daly[75] in recasting economics as a life science—akin to biology and especially ecology, rather than a physical science like chemistry or physics. The importance of this shift in "pre-analytic vision"[76] cannot be overemphasized. It implies a fundamental change in the perception of the problems of resource allocation and how they should be addressed. More particularly, it implies that the focus of analysis should be shifted from marketed resources in the economic system to the biophysical basis of interdependent ecological and economic systems[77].

Daly further elaborated on this theme with his work on "steady state economics"[78] which worked out the implications of acknowledging that the Earth is materially finite and non-growing, and that the economy is a subset of this finite global system. Thus the economy cannot grow forever (at least in a material sense) and ultimately some sort of sustainable steady state is desired. This steady state is not necessarily absolutely stable and unchanging. Like in ecosystems, things in a steady-state economy are changing constantly in both periodic and a periodic ways. The key point is that these changes are bounded and there is no long-term trend in the system. Daly's work in steady-state economics can be seen as one of the direct antecedents of ecological economics.

Adaptive Environmental Management

In the late 1970s, Canadian ecologist C. S. Holling became director of the International Institute for Applied Systems Analysis (IIASA). His earlier work on spruce budworm outbreaks in northern boreal forests had led him to a complex and dynamic view of ecosystems that eventually took over from the more "equilibrium" concepts that had held sway earlier. He was also concerned with how humans interacted with ecosystems and why their attempts at "management" failed so miserably (the spruce budworm/boreal forest was only one example). This all led to a groundbreaking book published in 1978 titled *Adaptive Environmental Assessment and Management*[79].

Adaptive environmental management redraws conventional boundaries by integrating science and management. Holling realized that laboratory and controlled field experiments on parts of ecological systems could not be aggregated to an understanding of the whole. At best, we experiment when we manage ecosystems. Of course, we only learn from experiments if we monitor them well, undertake a fair number of them, and are prepared to learn from them. Thus, environmental management agencies, rather than looking to science to determine for them what good management practice is, must consciously become a part of the experimentation and learning process. Furthermore, Holling argued, ecosystems do not have a single equilibrium state that they prefer. Rather, they have multiple equilibriums and evolve over time as well. This being the case, the scientists and agencies working with ecosystems must constantly adapt their management experiments to understand a changing system[80]. This means that models and policies based on them are not taken as the ultimate answers, but rather as guiding an adaptive experimentation process within the regional system. More emphasis is placed on monitoring and feedback to check and improve the model rather than using the model to obfuscate and defend a policy that is not corresponding to reality.

Adaptive environmental management has proved to be an effective approach to understanding and managing complex, changing systems with large uncertainties. While this approach emerged out of ecology and its application to management, it has tremendous implications for social organization. Environmental managers, people in associated communities, and those in the broader public who are especially interested in environmental issues should question, assist in the monitoring, and share in the learning. This is a very different vision than that of objective scientists determining the truth about environmental systems, managers applying it, and the people being passive beneficiaries. The approach acknowledges the co-evolutionary nature of ecological and economic systems (as discussed below) and is a key concept in ecological economics.

Co-evolution of Ecological and Economic Systems

One of the strongest barriers to the union of economics and ecology has been the presumption that ecological and economic systems are separable and do not need to be understood together. Economists think of economic systems as separate from nature, while the vast majority of natural scientists think of natural systems as apart from people. Indeed, social scientists generally have thought that all social phenomena are culturally determined. When natural scientists do consider social phenomena, they "naturally" look to natural law to explain it. And so a "line in the sand" is frequently found between cultural and environmental determinists with economists among the cultural determinists and ecologists among the environmental determinists. As we have noted, this line reflects historic Western beliefs about systems and about science that had become a part of our problem, an explanation for the un-sustainability of modern societies.

Evolutionary ecologists Paul Ehrlich and Peter Raven first alerted the scientific community to the importance of co-evolution between species[81]. The niche to which species evolve has most frequently been described as a fixed, physical niche. With the characteristics of the niche fixed, evolution acquires a direction, and evolutionary stories usually entail the species progressively fitting the characteristics better and better. Hence evolutionary stories are frequently stories of progress, with human evolution providing the ultimate story of progress. Co-evolution simply acknowledges that the characteristics of a species' niche at any one time are predominantly other species and their characteristics. Hence, the characteristics of any one species are selected in the context of the characteristics of other species and vice versa; species coevolves. Even as evolutionary direction and the analog to Western beliefs in progress are lost, co-evolution helps explain why species fit together into ecosystems while at the same time species and ecosystems continue to change.

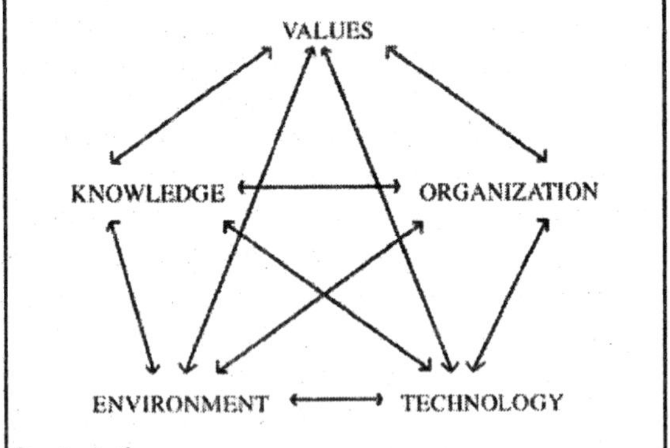

Source: Authors

Figure 8: The Coevolutionary Development Process

Norgaard[82] illustrates how understanding the co-evolutionary process can help us to understand how natural and social systems interconnect and change. From this, he suggests new directions for social organization to enhance environmental sustainability, social justice, and human dignity. Consider development as a process of co-evolution between knowledge, values, organization, technology, and the environment (Figure 1.8). Each of these subsystems is related to each of the others, yet each is also changing and affecting change in the others through selection. Deliberate innovations, chance discoveries, and random changes occur in each subsystem that affect, through natural selection, the distribution and qualities of components in each of the other subsystems. Whether new components prove fit depends on the characteristics of each of the subsystems at the time. With each subsystem putting selective pressure on each of the others, they co-evolve in a manner whereby each reflects the other. Thus everything is coupled, yet everything is changing.

Environmental subsystems are treated symmetrically with the subsystems of values, knowledge, social organization, and technology in this co-evolutionary explanation of development. New technologies, for example, exert new selective pressures on species, while newly evolved characteristics of species, in turn, select for different technologies. Similarly, transformations in the biosphere select for new ways of understanding the biosphere. For example, the use of pesticides induces resistance and secondary pest resurgence, selecting both for new pesticides and for more systematic ways of thinking about pest control. Pests, pesticides, pesticide production, pesticide institutions and policy, how we understand pest control, and how we value chemicals in the environment demonstrate an incredibly tight and rapid co-evolution in the second half of this century. In the short run, people can be thought of as interacting with the environment in response to market signals or their absence. The co-evolutionary model, however, incorporates longer-term evolutionary feedbacks. To emphasize co-evolutionary processes is not to deny that people directly intervene in and change the characteristics of environments. The co-evolutionary perspective puts its emphasis on the chain of events thereafter, and how different interventions alter the selective pressure and hence the relative dominance of environmental traits which, in turn, select for values, knowledge, organization, and technology and hence subsequent interventions in the environment.

While the co-evolutionary perspective treats changes in the various subsystems symmetrically, let us use this model to address technology in particular. People have interacted with their environments over millennia in diverse ways, many of them sustainable over very long periods, many not. Some traditional agricultural technologies, at the intensities historically employed, probably increased biological diversity. There is general evidence that traditional technologies, again at the level employed, included biodiversity-conserving strategies as a part of the process of farming. Technology today, however, is perceived as a leading culprit in the process of biodiversity loss. Modern agricultural technologies override nature, but do so only locally and temporarily. They do not "control" nature. Pesticides kill some pests, solving the immediate threat to crops. But the vacant niche left by the pest is soon filled by a second species of pest (or the original pests evolve resistance), pesticides drift to interfere with the agricultural practices of other farmers, and pesticides and their by-products accumulate in soil and groundwater aquifers to plague production and human health for years to come. Each farmer strives to control nature but creates new problems beyond his or her farm and in subsequent seasons for others. Because of all the new problems created beyond the individual farm in space and time, pre-harvest crop losses due to pests since World War II have remained around 35% while pesticide use has increased dramatically.

New technologies that work with natural processes rather than override them are sorely needed. During the past two centuries, technologies have largely descended from physics, chemistry, and, at best, microbiology. Ecologists and evolutionary biologists were never given the opportunity to systemically review such technologies, nor is it clear that our ecological and evolutionary understanding are sufficient to review them adequately now. A few agricultural technologies, such as the control of pests in agriculture through the use of other biological, have descended from ecological thinking. But research and technological development in biological control was nearly eliminated with the introduction of DDT in agriculture after World War II. Research on and development of agricultural technologies requiring fewer energy and material inputs eventually received considerable support in industrial countries after the rise in energy prices during the 1970s and the farm financial crises in the United States during the early 1980s. Support for agro-ecology, for technologies based on the management of complementarities between multiple species including soil organisms, however, is still minimal. Learning how to use renewable energy sources will be long and difficult since most of our knowledge has developed to capture the potential of fossil energy. Our universities and other research institutions are still structured around disciplinary rather than systemic thinking, and public understanding of the shortcomings of current technologies and possibilities for ecologically based technologies is weak. Scientists and technologists reproduce themselves and their institutions through direct control and education; hence science and technology sometimes respond slowly to changes in the social awareness of environmental problems.

From the co-evolutionary perspective, we can see more clearly how economies have transformed from coevolving with their ecosystems to coevolving around the combustion of fossil hydrocarbons. In this transformation, people have been freed from the environmental feedbacks on their economic activities that they experienced relatively quickly as individuals and communities. The feedbacks that remain, however, occur over longer periods and greater distances and are experienced collectively, even globally, by many people's making them more difficult to perceive and counteract[83]. By tapping into fossil hydrocarbons, Western societies freed themselves, at least for the short to medium term, from many of the complexities of interacting with environmental systems. Co-evolution occurred around fossil hydrocarbons. Tractors replaced animal power, fertilizers replaced the complexities of inter-planting crops that were good hosts of nitrogen-fixing bacteria with those which were not, and pesticides replaced the biological controls provided by more complex agro ecosystems. Furthermore, inexpensive energy meant crops could be stored for longer periods and transported over greater distances. Social organization coevolved around these new possibilities very quickly. Each of these accomplishments was based on the partial understanding of separate sciences and separate technologies. At least in the short run and "on the farm," separate adjustments of the parts seemed to fit into a coherent, stable whole. Agriculture transformed from an agro ecosystem culture of relatively self-sufficient communities to an agro industrial culture of many separate, distant actors linked by global markets. The massive changes in technology and organization gave people the sense of having control over nature and being able to consciously design their future while in fact problems were merely being shifted beyond the farm and onto future generations.

This co-evolutionary explanation of the un-sustainability of modern societies then is simply that development based on fossil hydrocarbons allowed individuals to control their immediate environments for the short run while shifting environmental impacts, in ways that have proven difficult to comprehend, to broader and broader publics (ultimately to the entire global polity) and on to future generations. These more distant impacts can select on our social organization as we realize their long-term and global implications and choose to respond in advance, or they can select directly as they are experienced in the future. Working with these collective, longer term, and more uncertain interrelationships is at least as challenging as environmental management had been historically. People's confidence in the sustainability of development is directly proportional to their confidence in our ability to address these new challenges.

The co-evolutionary perspective helps us see that the problem of humans interacting with their environment is not simply a matter of establishing market incentives or appropriate rules about the use of property. Our values, knowledge, and social organization have coevolved around fossil hydrocarbons. Our fossil fuel-driven economy has not simply transformed the environment, it has selected for individualist, materialist values; favored the development of reductionist understanding at the expense of systemic understanding; and preferred a bureaucratic, centralized form of control that works better for steady-state industrial management than for the varied, surprising dynamics of ecosystem management. And the co-evolutionary framing highlights how our abilities to perceive and resolve environmental problems within the dominant modes of valuing, thinking, and organizing are severely constrained.

The co-evolutionary framework elaborated by Norgaard complements the efforts of cultural ecologists in anthropology[84]. It has instigated new developments in thought among political economists[85], and is beginning to inspire ecological economics[86].

The Role of Neoclassical Economics in Environmental Economics

After all of this description of alternative paradigms, it is important to reiterate that ecological economics is methodologically pluralistic and accepts the framework of analysis of neoclassical economics along with other frameworks. Indeed, neoclassical market analysis is still an important pattern of thinking within ecological economics. There are, however, differences between patterns of thinking and how the patterns are used with particular assumptions. We have already emphasized that most neoclassical economists assume that technological advance will outpace resource scarcity over the long run and that ecological services can also be replaced by new technologies. Ecological economists, on the other hand, assume that resource and ecological limits are critically important and are much less confident that technological advances will arise in response to higher prices generated by scarcities. This difference in worldview, however, does not prevent neoclassical and ecological economists from sharing the same pattern of reasoning.

There is another way in which neoclassical and ecological economists differ even while using the same patterns of thinking. As noted in the previous chapter, neoclassical economists have chosen to ignore how the initial distribution of rights to resources affects how markets subsequently allocate resources between end products and consumers. They have chosen to ignore this relationship since World War II largely for two reasons. First, Karl Marx focused on questions of the distribution of power, and the "other" side of the Cold War, the former USSR, China, India and other nations, invoked Marx's name to rationalize their approach to social relations and development. In the West, especially the U.S. during the 1950s, questioning the distribution of power was effectively an act of disloyalty. But neoclassical economists also had a second rationale for ignoring equity in the initial distribution of rights to resources. Growing economies could avoid the political difficulties of redistribution by making everyone better off. This became an important argument for increasing the rate of economic growth even in the countries that were already rich.

Concern over sustainability has led to new concerns with equity in an era when Cold War politics have become history. Clearly, sustainability is a matter of transferring assets to future generations. This is a question of equity between generations. To understand sustainability using neoclassical economic reasoning, the distribution of resources between generations, or intergenerational equity, must be central. But sustainability is not simply a matter of intergenerational equity. In a world of very rich and very poor, asset transfer between generations is likely to be at less than a sustainable level. The very rich can be so rich that they do not worry about their progeny having enough. The very poor, on the other hand, can be so poor that each generation has to exploit resources and degrade environmental systems merely to subsist. For many ecological economists, these extremes characterize the world we live in and account for much of the un-sustainability. The extremes internationally between rich and poor nations also make it very difficult to reach international understandings on managing the global commons. So sustainability is also a matter of intra-generational and international equity. The conventional stance of neoclassical economists remains that economic growth will provide the conditions to resolve these inequities. But there have been two generations of economic growth since the international development programs were established after World War II, and inequality has increased. Thus the conventional stance is wearing a little thin and is increasingly questioned.

There is yet a third reason why neoclassical economists historically have not included distribution in their arguments. Once distribution is taken into consideration, there are many possible efficient market allocations depending on how rights to resources are distributed between people. Since World War II, however, economists have undertaken analyses of the costs and benefits of alternative public projects and other public decisions so as to advise legislatures and public agencies as to which project or decision is best. The legislatures and agencies have asked them for "the" answer assuming the current distribution of rights to resources, not an array of answers depending on alternative distributions of rights to resources. Thus the tradition of not considering equity is firmly rooted in public practice.

The situation, however, is yet more complicated. Neoclassical economics cannot determine whether one distribution of resources between people is better than another. Moral criteria must be invoked and the decision must be made politically. But political decision making is more typically driven by the existing distribution of power than by moral discourse. To a large extent, economists were asked to undertake cost-benefit analysis in order to offset the politics of power. Economists see themselves as acting more in the public interest than the politicians responding to power and pressure groups. Yet, economists have been making their recommendations based on the existing distribution of power as well. So, it is difficult to see how things are going to change. If sustainability requires intergenerational and intra-generational redistribution, there will have to be a serious moral discourse and improvements in democratic politics to achieve sustainability. Paralleling this transition, economists will have to learn how to inform democratic debate with a working sense of trade-offs between options rather than undertaking cost-benefit analyses on behalf of the public.

The realization that economics must work with a more democratic politics complements another research style emerging within ecological economics. Acknowledging that economists need to understand ecology and vice versa further opens the door to asking whether anyone can possibly be excluded from sharing in the search for sustainability. Surely, to the extent that social and ecological systems differ from place to place, local, experiential knowledge will be essential to implementing specific solutions. For this reason, some ecological economists are beginning to experiment with participatory research methods that incorporate lay people with experiential knowledge[87].

Ecological economics, as a new assemblage of concerned economists and ecologists, is not bound by the historic traditions of neoclassical economics. It uses the framework of neoclassical economics but is not constrained to use only that framework, nor is it constrained by the worldviews, politics, or cultures of economists in the past.

Critical Connections

It is difficult to determine where ecological economics ends and other approaches to understanding start. Ecological economists have reached out to other patterns of thinking and pursued a broad range of questions. And people from many fields have reached toward ecological economics. In the future, these connections may prove the most important of all, but for now, it is appropriate to describe them as a little less central to the origins of ecological economists.

Increased Efficiency and Dematerialization

Entrepreneurs and consumers have always had an incentive to get more from less. At the same time, when an individual uses less, he or she typically reaps only a portion of the benefits because of the numerous ways we are connected through ecosystems. Furthermore, choosing to use less must frequently be done collectively through developing new technologies, changing infrastructure such as that which supports automobile use over public transit, and adjusting the rules of the game for all. One response to the energy crises of the 1970s was to invest in the development of energy-efficient technologies, label the efficiency of electric appliances, mandate increased fuel efficiency for automobiles, and encourage public utilities to help their customers use less electricity through home insulation. One individual, Amory Lovins, has been especially effective in arguing how the United States could substantially change its course and avoid the environmental consequences of fossil fuel dependence and the risks of nuclear technology by shifting dramatically toward energy efficiency and renewable energy sources[88].

A group of ecological economists are documenting the prospects for "dematerialization" at the Wuppertal Institute for Climate, Environment, and Energy in Germany[89]. Their arguments parallel those of Lovins while also picking up on Herman Daly's argument that we need to stabilize the rate of material throughput in the economy. They have calculated the material input per unit of service (or MIPS) for numerous consumption goods. Material flows consist of flows of consumer goods and materials such as ores, soil, sand, and gravel, but do not include water and air which had to be moved to produce the consumer goods. Materials flow amount to about 32 million tons per capita per year in Germany or about 1.2 kg per DM (1.75 lbs. per dollar) spent. But some rather insignificant consumer choices result in significant material flows relative to readily available alternatives, and in other cases flows could be reduced by increases in the efficiency with which materials are used or by increasing the longevity of the consumer product. Researchers at Wuppertal think material flows can be reduced by as much as a factor of 10. All of this may seem remote from an ecological management perspective, but the counterargument is that we are so far from a level of flow consistent with natural fluxes where management is even possible that the first step is massive reduction in human-induced material flows.

Ecosystem Health

To a considerable extent to date, while whole ecosystems have been protected, only individual species have been managed. Models have been derived from principles of population biology that suggest how, for example, Douglas fir trees or salmon can be harvested sustainably. But trees and the salmon do not thrive apart from other species and a myriad of other factors that affect ecosystem behavior. For this reason, efforts to manage individual species using these models have proven amazingly ineffective[90]. In light of both broader concerns with maintaining ecosystems per se and the failures of individual species models, a group of ecologists and social scientists joined together in the early 1990s to study and promote the concept of ecosystem health[91] and launched the journal *Ecosystem Health* in 1995. This group includes many participants from the field of ecological economics and, like ecological economics, is trans-disciplinary. "Health," the organizing metaphor, reminds us that for ecosystems, like people, "an ounce of prevention is worth a pound of cure." But it is more than a metaphor once we get serious about defining its meaning, try to agree to preferred states of ecosystems, and set out to develop management criteria across diverse ecosystems in anticipation of multiple possible disturbances[92]. Other ecologists are using the term "ecosystem integrity" to make new bridges between biology and policy. "Conservation biology" emerged as a field during the 1980s among biologists who were not content to simply study the decline of biodiversity and became intent on saving species from extinction. These multiple efforts include scientists who participate in ecological economics as well. They are all examples of groups of scientists who are using science effectively to new ends by shedding the old assumptions about how knowledge fits together and affects progress.

Environmental Epistemology

The field of philosophy that studies how we think we can learn "truth" is known as epistemology. Clearly, if *Homo sapiens* are so special because the species is smarter than other animals, then the special problems we have gotten ourselves into relative to other animals must in some sense also be related to how we think. And if we believe that science has indeed driven the technological, and even to some extent the institutional, changes that are behind development, then how we know things scientifically must also be partly responsible for the environmental consequences of development. In this sense, the environmental crises of the latter half of the 20th century are challenging the underlying premises of the dominant forms of Western science. To argue that separating economics from ecology is a mistake, a dominant premise of ecological economics, is to make an epistemological statement. Realizing this, several ecological economists have explored the history and philosophy of science to directly understand how environmental crises have developed[93]. One of the dominant premises of Western science, for example, has been the idea that nature behaves in a predictable manner according to universal principles that once discovered are applicable everywhere. If nature, however, is evolving and, furthermore, has evolved differently in different places, then the expectation that there can be a "physics" of nature can lead people to make a good number of mistakes. If it is such basic premises that are at the root of our crises, then it would be most effective to tackle them directly before trying to create new ways of understanding.

Political Ecology

As noted in the previous chapter, Karl Marx has had an important influence on the social sciences. Besides focusing our attention on power and inequity, Marx has helped us keep our attention on history. The environmental crises of the latter half of the 20th century have stimulated new critiques of capitalism and development by Marxist anthropologists, economists, historians, and sociologists. From these critiques, a new field known as political ecology has emerged[94]. Again, the overlap of participants between political ecology and ecological economics is strong[95]. While most of the arguments with respect to equity made in ecological economics are formally neoclassical[96], the concern with equity complements research in the area of political ecology on power, poverty, and environmental transformation using Marxian frames of analysis. In ecological economics, we are beginning to see the two historically separate strands of economic thought used to inform each other[97].

Conclusions

Environmental economics is evolving through the interaction of diverse patterns of thinking with multiple disciplinary roots. The founding practitioners of ecological economics have combined understandings from multiple fields of thought, questioned historical assumptions, and risked being ostracized by their disciplinary peers. The opportunity for many more combinations and questioning of assumptions waits whoever would like to join the field. Hopefully, disciplinary pressures will ease.

This introduction to the field of ecological economics from this point pursues one dominant approach to the field. While ecological economists are certainly diverse, the largest "cluster" works from the initial premise that the earth has a limited capacity for sustainably supporting people and their artifacts determined by combinations of resource limits and ecological thresholds. To keep the economy operating sustainably within these limits, specific environmental policies need to be established. And so first we document the "pre-analytic vision" of this strain of ecological economics and then we elaborate on potential existing and new institutions for achieving it.

References

1. Costanza, R., H.E. Daly, and J.A. Bartholomew (1991), Goals, Agenda, and Policy Recommendations for Ecological Economics. In R. Costanza (ed.), *Ecological Economics: The Science and*

Management of Sustainability, pp. 1–20. New York: Columbia University Press.

2. Knight, F.H. (1956), Statistics and Dynamics: Some Queries regarding the Mechanical Analogy in Economics. In *On the History and Method of Economics*. Chicago: University of Chicago Press.

3. Canterbury, E.R. (1987), *The Making of Economics* (3rd ed.). Belmont, CA: Wadsworth.

   —Nelson, R.H. 1991. *Reaching for Heaven on Earth: The Theological Meaning of Economics*. Savage, MD: Rowman and Littlefield.

4. Page, T. (1995), Harmony and Pathology. *Ecological Economics* 15:141–144.

5. Simon, J.L. (1981), *The Ultimate Resource*. Princeton: Princeton University Press.

6. Ehrenfeld, D. (1978), *The Arrogance of Humanism*. Oxford: Oxford University Press.

   —Meffe, G.K. (1992), Techno-arrogance and Halfway Technologies: Salmon Hatcheries on the Pacific Coast of North America. *Conservation Biology* 6(3):350–354.

7. Lux, K. (1990), *Adam Smith's Mistake: How a Moral Philosopher Invented Economics and Ended Morality*. Boston: Shambhala.

8. Bellah, R.N., R. Madsen, W.M. Sullivan, A. Swidler, and S.M. Tipton (1991), *The Good Society*. New York: Alfred A. Knopf.—Daly, H.E., and J. Cobb. 1989. *For the Common Good: Redirecting the Economy Towards Community, the Environment, and a Sustainable Future*. Boston: Beacon Press.—Etzioni, A. 1993. *The Spirit of Community: The Reinvention of American Society*. New York: Simon and Schuster.

   —Norgaard, R.B. (1994), *Development Betrayed: The End of Progress and a Coevolutionary Revisioning of the Future*. London: Routledge.

9. Malthus, T. 1963 [1798], *Principles of Population*. Homewood, IL: Richard D. Irwin.

10. Ricardo, D. (1926), *Principles of Political Economy and Taxation*. London: Everyman.

11. Odum, H.T. (1971), *Environment, Power and Society*. New York: John Wiley.

    —Georgescu-Roegen, N. (1971), *The Entropy Law and the Economic Process*. Cambridge, MA: Harvard University Press.—Hannon, B. 1973. The Structure of Ecosystems. *Journal of Theoretical Biology*

41:535–546. —Costanza, R. 1980. Embodied energy and economic valuation. *Science* 210:1219–1224.

12. See Norgaard, R.B. (1994), *Development Betrayed: The End of Progress and a Coevolutionary Revisioning of the Future*. London: Routledge, pp. 213–216 for a history of concern motivated by the broader implications of the second law of thermodynamics.

13. Arthur, W.B. (1988), Self-reinforcing Mechanisms in Economics. In P. W. Anderson, K. J. Arrow, and D. Pines (eds.), *The Economy as an Evolving Complex System*, pp. 9-31. Redwood City, CA: Addison Wesley. —Boulding, K. E. 1981. *Evolutionary economics*. Beverly Hills, CA: Sage.—Lindgren, K. 1991. Evolutionary phenomena in simple dynamics. In C. G. Langton, C. Taylor, J. D. Farmer, and S. Rasmussen, *Artificial life, SFI studies in the sciences of complexity*, Vol. X, pp. 295–312. Redwood City, CA: Addison-Wesley.

—Maxwell, T. and R. Costanza (1993). An Approach To modeling the Dynamics of Evolutionary Self Organization. *Ecological Modeling* 69:149–161.

14. Arthur, W.B. (1988), Self-reinforcing Mechanisms in Economics. In P.W. Anderson, K. J. Arrow, and D. Pines (eds.), *The economy as an evolving complex system*, pp. 9–31. Redwood City, CA: Addison Wesley.

15. Günther, F., and C. Folke (1993), Characteristics of Nested Living Systems. *Journal of Biological Systems* 1(3): 257-274. —Kay, J. J. 1991. A nonequilibrium thermodynamic framework for discussing ecosystem integrity. *Environmental Management* 15:483–495.

16. Day, R.H. (1989), Dynamical Systems, Adaptation and Economic Evolution. MRG Working Paper No. M8908, University of Southern California. —Day, R. H., and T. Groves (eds.). 1975. *Adaptive economic models*. New York: Academic Press. —England, R. W. (ed.). 1994. *Evolutionary concepts in contemporary economics*. Ann Arbor, MI: University of Michigan Press. —Nelson, R. R. and S. Winter. 1974. Neoclassical vs. evolutionary theories of economic growth: Critique and prospectus. *Economic Journal* 84:886–905.

17. Vitousek, P.M. et al. (1986), Human Appropriation of the Products of Photosynthesis. *BioScience* 34(6):368–373.

18. Arrow, K. (1962), The Economic Implications of Learning by Doing. *Review of Economic Studies* 29:155–173.

19. Kaitala, V. and M. Pohjola (1988), Optimal Recovery of a Shared Resource Stock: A Differential game Model with Efficient Memory equilibrium. *Natural Resource Modeling* 3:91–119.

20. Folke, C. (1991), Socioeconomic Dependence on the Life-Supporting Environment. In C. Folke and T. Kåberger (eds.), *Linking the natural environment and the economy: Essays from the Eco-Eco group*, pp. 77–94. Dordrecht, the Netherlands: Kluwer Academic Publishers.

21 Costanza, R. (1987), Social Traps and Environmental Policy. *BioScience* 37:407–412.

22. Daly, H.E. (1977), *Steady State Economics*. San Francisco: W. H. Freeman.

23. Blaikie, P. and H. Brookfield (1987), *Land Degradation and Society*. London: Metheun.

– Redclift, M. (1984), *Development and the Environmental Crisis: Red or Green Alternatives*. London: Metheun.

24. Bator, F. (1957), The Simple Analytics of Welfare Maximization. *American Economic Review* 47:22–59.

25. Howarth, R.B. and R.B. Norgaard (1992), Environmental Valuation under Sustainable Development. *American Economic Review* 82:473–477.

26. Allee, W.C., A. E. Emerson, O. Park, T. Park, and K. P. Schmidt (1949), *Principles of Animal Ecology*. Philadelphia: Saunders.

27. Goodland, R. (1975), The Tropical Origin of Ecology. *Oikos* 26:240–245.

28. Translated in Allee, W. C., A. E. Emerson, O. Park, T. Park, and K.P. Schmidt (1949), *Principles of Animal Ecology*. Philadelphia: Saunders.

29. Andrewartha, H.G. and L.C. Birch (1954), *The Distribution and Abundance of Animals*. Chicago: University of Chicago Press.

30. Odum, E.P. (1953), *Fundamentals of Ecology* (1st ed.). Philadelphia: Saunders.

31. McIntosh, R.P. (1985), *The Background of Ecology: Concept and Theory*. Cambridge: Cambridge University Press.

32. Lotka, A.J. 1956 [1925], *Elements of Mathematical Biology*. New York: Dover.

33. Kingsland, S.E. (1985), *Modeling Nature: Episodes in the History of Population Ecology*. Chicago: Chicago University Press.

34. Hanemann, M. (1988), Economics and the Preservation of Biodiversity. In E. O. Wilson (ed.), *Biodiversity*, pp. 193–199. Washington, DC: National Academy Press. –McNeely, J. A. 1988. *Economics and biological diversity: Developing and using economic incentives to conserve biological resources*. Gland, Switzerland: International Union for the Conservation of Nature and Natural Resources. –Randall, Alan. 1988. What mainstream economists have to say about the value of biodiversity. In E. O. Wilson (ed.), *Biodiversity*, pp. 217–223. Washington, DC: National Academy Press.

35. Sagoff, M. (1988), *The Economy of the Earth*. Cambridge: Cambridge University Press.

36. Mitchell, R.C. and R.T. Carson (1989), *Using Surveys to Value Public Goods: The Contingent Valuation Method*. Washington, DC: Resources for the Future.

37. Hotelling, H. (1931), The Economics of Exhaustible Resources. *Journal of Political Economy* 39:137–175.

38. Marglin, S.A. (1963), The Social Rate of Discount and the Optimal Rate of Investment. *Quarterly Journal of Economics* 77:95–112.

39. Coats, A.W. (1993), *The Sociology and Professionalization of Economics*. New York: Routledge.

40. Coats, A.W. (1993), *The Sociology and Professionalization of Economics*. New York: Routledge, p. 27.

41. Martinez-Alier, J. (1987), *Ecological Economics: Energy, Environment, and Society*. Cambridge, MA: Blackwell.

42. Jansson, A.-M., M. Hammer, C. Folke, and R. Costanza (eds.). (1994), *Investing in Natural Capital: The Ecological Economics Approach to Sustainability*. Washington, DC: Island Press.

    –Costanza, R. and H.E. Daly (eds.). (1987), Ecological Economics. *Ecological Modeling* [Special Issues] 38(1) and (2).

43. Hueting, R. (1980), *New Scarcity and Economic Growth*. Amsterdam: North Holland.

44. Ahmad, Y.J., S. El Serafy, and E. Lutz (1989), *Environmental Accounting for Sustainable Development*. A UNEP-World Bank Symposium. Washington, DC: The World Bank.

45. Costanza, R. (ed.). (1991), *Ecological Economics: The Science and Management of Sustainability*. New York: Columbia Press. —May, P. H. (ed.). 1995. *Economia ecologica: Applicações no Brasil*. Rio de Janeiro: Editora Campus. —Peet, J. 1992. *Energy and the ecological economics of sustainability*. Washington, DC: Island Press.

46. Norgaard, R.B. (1989), The Case for Methodological Pluralism. *Ecological Economics* 1:37–57.

47. Ayres, R.U. (1978), *Resources, Environment, and Economics: Applications of the Materials/Energy Balance Principle*. New York: John Wiley and Sons.

—Costanza, R. and R. A. Herendeen (1984), Embodied Energy and Economic Value in the United States Economy: 1963, 1967, and 1972. *Resources and Energy* 6:129–161.

—Hall, C.A. S., C.J. Cleveland, and R.Kaufman (1986), *Energy and Resource Quality: The Ecology of the Economic Process*. New York: John Wiley and Sons.

48. Weitzman, M. (1995), Diversity Functions. In C. Perrings, K. Goran-Maler, C. Folke, C. S. Holling, and B.-O. Jansson (eds.), *Biodiversity Loss: Economic and Ecological Issues*. Cambridge: Cambridge University Press.

49. Norgaard, R.B. (1981), Sociosystem and Ecosystem Coevolution in the Amazon. *Journal of Environmental Economics and Management* 8:238–254.

50. Boulding, K.E. (1978), *Ecodynamics: A New Theory of Societal Evolution*. Beverly Hills, CA: Sage Publications. —Boulding, K. E. 1985. *The world as a total system*. Beverly Hills, CA: Sage Publications.

51. Allen, T.F.H. and T.B. Starr (1982), *Hierarchy: Perspectives for Ecological Complexity*. Chicago: University of Chicago Press.—O'Neill, R. V., D. L. DeAngelis, J. B. Waide, and T. F. H. Allen. 1986. *A Hierarchical Concept of Ecosystems*. Princeton, NJ: Princeton University Press.

52. Von Bertalanffy, L. (1968), *General System Theory: Foundations, Development, Applications*. New York: George Braziller, p. 18.

53. Weiner, N. (1948), *Cybernetics: Or Control and Communication in the Animal and the Machine*. Cambridge, MA: MIT Press.

54. Leontief, W. (1941), *The Structure of American Economy 1919–1939*. New York: Oxford University Press.

55. Von Neumann, J. and O. Morgenstern (1953), *Theory of Games and Economic Behavior*. Princeton, NJ: Princeton University Press.

56. Forrester, J.W. (1961), *Industrial Dynamics*. Cambridge, MA: MIT Press.

57. Odum, H.T. (1971), *Environment, Power and Society*. New York: John Wiley.

58. Patten, B.C. (1971–1976), *Systems Analyses and Simulation in Ecology*, Vols. 1–4. New York: Academic Press.

59. Hannon, B. (1973), The Structure of Ecosystems. *Journal of Theoretical Biology* 41:535–546.

60. Innis, G. (1978), *Grassland Simulation Model, Ecology Studies No. 26*. New York: Springer-Verlag.

61. Meadows, D.H., D.L. Meadows, J. Randers, and W.W. Behrens (1972), *The Limits to Growth*. New York: Universe.

62. Cole, H.S. D., C. Freeman, M. Jahoda, and K.L.R. Pavitt. (eds.). (1973), *Models of Doom: A Critique of the Limits to Growth*. New York: Universe Books.

—Oltmans, W.L. (1974), *On growth*. New York: Capricorn.

63. Ehrlich, P.R., and J.P. Holdren (1988), *The Cassandra Conference: Resources and the Human Predicament*. College Station, TX: Texas A & M University Press.

—Meadows, D.H., D.L. Meadows, and J. Randers (1992), *Beyond the Limits: Confronting Global Collapse, Envisioning a Sustainable Future*. Post Mills, VT: Chelsea Green. —Mesarovic, M., and E. Pestel. 1974. *Mankind at the turning point: The second report to the club of Rome*. New York: Dutton. —Pestel, E. 1989. *Beyond the limits to growth: A report to the club of Rome*. New York: Universe Books.

64. Hardin, G. (1968), The Tragedy of the Commons. *Science* 162:1243–1248.

65. Berkes, F. (ed.). (1989), *Common Property Resources: Ecology and Community-based Sustainable Development*. London: Bellhaven Press.

66. Gordon, H.S. (1954), The Economic Theory of a Common Property Resource. *Journal of Political Economy* 62:124–142.

67. Hanna, S. and M. Munasinghe (eds.). (1995a), *Property Rights and the Environment: Social and Ecological Issues*. Washington, DC: The Beijer Institute of Ecological Economics and The World Bank.

—Hanna, S. and M. Munasinghe (eds.). 1995b. *Property rights in a social and ecological context: Case studies and design applications.* Washington, DC: The Beijer Institute of Ecological Economics and The World Bank.

68. Odum, H.T. and E.C. Odum (1976), *Energy Basis for Man and Nature.* New York: McGraw-Hill.—Hall, Charles A. S., Cutler J. Cleveland, and Robert Kaufman. 1986. *Energy and resource quality: The ecology of the economic process.* New York: John Wiley and Sons.

69. See, for example, Chapter 3 of Ayres, R.U. (1978), *Resources, Environment, and Economics: Applications of the Materials/Energy Balance Principle.* New York: John Wiley and Sons.; and Chapters 6 and 7 in Faber, M., R. Manstetten, and J. Proops. 1996. *Ecological economics: Concepts and methods.* Cheltenham, U.K.: Edward Elgar.

70. Odum, H.T. (1957), Trophic Structure and Productivity of Silver Springs, Florida. *Ecological Monographs* 27:55–112.

71. Odum, E.P. (1953), *Fundamentals of Ecology* (1st ed.). Philadelphia: Saunders.

72. Hannon, B. (1973), The Structure of Ecosystems. *Journal of Theoretical Biology* 41:535–546. —Ayres, R.U. 1978. *Resources, environment, and economics: Applications of the materials/energy balance principle.* New York: John Wiley and Sons. —Costanza, R. 1980. Embodied energy and economic valuation. *Science* 210:1219–1224.

    —Cleveland, C.J., R. Costanza, C.A.S. Hall, and R. Kaufmann. (1984), Energy and the United States economy: A biophysical perspective. *Science* 225:890–897.

73. Costanza, R., F. H. Sklar, and M.L. White (1990), Modeling Coastal Landscape Dynamics. *BioScience* 40:91–107. —Bockstael, N., R. Costanza, I. Strand, W. Boynton, K. Bell, and L. Wainger. 1995. Ecological economic modeling and valuation of ecosystems. *Ecological Economics* 14:143–159.

74. Boulding, K.E. (1966), The Economics of the Coming Spaceship Earth. In H. Jarrett (ed.), *Environmental Quality in a Growing Economy*, pp. 3–14. Baltimore, MD: Resources for the Future/ Johns Hopkins University Press.

75. Daly, H.E. (1968), On Economics as a Life Science. *Journal of Political Economy* 76:392–406.

76. Schumpeter, J.A. (1950), *Capitalism, Socialism and Democracy.* New York: Harper & Row.

77. Clark, C.W. (1973), The Economics of Overexploitation. *Science* 181:630–634.

—Martinez-Alier, J. (1987), *Ecological Economics: Energy, Environment, and Society*. Cambridge, MA: Blackwell. —Cleveland, C. J. 1987. Biophysical economics: Historical perspective and current research trends. *Ecological Modelling* 38:47–74.

—Christensen, P. (1989), Historical Roots for Ecological Economics: Biophysical Versus Allocative Approaches. *Ecological Economics* 1:17–36.

78. Daly, H.E. (1973), The Steady State Economy: Toward a Political Economy of Biophysical Equilibrium and Moral Growth. In H. E. Daly (ed.), *Toward a steady state economy*, pp. 149–174. San Francisco: W. H. Freeman.—Daly, H. E. 1977. *Steady state economics*. San Francisco: W. H. Freeman.—Daly, H. E. 1991a. Ecological economics and sustainable development. In C. Rossi and E. Tiezzi (eds.), *Ecological physical chemistry*, pp. 185–201. Amsterdam: Elsevier.—Daly, H. E. 1991b. Elements of environmental macroeconomics. In R. Costanza (ed.), *Ecological economics: The science and management of sustainability*, pp. 32–46. New York: Columbia Press.

—Daly, H.E. (1991c), Sustainable Development: From Conceptual Theory towards Operational Principles. *Population and Development Review* 16: supplement.

—Daly, H.E. (1991d), *Steady-state Economics* (2nd ed.). Washington, DC: Island Press.

79. Holling, C.S. (ed.). (1978), *Adaptive Environmental Assessment and Management*. Chichester: Wiley.

80. Gunderson, L., C.S. Holling, and S. Light (eds.). (1995), *Barriers and Bridges to the Renewal of Ecosystems and Institutions*. New York: Columbia University Press.

—Holling, C.S. (ed.). (1978), *Adaptive Environmental Assessment and Management*. Chichester: Wiley.—Lee, K. 1993. *Compass and the gyroscope: Integrating science and politics for the environment*. Washington, DC: Island Press. —Walters, C. J. 1986. *Adaptive environmental management of renewable resources*. New York: McGraw-Hill.

81. Ehrlich, P.R., and P.H. Raven (1964), Butterflys and Plants: A Study in Coevolution. *Evolution* 18:586–608.

82. Norgaard, R.B. (1994), *Development Betrayed: The End of Progress and a Coevolutionary Revisioning of the Future*. London: Routledge.

83. Norgaard, R.B. (1994), *Development Betrayed: The End of Progress and a Coevolutionary Revisioning of the Future*. London: Routledge.

84. Boyd, R. and P.J. Richerson (1985), *Culture and the Evolutionary Process*. Chicago: University of Chicago Press. – Durham, W. H. 1991. *Coevolution: Genes, culture, and human diversity*. Stanford, CA: Stanford University Press.

85. Stokes, K.M. (1992), *Man and the Biosphere: Toward a Coevolutionary Political Economy*. Armonk, NY: M. E. Sharpe.

86. Gowdy, J.M. (1994), *Coevolutionary Economics: The Economy, Society and the Environment*. Dordrecht: Kluwer.

87. e.g., van den Belt, M., L. Deutsch, and A. Jansson (1997), A Consensus-based Simulation Model for Management in the Patagonia Coastal Zone. *Ecological Modeling* 110: 79-103.

88. Lovins, A.B. (1977), *Soft Energy Paths*. Friends of the Earth International. Cambridge, MA: Ballanger. – Lovins, A. B. 1996. *Megawatts – Twelve transitions, eight improvements and one distraction*. Energy Policy 24(4):331–343.

89. Hinterberger, F. and W.R. Stahel (1996), *Eco-efficient Services*. Boston: Kluwer.

90. Botkin, D.B. (1990), *Discordant Harmonies: A New Ecology for the Twenty-first Century*. Berkeley: University of California Press. – Holling, C. S. (ed.). 1978. *Adaptive environmental assessment and management*. Chichester: Wiley. – Meffe, G. K. 1992. Techno-arrogance and halfway technologies: Salmon hatcheries on the Pacific Coast of North America. *Conservation Biology* 6(3):350–354.

91. Costanza, R., B.G. Norton, and B.D. Haskell (1992), *Ecosystem Health: New Goals for Environmental Management*. Washington, DC: Island Press.

92. Rapport, D. (1995), Editorial: More than a Metaphor. *Ecosystem Health* 1:197.

93. Funtowicz, S.O. and J.R. Ravetz (1991), A New Scientific Methodology for Global Environmental Problems. In R. Costanza (ed.), *Ecological economics: the science and management of sustainability*, pp. 137–152. New York: Columbia University Press.

– Norgaard, R.B. (1989), The Case for Methodological Pluralism. *Ecological Economics* 1:37–57. – Norgaard, R. B. 1994. *Development betrayed: The end of progress and a coevolutionary revisioning of the future*. London: Routledge. – O'Connor, M., S. Faucheux, G. Froger, S. Funtowicz, and G. Munda. 1996. Emergent complexity and procedural rationality: post-normal science for sustainability. In R. Costanza, O. Segura, and J. Martinez-Alier (eds.), *Getting down to earth: practical applications of ecological economics*, pp. 223–248. Washington, DC: Island Press.

94. e.g., Blaikie, P. (1985), *The Political Economy of Soil Degradation in Developing Countries*. London: Longman.

95. See, for example, the contributors to O'Connor, M. (ed.). (1995), *Is Capitalism Sustainable: Political Economy and the Politics of Ecology*. New York: Guilford Press.

96. e.g., Howarth, Ri. B. and R.B. Norgaard (1992), Environmental Valuation under Sustainable Development. *American Economic Review* 82:473–477.

97. Martinez-Alier, J. and M. O'Connor (1996), Ecological and Economic Distribution Conflicts. In R. Costanza, O. Segura, and J. Martinez-Alier (eds.), *Getting Down to Earth: Practical Applications of Ecological Economics*, pp. 153–183. Washington, DC: Island Press.

2

Human and Environment: A Journey of Development

"... It took Britain half the resources of the planet to achieve its prosperity; how many planets will a country like India require ...?"
– Mahatma Gandhi, when asked if, after independence, India would attain British standards of living

Historically, the recognition by humans of their impact upon the earth has consistently lagged behind the magnitude of the damage they have imposed, thus seriously weakening efforts to control this damage. Even today, technological optimists and others ignore the mounting evidence of global environmental degradation until it intrudes more inescapably upon their personal welfare. Even some serious students draw comfort from the arguments that: GDP figures are increasing throughout much of the world, Life expectancies are increasing in many nations, Evidence of greenhouse warming is ambiguous, Some claims of environmental damage have been exaggerated and Previous predictions of environmental catastrophe have not been borne out.

Each of these statements is correct. However, not one of them is a reason for complacency, and indeed, taken together, they should be viewed as powerful evidence of the need for an innovative approach to environmental analysis and management. GDP and other current measures of national income accounting are notorious for overweighting market transactions, understating resource depletion, omitting pollution damage, and failing to measure real changes in well-being. For example, the Index of Sustainable Economic Welfare[2] shows much reduced improvement in real gains, despite great increases in resource depleting throughput. Increases in life expectancies in many nations, by contrast, clearly indicate improvements in welfare; but unless accompanied by corresponding decreases in birth rates, they are warnings of acceleration in population growth, which will compound all other environmental problems. In the former USSR, sharply increasing infant mortality rates and actual declines in life expectancy attest to the dangers of massive accumulations of pollution stocks and neglect of public health[3].

The divergence in views among scientists concerning the greenhouse effect underscores the pervasiveness of uncertainty about the basic nature of our ecological life-support systems and emphasizes the need for building precautionary minimum safe standards into environmental policies. The fact that some environmental problems have been overestimated and that the magnitude of any one of these problems can be denied or debated does not reduce the urgency of our responsibility to seek the underlying patterns from many indicators of what is happening to the "balance of the earth"[4].

Only recently, with advances in environmental sciences, global remote sensing, and other monitoring systems, has a more comprehensive assessment of local and global environmental deterioration become possible. Evidence is accumulating with respect to accelerating loss of vital rain forests, species extinction, depletion of ocean fisheries, shortages of fresh water in some areas and increased flooding in others, soil erosion, depletion and pollution of underground aquifers, decreases in quantity and quality of irrigation and drinking water, and growing global pollution of the atmosphere and oceans, even in the polar regions[5]. Obviously the exponential growth of human populations is rapidly crowding out other species before we have begun to understand fully our dependence upon species diversity. Although post-Cold War conflicts such as those in Haiti, Somalia, Sudan, and Rwanda are characterized in part by ethnic differences, territorial overcrowding and food shortages are contributing factors and consequently provide additional early warning of accumulating global environmental problems.

Clearly, remedial policy responses to date have been local, partial, and inadequate. Early policy discussions and the resulting responses tended to focus on symptoms of environmental damage rather than basic causes and policy instruments tended to be ad hoc rather than carefully designed for efficiency, fairness, and sustainability. For example, in the 1970s emphasis centered on end-of-pipe pollution control which, while a serious problem was actually a symptom of expanding populations and inefficient technologies that fueled exponential growth of material and energy throughput while threatening the recuperative powers of the planet's life-support systems.

As a result of early perceptions of environmental damage, much was learned about policies and instruments for attacking pollution. These insights will help in dealing with the more fundamental and intractable environmental issues identified here.

The basic problems for which we need innovative policies and management instruments include:

- unsustainably large and growing human populations that exceed the carrying capacity of the earth
- highly entropy-increasing technologies that deplete the earth of its resources and whose unassimilated wastes poison the air, water, and land
- land conversion that destroys habitat, increases soil erosion, and accelerates loss of species diversity.

As emphasized throughout this work, these problems are all evidence that the material scale of human activity exceeds the sustainable carrying capacity of the earth. We argue that in addressing these problems, we should adopt courses based upon a fair distribution of resources and opportunities between present and future generations as well as among groups within the present generation. These strategies should be based upon an economically efficient allocation of resources that adequately accounts for protecting the stock of natural capital. This section examines the historical record and the emerging trans-discipline of ecological economics for guidance in designing policies and instruments capable of dealing with these problems.

Historically, severe anthropogenic damage to some regions of the earth began as soon as humans learned to apply highly entropy-increasing technological processes to agriculture and was sharply escalated by factory production in Europe during the industrial revolution. Early public policy responses were feeble to nonexistent, allowing polluters whose political and economic power began to eclipse that of the feudal magnates to gain de facto property rights to emit wastes into the common property resources of air and water. In England, it was not until urban agglomeration in London with its choking smog from coal fires so discomforted Parliament that forceful action was taken. In the mid-twentieth century, incidents of deaths from smog, the result of automobiles and modern industry, began to occur. In Donora, Pennsylvania, in the U.S. in 1948 a "killer smog" produced by a steel mill operating during a week-long temperature inversion killed several people and caused illness in the thousands. In London several thousand people were killed during one winter night in 1952 as a result of the smog from domestic and industrial coal burning. Eventually these incidents led to the passage of clean air legislation and improved technologies.

Even more massive loss of life from the spread of water-borne diseases continued to be accepted as part of the human condition until advances in scientific knowledge concerning the role of microorganisms prompted sewage treatment and water purification systems. Vast urban expenditures on such systems eventually reduced the enormous loss of human life from the uncontrolled discharge of human waste into common property waterways. The application of appropriate science, appropriate technology, and community will was necessary to reduce the costly loss of human life that had resulted from unprecedented population expansion, the concentration of humans into unplanned urban areas, and uncompensated appropriation of common property resources for waste disposal.

Homo sapiens are at another turning point in its relatively long and (so far) inordinately successful history. Our species' activities on the planet have now become of so large a scale that they are beginning to affect the ecological life-support system itself. The entire concept of economic growth (defined as increasing material consumption) must be rethought, especially as a solution to the growing host of interrelated social, economic, and environmental problems. What we need now is real economic and social development (qualitative improvement without growth in resource throughput) and an explicit recognition of the interrelatedness and interdependence of all aspects of life on the planet. We need to move from an economics that ignores this interdependence to one which acknowledges and builds upon it. We need to develop an economics that is fundamentally ecological in its basic view of the problems that now face our species at this crucial point in its history.

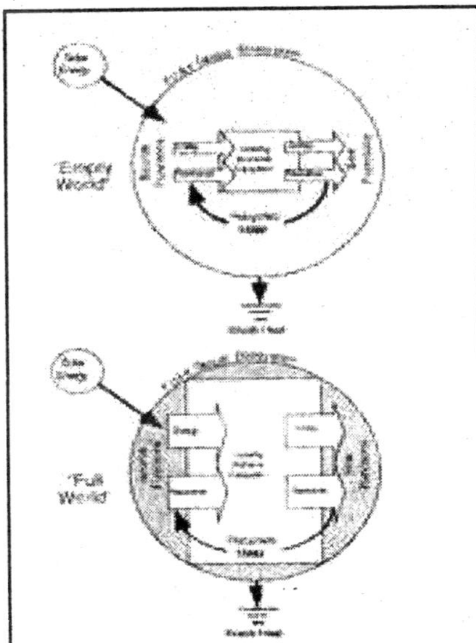

Source: Goodland, Daly and El Serafy 1992[1]

Figure 1: The Finite Global Ecosystem Relative to the Economic Subsystem.

As we show, this new ecological economics is, in a very real sense, a return to the classical roots of economics. It is a return to a point when economics and the other sciences were integrated rather than academically isolated as they are now. Ecological economics is an attempt to transcend the narrow disciplinary boundaries that have grown up in the last 90 years in order to bring the full power of our intellectual capital to bear on the huge problems we now face.

The current dilemma of our species can be summarized in ecological terms as follows: We have moved from an early succession "empty world" (empty of people and their artifacts, but full of natural capital) where the emphasis and rewards were on rapid growth and expansion, cutthroat competition, and open waste cycles, to a maturing "full world" (see Figure 1) where the needs, whether perceived by decision makers or not, are for qualitative improvement of the linkages between components (development), cooperative alliances, and recycled "closed loop" waste flows.

Can we recognize these fundamental changes and reorganize our society rapidly enough to avoid a catastrophic overshoot? Can we be humble enough to acknowledge the huge uncertainties involved and protect ourselves from their most dire consequences? Can we effectively develop policies to deal with the tricky issues of wealth distribution, population prudence, international trade, and energy supply in a world where the simple palliative of "more growth" is no longer a solution? Can we modify our systems of governance at international, national, and local levels to be better adapted to these new and more difficult challenges?

Homo sapiens has successfully adapted to huge challenges in the past. We developed agriculture as a response to the limits of hunting and gathering. We developed an industrial society to adapt to the potential of concentrated forms of energy. Now the challenge is to live sustainably and well but within the material limits of a finite planet. Humans have an ability to conceptualize their world and foresee the future that is more highly developed than that of any other species. We the authors hope that we, the human species, can use this skill of conceptualization and forecasting to meet the new challenge of sustainability. Ecological economics seeks to meet that challenge.

The Global Ecosystem and the Economic Subsystem

A most useful indicator of the magnitude of our environmental predicament is population times per capita resource consumption[6]. This is the scale of the human economic subsystem with respect to that of the global ecosystem on which it depends, and of which it is a part. The global ecosystem is the source of all material inputs feeding the economic subsystem, and is the sink for all its wastes. Population times per capita resource consumption is the total flow—throughput—of resources from the ecosystem to the economic subsystem then back to the ecosystem as waste, as shown in Figure 1. The upper diagram illustrates the bygone era when the economic subsystem (depicted by a square) was small relative to the size of the global ecosystem. The lower diagram depicts a situation much nearer to today in which the economic subsystem is very large relative to the global ecosystem.

The global ecosystem's source and sink functions have large but limited capacity to support the economic subsystem. The imperative, therefore, is to maintain the size of the global economy to within the capacity of the ecosystem to sustain it. It took all of human history to grow to the $600 billion/yr scale of the economy of 1900. Today, the world economy grows by this amount every two years. Unchecked, today's $16 trillion/yr global economy may be five times bigger only one generation or so hence.

It seems unlikely that the world can sustain a doubling of the material economy, let alone the Brundtland Commission's called for "five- to ten-fold increase"[7]. Throughput growth is not the way to reach sustainability; we cannot "grow" our way into sustainability. The global ecosystem, which is the source of all the resources needed for the economic subsystem, is finite and has limited regenerative and assimilative capacities. While it now looks inevitable that the next century will be occupied by double the number of people in the human economy consuming resources and burdening sinks with their wastes, it seems doubtful that these people can be supported sustainably at anything like current Western levels of material consumption. We have already begun to bump up against various kinds of limits to continued material expansion. The path to sustainable future gains in the human condition will be through qualitative improvement rather than quantitative increases in throughput.

From Localized Limits to Global Limits

The economic subsystem has already reached or exceeded important source and sink limits. We have already fouled parts of our nest and there is practically nowhere on this earth where signs of the human economy are absent. From the center of Antarctica to Mount Everest human wastes are obvious and increasing. It is not possible to find a sample of ocean water with no sign of the 20 billion tons of human wastes added annually. PCBs (polychlorinated-biphenyls), other persistent toxic chemicals like DDT, and heavy metal compounds have already accumulated throughout the marine ecosystem. One fifth of the world's population breathes air more poisonous than World Health Organization (WHO) standards recommend, and an entire generation of Mexico City children may be intellectually stunted by lead poisoning.

Since the Club of Rome's 1972 "Limits to Growth," the emphasis has shifted from source limits to sink limits. Source limits are more open to substitution, are more amenable to private ownership, and are more localized. Consequently, they are more amenable to control by markets and prices. Sink limits involve common property where markets fail. Since 1972, the case has substantially strengthened that there are limits to throughput growth on the sink side[8]. Some of these limits are tractable and are being tackled, such as the CFC phase-out under the Montreal Convention. Other limits are less tractable, such as increasing CO_2 emissions and the massive human appropriation of biomass. Another example is landfill sites, which are becoming extremely difficult to find. Garbage is now shipped thousands of miles from industrial to developing countries in search of unfilled sinks. It has so far proved impossible for the U.S. Nuclear Regulatory Commission to rent a nuclear waste site for US$100 million. Germany's Kraft-Werk Union signed an agreement with China in 1987 to bury nuclear waste in Mongolia's Gobi Desert. These facts confirm that landfill sites and toxic dumps—aspects of sinks—are increasingly hard to find. One important limit is the sink constraint of fossil energy use. Therefore, the rate of transition to renewable energy sources, including solar energy, parallels the rate of the transition to sustainability. Technological optimists also add the possibility of cheap fusion energy by the year 2050. In the face of such high-stakes uncertainty, we should be agnostic on technology. We should encourage sustainable technological development but not bank on it to solve all environmental problems. Since research has only just begun to focus on input reduction and has focused even less on sink management, there is probably the most scope for dramatic technological improvements in these areas.

First Evidence of Limits: Human Biomass Appropriation

The best evidence that there are imminent limits is the calculation by Vitousek et al.[9] that the human economy uses—directly or indirectly—about 40% of the net primary product of terrestrial photosynthesis today. (This figure drops to 25% if the oceans and other aquatic ecosystems are included.) And desertification, urban encroachment onto agricultural land, blacktopping, soil erosion, and pollution are increasing, as is the search for food by expanding populations. This means that in only a single doubling of the world's population (say 40–45 years) we will use 80% and 100% shortly thereafter. As Daly[10] points out, 100% appropriation is ecologically impossible, but even if it were possible, it would be socially undesirable. The world will go from half-empty to full in one doubling period, irrespective of the sink being filled or the source being consumed.

Second Evidence of Limits: Climate Change

The second evidence that limits have been exceeded is climate change. The year 1990 was the warmest year in more than a century of record-keeping. Seven of the hottest years on record all occurred in the last 11 years. The 1980s were 1ÚF warmer than the 1880s, while 1990 was 1.25ÚF warmer. This contrasts alarmingly with the preindustrial constancy in which the earth's temperature did not vary more than 2Ú–4ÚF in the last ten thousand years. Humanity's entire social and cultural infrastructure over the last 7000 years has evolved entirely within a global climate that never deviated as much as 2ÚF from today's climate[11].

It is too soon to be absolutely certain that global change has begun; normal climatic variability is too great for absolute certainty. There is even greater uncertainty about the possible effects. But all the evidence suggests that global change may well have started, that CO_2 accumulation started years ago as postulated by Svante Arrhenius in 1896, and that it is worsening fast. Scientists now practically universally agree that such change will occur, although differences remain on the rates and impacts. The U.S. National Academy of Science warned that global change may well be the most pressing international issue of the next century. A dwindling minority of scientists remain agnostic. The dispute concerns policy responses much more than the predictions.

The scale of today's fossil fuel-based human economy is the dominant cause of greenhouse gas accumulation. The biggest contribution to greenhouse warming, carbon dioxide released from burning coal, oil, and natural gas, is accumulating in the atmosphere. Today's 5.8 billion people annually burn the equivalent of more than one ton of coal each.

Next in importance contributing to climate change are all other pollutants released by the economy that exceed the biosphere's absorptive capacity: methane, CFCs, and nitrous oxide. Relative to carbon dioxide these three pollutants are orders of magnitude more damaging, although their amount is much less. Today's market price to polluters for using atmospheric sink capacity for carbon dioxide disposal is zero, although the real opportunity cost may turn out to be astronomical. Economists are almost unanimous in persisting in externalizing the costs of CO_2 emissions, even though by

1993 more than 180 nations had signed a treaty to internalize such costs.

There may be a few exceptions to the negative impacts of global warming, such as plants growing faster in CO_2-enriched laboratories where water and nutrients are not limiting. However, in the real world, it seems more likely that crop belts will not shift quickly enough with changing climate, nor will they grow faster because some other factor (e.g., suitable soils, nutrients, or water) will become limiting. The prodigious North American breadbasket's climate may indeed shift north, but this does not mean the breadbasket will follow because the deep, rich prairie soils will stay put, and Canadian boreal soils and muskeg are very infertile.

The costs of rejecting the greenhouse hypothesis, if true, are vastly greater than the costs of accepting the hypothesis if it proves to be false. By the time the evidence is irrefutable, it is sure to be too late to avert unacceptable costs, such as the influx of millions of refugees from low-lying coastal areas (55% of the world's population lives on coasts or estuaries), damage to ports and coastal cities, increases in storm intensity, and most important of all, damage to agriculture. The greenhouse threat is more than sufficient to justify action now, even if only in an insurance sense. The question now to be resolved is how much insurance to buy.

Admittedly, uncertainty prevails. But uncertainty cuts both ways. Given the size of the stakes involved, "business as usual" or "wait and see" is an imprudent, if not foolhardy, strategy. Although underestimation of climate change or ozone shield risks is just as likely as overestimation, recent studies suggest we are consistently underestimating risks. In May 1991, the U.S. EPA upped by 20-fold their estimate of UV-cancer deaths, and the earth's ability to absorb methane was revised downwards by 25% in June 1991. In the face of uncertainty about global environmental health, prudence should be paramount.

The relevant component here is the tight relationship between carbon released and the scale of the material economy. Global carbon emissions have increased annually since the industrial revolution, they are now at nearly 4%/yr. To the extent energy use parallels economic activity, carbon emissions are an index of the scale of the material economy. Fossil fuels account for 78% of U.S. energy.

Reducing fossil energy intensity is possible in all industrial economies and in the larger developing economies such as China, Brazil, and India. Increasing energy use without increasing CO_2 means primarily making the transition to *renewable:* biomass, solar, and hydroelectric power. The other major source of carbon emissions—deforestation—also parallels the scale of the economy. More people needing more land push back the frontier. But such geopolitical frontiers are rapidly vanishing today.

The seven billion tons of carbon released each year by human activity (from fossil fuels and deforestation) accumulate in the atmosphere, and carbon accumulation appears for all practical purposes to be irreversible. Hence it is of major concern for the sustainability of future generations. Removal of carbon dioxide by liquefying it or chemically scrubbing it from stacks might double the cost of electricity. At best, technology may reduce, but not eliminate, this major cost.

Third Evidence of Limits: Ozone Shield Rupture

The third evidence that global limits have been reached is the rupture of the ozone shield. It is difficult to imagine more compelling evidence that human activity has already damaged our life-support systems than the cosmic holes in the ozone shield. That CFCs (chloro fluro carbons) would damage the ozone layer was predicted as far back as 1974 by Sherwood Rowland and Mario Molina. But when the damage was first detected—in 1985 in Antarctica—disbelief was so great that the data were rejected as coming from faulty sensors. Retesting and a search of hitherto undigested computer printouts confirmed that not only did the hole exist in 1985, but that it had appeared each spring since 1979. The world had failed to detect a vast hole that threatened human life and food production and that was more extensive than the United States and taller than Mount Everest.

The single Antarctic ozone hole has now gone global. All subsequent tests have proved that the global ozone layer is thinning far faster than models predicted. A second hole was subsequently discovered over the Arctic, and recently ozone shield thinning has been detected over both North and South temperate latitudes, including over northern Europe and North America. Furthermore, the temperate holes are edging from the less dangerous winter into the spring, thus posing more of a threat to sprouting crops and to humans.

The relationship between the increased ultraviolet "b" radiation let through the impaired ozone shield and skin cancers and cataracts is relatively well known: every 1% decrease in the ozone layer results in 5% more of certain skin cancers. This is already alarming in certain regions (e.g., Queensland). The world seems destined for 1 billion additional skin cancers, many of them fatal, among people alive today. The possibly more serious human health effect is depression of our immune systems, increasing our vulnerability to an array of tumors, parasites, and infectious diseases. In addition, as the shield weakens, crop yields and marine fisheries decline. But the gravest effect may be the uncertainty, such as upsetting normal balances in natural vegetation. Keystone species – those on which many others depend for survival – may decrease, leading to widespread disruption in environmental services and accelerating extinctions.

The one million or so tons of CFCs annually dumped into the biosphere take about 10 years to waft up to the ozone layer, where they destroy it with a half-life of about one century. Today's damage, although serious, only reflects the relatively low levels of CFCs released in the early 1980s. If CFC emissions cease today, the world still will be gripped in an unavoidable commitment to ten years of increased damage. This would then gradually return to pre-damage levels over the next century.

This shows that the global ecosystem's sink capacity to absorb CFC pollution has been exceeded. Since the limits have been reached and exceeded, mankind is in for damage to environmental services, human health, and food production. Eighty-five per cent of CFCs are released in the industrial north, but the main hole appeared in Antarctica in the ozone layer 20 kilometers up in the atmosphere, showing the damage to be widespread and truly global in nature.

Fourth Evidence of Limits: Land Degradation

Land degradation is not new. Land has been degraded by civilization for thousands of years, and in many cases previously degraded land remains unproductive today. But the scale has mushroomed and is important because practically all (97%) of our food comes from land rather than from aquatic or ocean systems. Since 35% of the earth's land already is degraded, and since this figure is increasing and largely irreversible in any time scale of interest to society, such degradation is a sign that we have exceeded the regenerative capacity of the earth's soil source.

Pimentel et al.[12] and Kendall and Pimentel[13] found soil erosion to be serious in most of the world's agricultural areas and that this problem is worsening as more marginal land is brought into production. Soil loss rates, generally ranging from 10 to 100 hectares per year, exceed soil formation rates by at least tenfold. Agriculture is leading to erosion, Stalinization, or water logging of possibly 6 million hectares per year. This is a crisis that may seriously affect the sustainability of the world's food supply.

Exceeding the limits of this particular environmental source function raises food prices and exacerbates income inequality at a time when one billion people are already malnourished. As one third of developing country populations now face fuel wood deficits, crop residues and dung (needed for fertilizer) are diverted from agriculture to fuel. Fuel wood overharvesting and this diversion intensify land degradation, hunger, and poverty.

Fifth Evidence of Limits: Biodiversity Loss

The scale of the human economy has grown so large that there is no longer room for all species in the ark. The rates of takeover of wildlife habitat and of species extinctions are the fastest they have ever been in human history and are accelerating. The world's richest species habitat, tropical forest, has already been 55% destroyed, and the current rate of loss exceeds 168,000 square kilometers per year. As the total number of species extant is not yet known to the nearest order of magnitude (5 million or 30 million or more), it is impossible to determine precise extinction rates. However, conservative estimates put the rate at more than 5000 species of our inherited genetic library irreversibly extinguished each year. This is about 10,000 times as fast as pre-human extinction rates. Less conservative estimates put the rate at 150,000 species per year[14]. Many find such anthropocentrism to be arrogant and immoral. It also increases the risks of overshoot. Built-in redundancy is a part of many biological systems, but we do not know how near we are to the thresholds.

Climate Change

India's Carbon free Technology

The Intergovernmental Panel on Climate Change (IPCC) recently released its Fourth Assessment Report and the United Nations published its Human Development Report 2007.

Both these reports gave a stern warning on the serious dangers of climate change facing the world and linked it to human activity. Depending on the amount of carbon emitted, the IPCC report estimates a global temperature rise of 1.8-4C and sea level rise of 18-59cm by the end of the century. Further, the impacts could be abrupt and irreversible.

The IPCC report calls for deployment of renewable or carbon-free technologies that are currently available or will be commercialised in coming decades. This requires moving away from the coal and oil based economy to one in which a "significant" fraction of energy supply comes from carbon-free technologies such as solar, wind, nuclear, biofuels, hydroelectricity, fuel cells, batteries, hybrid cars, carbon capture and sequestration, etc. There are also some outlier suggestions such as building giant space mirrors to reflect solar radiation back into space.

Should India be concerned with the problem of global warming at all? The UN report calls for developed countries to cut carbon dioxide (CO_2) emissions by 80 per cent by 2050 and developing countries by 20 per cent from 1990 levels. India has strongly objected to this since most of the build-up of CO_2 is due to industrialisation of the west and India has low per capita CO_2 emissions[15]. However, global warming is not going to be selective. If anything, it will affect the countries near the equator far more than those in higher latitudes and the poor will be the worst affected. Moreover, India's CO_2 emissions are growing rapidly and it is poised to become the world's third largest emitter by 2030 (after China and the US). Consequently, there will be growing pressure on India for proactive action. Since India has rejected mandatory CO_2 cuts, what are the other options? As we see presently, carbon credit trading and carbon-free technologies are other opportunities.

Can India develop carbon-free technologies to meet a part of its future energy requirements? India's present total commercial energy supply is about 4,000 billion kwh[16]. The Planning Commission estimates it to grow to 20,000 billion kwh by 2030[17]. How India achieves this steep growth is in itself a challenge. It is further compounded by the fact that a "reasonable" fraction of this energy should be from carbon-free sources. How much is "reasonable"? Coal, oil and gas presently supply 97 per cent of India's commercial energy and many new carbon-free technologies are still to become mature for large-scale implementation. It is therefore, nearly impossible to make a major switch. In one possible scenario, India could plan to meet 15 per cent of its future energy needs from carbon-free technologies[18]. This implies by 2030, carbon-free sources contribute about 2,500 billion kwh out of 20,000 billion kwh. (Of course, no technology is totally "carbon-free" since there are CO_2 emissions over the total life cycle of any technology.)[19]

In this article, we examine the potential from several energy sources. We estimate the maximum possible potential from these options and so the actual may turn out to be lower.

Wind

Wind power is a reasonably mature technology and India with its installed capacity of 7,600 MW, is the fourth largest in the world. Wind power potential in India is estimated at 45,000 MW. However, wind power is location specific and intermittent. This intermittency is now causing some scarcity of electric power in Tamil Nadu, which has a sizeable fraction of wind energy. Wind speeds in India are in general lower than those in Europe and the US and consequently wind turbines operate at less than 20 per cent load factor. If India achieves the estimated potential of 45,000 MW, wind can generate about 100 billion kwh, which is less than 1 per cent of India's desired energy supply of 20,000 billion kwh.

Biofuels

Oil bearing crops such as jatropha, pongamia pinnata and mahua can be used to produce biodiesel, which is an effective substitute for diesel. Likewise, ethanol can be produced from sugar cane juice, molasses and sweet sorghum. An enticing option would be to produce fuel from any cellulosic biomass such as wood chips, rice husk and sugarcane bagasse though the technology is yet to be commercially proven. However, as shown by recent experience in US, Mexico and Thailand, large-scale biofuel production requires careful planning. Use of land for biofuels should not in any way compromise with production of food grain or animal feed. Diversion of agricultural land for producing fuel should therefore be discouraged.

India has an estimated 30 million hectares of cultivable wastelands out of a total area of 328 million hectares. It is debatable whether to plant such a large area with bio-fuels given the pressures of population. However, if all of this is used to grow bio-fuel producing crops, India can produce about 40 million tonnes of oil, equivalent to 525 billion kwh of energy[20]. India could also produce up to 10 billion litres of ethanol, (50 billion kwh) if it develops cellulosic ethanol technology and improves yield of sugar cane using drip irrigation and fertigation technologies[21]. The total contribution of bio-fuels will be about 3 per cent of India's energy supply.

Hydroelectricity

India's hydroelectric potential is estimated to be 84,000 MW (at 60 per cent load factor). Present generation capacity is about 34,000 MW operating at an average 29 per cent load factor. Most of the untapped potential is in Arunachal Pradesh and it is not clear how much of this can be tapped given the social problems of rehabilitation and resettlement of people affected by large hydro projects. If India can achieve the full potential of 84,000 MW, it will generate about 400 billion kwh, 2 per cent of the desired total energy supply.

Therefore even in the most optimistic scenario, wind, hydro and biofuels contribute about 1,100 billion kwh, which is effectively the upper limit from these sources. This is less than 6 per cent of India's expected commercial energy by 2030 and therefore it appears that these sources will remain marginal in India's future energy mix. Bulk of carbon-free energy will have to depend on sources such as coal (with carbon capture), nuclear and solar.

Coal (with Carbon Capture)

India has abundant and cheap coal reserves and coal accounts for 51 per cent of the present commercial energy supply. Therefore, coal will continue to dominate the energy mix in near future. However, every kwh of electricity from coal also releases about 1 kg of CO_2 into the atmosphere. An emerging option is therefore to capture the CO_2 from coal power plants and bury it deep underground. This sequestration technology requires modern coal gasification and combined cycle power plants[22]. All these ancillaries will make coal power expensive, almost doubling the cost of electricity. At present there are only a few pilot plant experiments for sequestration underway in North America. A major research programme is necessary to prove CO_2 capture and sequestration for Indian conditions. If we assume that 40 per cent of India's future energy is from coal then annual coal-based CO_2 emissions would be about 2,500 million tonnes. Out of this, at least 400 million tonnes of CO_2 would have to be captured and sequestered annually and this is a huge challenge. It will require successful commercialisation of the technology and proper site selection for long-term sequestration.

Nuclear

India's installed nuclear power is 4,120 MW and contributes less than 3 per cent of the electricity generation. Domestic uranium reserves being limited, India is pursuing the three-phase programme with the objective of developing breeder reactors using plutonium and later thorium derived reactor technology. The proposed Indo-US nuclear agreement provides the opportunity for importing light water reactors with fuel. India could then add up to 24,000 MW from this route by 2030. Large-scale deployment of breeder reactors is still at least several years away and depends on a successful demonstration of the prototype reactor presently being built. It also depends on the building of large-scale spent fuel reprocessing facilities since every 500 MW breeder reactor requires 3 tonnes of plutonium that has to be reprocessed from spent fuel from the reactor. Given international collaboration, it is possible for India to install 35,000 MW of nuclear power by 2030, which will generate 260 billion kwh, 1.3 per cent of total energy supply. However, the crucial point is that this is just the beginning; the fruits of breeder and thorium reactors will be realised only in the years after 2030.

Solar

Most parts of India receive a good average daily solar radiation of 5-6 kwh/m^2. Therefore, if solar generation technologies are deployed on 20 million hectares, India can generate about 24,000 billion kwh even at a modest 10 per cent efficiency. This is more than India's expected total energy supply and several times the desired carbon-free energy. Solar energy evidently is a crucial option for a long-term solution to the climate problem. It is a more efficient option than biofuels since the latter utilise sunlight indirectly through photosynthesis. The overall efficiency of making biofuel from sunlight is less than 1 per cent.[23] As against this, the efficiency of present generation silicon cells is about 20 per cent. Unfortunately, these continue to be expensive and the challenge is to make them cost competitive. Solar thermal power using concentrators is another attractive option for utility scale power generation. A single stretch of land measuring 20 km X 20 km, say in sun-drenched Ladakh, can generate over 20,000 MW of electric power contributing 50 billion kwh of energy (equivalent to eight coal power plants).

India's total commercial energy supply is expected to be 20,000 billion kwh by 2030, out of which 2,500 billion kwh is desired from "carbon-free" sources. Wind, biofuels and hydro will be marginal players contributing less than 6 per cent of India's future needs even if they are developed to the maximum potential.

This analysis suggests that India must use all the resources discussed here and technologies to the limits of their potential to generate a "reasonable" fraction of carbon-free energy. Wind, hydro and biofuels have limitations and can contribute only to an extent. Nuclear, solar and coal (with carbon capture and sequestration) are vital for India's long-term energy security in a climate-friendly manner.

A large number of research and development programmes are required to prove several of these technologies for large scale implementation. While India has a large and ongoing nuclear power programme, a similar major effort is lacking in solar energy and carbon capture and sequestration. Indian R&D investments in these areas are still modest and have to be scaled up dramatically, almost on a war footing.

Germany, despite not being so blessed with solar radiation leads the world in grid-corrected solar PV systems mainly because of government subsidies and investments for R&D. Japan also has sizeable subsidies. India's experience is limited to solar water heating systems and solar PV panels for niche applications. It is befitting for India to initiate major programmes in utility-scale solar power generation involving the government, industry and the scientific community. Efforts should also be made to make these projects attractive for talented and qualified research scientists and engineers. If India develops some of these technologies, it will enable other developing countries to adopt these as well in their effort to combat climate change.[24]

Some Unanswered Questions in the Climate Change Regime

The climate change regime is the sum total of the United Nations Framework Convention on Climate Change (UNFCCC) 1992 and the decisions taken by the annual conference of parties (CoP) to the UNFCCC aimed at fleshing out the skeletal provisions contained in the convention which sets forth a long-term policy structure to address climate change and short-term emission reduction commitments of greenhouse gases. Some of the landmark decisions of the CoP, which include adoption of the Kyoto Protocol at its third annual meeting in 1997, and adoption of the Kyoto rule book at its seventh annual meeting in Marrakech in 2001 leave a number of questions of crucial importance unanswered. The adoption of the Marrakech Accords by the first meeting of the Parties serving as the Conference of Parties to the Kyoto Protocol (hereinafter CoP/MoP1),[25] which was held in Montreal in late 2005, saw the formal launch of trading in emission reduction of greenhouse gases.[26]

The CoP has been lenient so far regarding specifying how much emission reduction of greenhouse gases should take place at the domestic level in Annex I countries (industrialised countries). Trading in greenhouse gases not only offers a chance of exploitation but it is also challenging to verify emission reduction.

The climate change regime is biased in favour of mitigation. It clearly says mitigation will result in the stabilisation of greenhouse gas concentrations at a sustainable level, which will allow sufficient time for ecosystems to "adapt" naturally to climate change. It is inherent in this logic that mitigation will pave the way for adaptation. But it obscures one thing: the capacity to adapt to rapid changes and this new variability differs significantly from one country to another. The small islands, being vulnerable to the effects of climate change, warrant a concrete adaptation policy. Unfortunately, the response of the CoP has been insufficient to take the law on adaptation from its infancy to centre stage, which would have helped the small-island states get enough money from the financial mechanism to prepare for the adverse effects of climate change.

In terms of fairness, it is good that countries which have not joined the protocol or have no intention of doing so do not benefit from the protocol's emission trading regime. The rules for the Clean Development Mechanism (CDM) bar non-parties to the Kyoto Protocol from participating in CDM projects. It is however possible that CDM rules are seen to conflict with international investment law, which prescribes non-discriminatory standards of treatment for foreign investors.

Article 6 of the protocol allows for and outlines emissions trading in which a party included in the Annex I countries "may transfer, or acquire from, any other such Party emission reduction units resulting from projects aimed at reducing anthropogenic emissions by sources or enhancing anthropogenic removals by sinks of greenhouses gases."[27] These projects, however, can only be used as supplemental measures to domestic actions. It does not specify a minimum amount of emission reduction of greenhouse gases to be made through domestic action. The principle is retained in the decision of the CoP/MoP I without any change, which says that emission trading in greenhouse gases should be supplementary to domestic action and that domestic action should thus constitute a significant element of effort made by each party included in Annex I to meet its emission reduction targets under Article 3(1).[28] The words "significant element" do not imply a fixed percentage of domestic reduction out of their worldwide reduction target of 5.2 per cent to be achieved by the industrialised countries between 2008 and 2012. The developed countries might use this loophole to fulfill their entire obligations through emission trading. Likewise at the CoP-3 in Kyoto in 1997, in the fixing of a greenhouse gas reduction target of an individual developed country the CoP/MoP 1 should have taken the opportunity to fix minimum domestic cuts of greenhouse gases of an individual developed country.

In the CoP-4 meeting in Buenos Aires, in 1998, the issue of how much of a country's emission reduction of greenhouse gases could be met through trading was discussed. The US argued that it should be limitless while the European Union felt should be supplementary to domestic reductions. The sharp division between the EU and the US at the CoP-4 did signal that not specifying the extent of emission reduction to be made through domestic action might be misconstrued to mean that the entire obligations could be fulfilled through trading routes only. Fulfillment of the obligations through trading routes may be described as their attempt to buy their way out of their environmental responsibilities.

The trading route to meet the obligations offers the prospect of commercial exploitation. The investors from the developed countries may invest in greenhouse gas absorbing projects and they may sell the emission reduction credits in the future at a higher rate.[29]

Ignoring the Rio Agenda

The developed countries had agreed at the Earth Summit at Rio de Janeiro in 1992 to take the initiative in making the earliest and deepest domestic cuts in the emissions. Not making deep domestic cuts waters down the obligations on the part of the developed countries under the principle of common but differentiated responsibilities.[30] The developed countries making a cut also part of the leadership principle to be shown by the developed countries. They are strongly tempted to achieve the major portion of their emission reduction targets by trading since the cost of abatement of greenhouse gases is much less in developing countries.

Trading in emission reduction through CDM projects allows industrialised countries to claim credit for funding reductions in developing countries. In other words, emission trading enables industrialised countries to "double count" trades as both domestic reduction and assistance to developing countries required by the leadership principle.[31]

There is genuine fear that emission trading would undermine one of the objectives of Agenda 21 of the Rio Summit and the UNFCCC relating to maximisation of new and additional resources,[32] which is supposed to cover that portion of the cost of environment protection measures taken by the developing countries as per the obligations under the UNFCCC. Money for emission trading under CDM can come from both the public as well as private sectors. But investment in a CDM project coming from the public sector should not be diverted from official development assistance (ODA). The industrialised country governments may prefer diverting public funds, which have traditionally gone through ODA, to CDM projects with a view to earning Certified Emission Reduction Units (CERUs) thereby helping them meet a part of their reduction obligations under the Kyoto Protocol. One of the likely sufferers may be the publicly funded Global Environment Facility (GEF) since, unlike CDM projects, GEF projects do not earn any credits for the industrialised countries.[33]

Verification of Greenhouse Gases

Despite rigorous monitoring of CDM project activity by the designated operational entity, there is an inherent uncertainty in verifying greenhouse gas emission reduction.[34] Even the best scientific methods do not eliminate the uncertainty in the measurements. The question then arises as to how to account for this uncertainty in the measurements. One of the reasonable suggestions is that parties should only be able to trade in emission reduction projects, which represent demonstrable reductions in emissions or that are associated with sources and sectors for which there is a higher level of scientific certainty in determining emission level. The decision taken by CoP/MoP I includes a measure to prevent fraud, malfeasance or incompetence of the designated operational entities regarding proposed issuance of certified emission reduction units to an entity involved in a CDM project, which has not actually reduced the emission level of greenhouse gases from the level prior to the project. The measure is meant to review the proposed issuance of certified emission reduction units by the designated operational entities. A party involved in the project activity or at least three members of the "Executive Board" request a review of the issuance of the proposed CERUs.[35] In such cases, the role of non-state entities having long experience in the field becomes crucial; future meetings of parties serving as CoP to the protocol should include in the Kyoto rule book, authorising such bodies to review proposed issuance of CERUs.

Adaptation Issues

The international climate change regime is aimed at realising two goals: (1) mitigation of greenhouse gases, and (2) adaptation. Mitigation of greenhouse gases will result in the stabilisation of greenhouse gas concentrations at a sustainable level, which will allow sufficient time to ecosystems to "adapt" naturally to climate change.[36] Mitigation of greenhouse gas is integral to the goal of sustainable development. One of the imperatives of the goal is to build up "adaptive capacity" particularly in the small island states and the least developed countries as they are faced with the threat of irreversible damage.[37] The building of adaptive capacity may include such measures as building sea walls to combat sea-level rise and developing heat-and drought resistant crops. These measures would incur a huge amount of money. The sixth CoP decided to set up an adaptation fund to meet adaptation costs. Money for this fund would come from 2 per cent of the share of proceeds of the implementation of the CDM projects.[38] The Global Environment Facility (GEF) was entrusted with the task of running the fund. During the CoP/MoP 1, the Philippines, on behalf of the G-77/China, questioned whether the GEF council had a mandate to decide that the World Bank would be the trustee for the adaptation fund.[39] The developing countries emphasised that having the GEF, and the World Bank acting as the trustee, would not be the best option for managing the fund. They preferred that the CoP control the fund. Their opposition can be traced to two reasons:[40] First, the World Bank already exercises some form of influence over the financial policies of many developing countries and they prefer an alternative "window" for assistance on environmental issues. Second, they doubt the ability of the World Bank to address environmental issues and are afraid that such issues may be dealt with at the cost of social aspects. They fear a conflict of interest between the Bank's role as lender and its role in financing the reduction of greenhouse gas emissions.

The amount of money that will accumulate from a share of the proceeds of CDM projects cannot be determined at this stage. Moreover, given the number of eligible countries involved, any allocation will only make a marginal contribution to a country's overall effort. There is an idea that a levy on the other two mechanisms namely Joint Implementation and Emission Trading on the pattern of the CDM should be charged, which may result in more resources at the disposal of the Adaptation Fund.[41]

The UNFCCC assigns the developed countries the responsibility for assisting developing country parties that are "particularly vulnerable" to the adverse effects of climate change to meet the costs of adaptation without defining the term particularly vulnerable.[42] Ability to adapt is severely constrained by poverty. It is generally understood that particularly vulnerable countries are the small-island developing states because they are more susceptible to the effects of a rising sea-level.

The mandate of the GEF restricts it to funding activities at the planning stage, which includes studies of possible impacts of climate change, to identify particularly vulnerable countries or regions and develop policy options for adaptation and appropriate capacity-building. The actual adaptation work aimed at building adaptive capacity, like building sea walls to combat sea-level rise and developing heat-and-drought resistant crops, cannot be funded by the GEF. The GEF funds the incremental cost or additional costs of activities that provide "global benefits". GEF funding cannot be spent on any activities, the benefits of which are intended to accrue at the local or national level. The activities aimed at building adaptive capacity qualify as general development measures.

The recent policy decision of the GEF council namely, development of a "Resource Allocation Framework" (RAF), is going to affect the funding of adaptation measures. The RAF says that resources from GEF will be governed by two criteria: (1) a country's potential to generate global environmental benefits, and (2) country performance. The first criterion conveys clearly that the GEF will provide funds after measuring the potential of each country to generate global environmental benefits in a particular area. The second criteria imply that GEF will measure each country's policies and practices relevant to a successful implementation of GEF programmes and projects. The criterion may be helpful to an extent in projects where it is demonstrable that replacing a particular component of a greenhouse gas or ozone depleting substance mitigation project is going to have global environmental benefits.

The CoP/MoP I merely requested the GEF to report to it on how its recent policy decision will influence the funding available to developing countries for the implementation of their commitments under UNFCCC.[43] The financial mechanism has to function under the guidance of the CoP. It is important to note that the GEF is guided not only by its operational policy but also by the decisions of the CoP. The GEF is obligated as per the provisions of the UNFCCC to conform to the guidance of the CoP. At CoP 1, parties to the UNFCCC decided to adopt a three-stage process for adaptation measures and planning to be covered by GEF funding.[44] Stages one and two deal with studies regarding possible impacts of climate change and planning required in particular regions and policy options for adaptation and capacity building. Stage three suggests measures to facilitate adequate adaptation as envisaged by Article 4(1)(b) and Article 4(4) of the convention.[45] Stage three funding is contingent on the fact that the previous two stages have already been complied with. What is meant by adequate adaptation is not defined in the convention. It is being generally considered to include measures like increasing the height of sea-walls, building irrigation systems to protect agriculture from salt intrusion, or installing of air conditioning systems to avoid heat related illness or death. But the GEF does not have enough resources to meet these costs as its resources are becoming more and more inadequate as more and more areas are being assigned to it for funding.[46] Another reason is that there is no objective criterion for defining a donor's obligation. Being mandated by Article 11 of the UNFCCC to decide on the policy of the financial mechanism, the CoP may try to correct this situation by setting objective criteria for defining a donor's obligation to provide funds.

Clean Development Mechanism

Under the Clean Development Mechanism, there will be flow of investment finance from the industrialised to developing countries for projects that reduce greenhouse gas emissions. The projects owned in whole or in part by a foreign investor would be treated as "investments" within the meaning of international investment agreement. The CDM rules bar non-parties to the Kyoto Protocol from participating in CDM projects. The eligibility to participate in the mechanism by a party included in Annex I is dependent on its methodological and reporting requirements under Article 5(1) and 2,[47] and Article 7 paragraphs 1 and 4 of the Kyoto Protocol.[48] This rule runs counter to non-discriminatory standards of treatment found in international investment agreements.

The goal of the CDM project is to achieve sustainable development.[49] The host is sovereign to give consent to a project. It may reject a project if it is not going to achieve sustainable development. This is a kind of performance requirement. This kind of restriction is prohibited by international investment rules. Private entities can also participate in CDM projects that are authorised by the CoP. But it is not clear whether authorisation is mandatory and if it is, whether any party can authorise a private entity from a non-party. The adoption of the Kyoto rulebook without addressing this issue might run into rough weather, as the US being a potential source of investment in the field of renewable energy happens to be a non-party to the Kyoto Protocol.

Meeting obligations through emission trading will do nothing to benefit the atmosphere unless a major share of the reductions is made inside the territory. Moreover, there is uncertainty involved in measuring emission reduction through trading. In such a situation, only projects having very little uncertainty should be permitted under CDM. The small-island states are definitely facing the threat of irreversible damage. Measures, which are aimed at building their adaptive capacity, should be initiated now as per the "precautionary principle". The financial mechanisms should not be tied to the concept of global environmental benefits where only adequate adaptation measures can reduce the damage. Keeping in view the issue of climate change at the centre, only parties to the Kyoto Protocol should be given permission for emission trading. Otherwise if non-parties are permitted to trade, they will forget the basic obligations under Article 5(1) of the Kyoto Protocol.[50]

Climate Change and India

With regard to climate change, India has some real tough tight-rope walk before it. With temperatures poised to rise by 2.5 to 5 degrees Celsius over the century, monsoon patterns threatening to go haywire and sea levels likely to rise, as it is there will be problems of food security, water scarcity, livelihood, and health to reckon with. To be balanced with this are the imperatives of sustaining a high economic growth as a prerequisite to poverty alleviation, and the need to raise per capita energy consumption to provide a minimally acceptable level of wellbeing.

India has rightly been looking both inward and outward in its efforts to balance its varied and often seemingly contradictory concerns. This is reflected in our comprehensive domestic agenda for mitigating climate change, adapting to it and aiming to cut the emission intensity of GDP by 20-25% of the 2005 level by 2020. This is also reflected in our proactive climate negotiations in international floor where we have persistently been upholding the principle of common but differentiated responsibility, fighting for the rights of the developing countries to economic growth without the impediments of immediate formal caps on emissions, and insisting that developed countries respect their obligations to reduce emission and help developing countries to get on to the path of sustainable development.

Climate change is not just about the environment. As Copenhagen has proved, for some it means clinging on to their high consumption lifestyles while finding out ways to sweep the products of such lifestyles under the carpet. For others it means safeguarding their rights to grow, and for yet others it is a question of their very existence. Certainly it is not the best backdrop for world consensus. India and the other Basic group of countries have however, done the best they could have under the circumstances. Emerging as a powerful force in the climate change negotiations, the coordinated efforts of this quartet has ensured that the negotiations under UNFCCC will continue on the two tracks laid out at Bali—one leading to long-term cooperative action and the other leading to the second commitment period of Annex I Parties under the Kyoto Protocol. The 30 billion dollar "Copenhagen Green Climate Fund" for the period 2010-12 would also be a useful support for adaptation and mitigation efforts in the lesser developed and more vulnerable countries.

Facing the Challenge

Climate change is primarily caused by the building up of greenhouse gases (GHG) e.g. carbon dioxide, methane, nitrous oxide and others in the atmosphere. The global increases in carbon dioxide concentration which have been responsible for the largest part of this build-up, are due primarily to fossil fuel use and land-use change, owing to human activities taking place since pre-industrial times, while those of methane and nitrous oxide are primarily due to agriculture.

Climate change can be accompanied by higher average temperatures near earth's surface, changed rainfall patterns, and increased severity and frequency of floods, droughts and cyclones, which can severely impact livelihoods, especially of the poor in developing countries. The change in climate could lead to impacts on freshwater availability, oceanic acidification, food production, flooding of coastal areas and increased burden of vector borne and water borne diseases associated with extreme weather events, etc.

The Challenge of Climate Change

Climate change can slow down the pace of development either directly through increased exposure to climate variability or indirectly through erosion of the capacity to adapt.

Climate change necessitates that the developing countries, though not responsible for climate change, adapt to it and implement response strategies so as to minimize impacts on livelihoods and natural resources. Further, mitigation measures have to be adopted at the global level with a view to minimise further change in climate, and eventually stabilize it. Both these strategies cast additional social, human, and economic burdens on developing countries. Large amount of national resources have to be committed for adaptation measures. Besides, actions for mitigating climate change that may involve emissions reduction have huge implications for the growth of developing countries, particularly in those sectors e.g. energy generation, and transport where emissions emanate largely from consumption of fossil fuels and the use of alternative sources of energy is limited by resources, technology and access/availability.

India's Vulnerability to Climate Change

India is already facing high degree of climate variability and may face additional challenge because of climate change. A significant part of the annual variation in India's GDP growth over the past half century is attributable to yearly variations in rainfall. The Himalayan ecosystem, so vital for our water security, is vulnerable to climate change. Moreover, increases in mean sea levels will affect large populations and communities in peninsular and coastal India.

Although there is no significant long term trend in monsoon rainfall or floods in the summer monsoon season at all-India level, a warming of 0.4°C in surface air temperature has been noticed over the period 1901-2000. Total frequency of cyclonic storms forming over Bay of Bengal has, however, remained almost constant over 1887-1997.

It has been noticed, on the other hand, that the Gangotri glacier, one of the largest in the Himalayas, has been retreating since long and more rapidly in recent decades. As the glaciers retreat, they become more fragmented and the smaller glaciers are more sensitive to global warming. As per the Geological Survey of India, glaciers are worldwide in a phase of recession is a natural cyclic process. The accelerated melting which these glaciers are experiencing as a result of the earth's warming may have a profound effect on future water availability.

It is projected that, by the end of 21st century, rainfall in India may increase by 15-40% with high regional variability. Warming may be more pronounced over land areas with northern India experiencing maximum increase. The warming could be relatively greater in winter and post-monsoon seasons. The annual mean temperature could increase by 3°C to 6°C over the century. Under these circumstances, it is projected that India may suffer huge losses due to the increased incidence of extreme weather events and additional risks to the livelihoods of people.

Global Regime for Addressing Climate Change

In response to the concerns about the potential impacts of accumulated and rising stock of GHG emissions and the need to address climate change, an international regime of actions was agreed in from of the United Nations Framework Convention on Climate Change (UNFCCC), 1992. The Convention seeks to achieve stabilization of greenhouse gas concentrations in the atmosphere at a level that would prevent dangerous anthropogenic interference with the climate system. The Convention affirms that climate change is a global problem requiring global efforts from all countries, but also recognizes the primary contribution of the developed countries to the high stock of CO_2 emissions in the atmosphere, and expects the developed countries to necessarily take the lead. This principle of, "common but differentiated responsibilities and respective capabilities", is the basis of burden sharing between Parties while working towards reaching the objectives of the Convention.

As per the principle of 'common but differentiated responsibilities and respective capabilities', developing countries including India have no obligation to reduce the green house gas emissions. The Convention recognises that the economic and social development and poverty eradication are the first and overriding priorities of the developing countries parties, and that, in course of meeting the developmental needs, the emissions of developing countries are bound to rise. Any mitigation action by the developing countries must, therefore, be taken in the context of sustainable development and be consistent with their national priorities. Further, the Convention also recognises that the extent to which developing countries parties will effectively implement their commitments i.e. taking actions to mitigate emissions under the convention will depend on the effective implementation by developed countries parties of their commitments relating to provision of financial resources and transfer of technology.

All industrialized countries are required under the Convention to have binding commitments to reduce their emissions. Kyoto Protocol was signed by the Parties to UNFCCC in 1997 to agree on quantified and specific emission reduction targets for each of the 37 industrialised countries that are listed in Annex-I of the Convention. The Kyoto Protocol lays down binding quantified emission reduction targets for all industrialised countries for the first commitment period of 2008-2012, although the US, the world's biggest emitter of greenhouse gases, did not ratify the Kyoto Protocol.

In December 2007, after the publication of the 4th Assessment Review of the Inter Governmental Panel on Climate Change which established that climate change is unequivocal, the Parties to UNFCCC adopted the Bali Action Plan to enhance the implementation of the Convention. The Bali Action Plan (BAP) calls for full, effective and sustained implementation of the UNFCCC through long-term cooperative action, now, up to and beyond 2012. It is a comprehensive dialogue to address the four major building blocks of climate change, i.e. GHG mitigation, adaptation to climate change impacts; technology development and cooperation; and finance. In pursuance of the Bali Action Plan, negotiations to define the aggregate targets of emission reduction for developed countries including the US and other issues relating to adaptation and financing of adaptation, mitigation and technology in developing countries are underway. On a parallel track, the negotiations to determine the individual quantified emission reduction targets of the Parties to Kyoto Protocol for the second commitment period beginning from 2013 are continuing.

International Negotiations on Climate Change

In the recent international negotiations conducted under the UNFCCC, the industrialized countries have called upon developing countries to contribute to the global effort to address climate change. Specifically, it has been suggested that while the developed countries will take appropriate emission reduction targets in the midterm, the developing countries should follow a low carbon development path and deviate in terms of GHG emission from business as usual scenario. It has also been suggested that the developing countries should place their domestic mitigation commitments of developed countries. Implicit in the arguments of the developed countries is the suggestion that the international support for adaptation to and mitigation of climate change in developing countries will depend on the willingness of the developing countries to subject their national action plans to review and progress in terms of low carbon development.

India's approach to the negotiations is fully anchored in the UNFCCC and Kyoto Protocol. India has argued in the international negotiating floor that the developed country parties must take actions in accordance with the principle of equity and 'common but differentiated responsibilities and respective capabilities' in order to achieve the objectives of the convention. Such actions of the developed countries should include deep and ambitious targets for emission reduction in the second commitment period (post 2012) of the Kyoto Protocol. The starting point for a fair and equitable agreement in the climate change negotiations is, therefore, the acceptance by developed countries of the principle of per capita equity, their historical responsibility, and their undertaking to make credible cuts in GHG emissions of 25-40% by 2020 over 1990 reference levels.

India has stated that the actions of the developing countries will depend on the support in terms of finance and technology provided by the developing countries. While India is willing to accept monitoring, reporting and verification (MRV) as per agreed procedures for those actions that are supported by the international community in terms of finance and technology through agreed channels, its voluntary actions financed from its own domestic resources cannot be subjected to international review. While India has taken a number of steps, on her own, to adapt to climate change and mitigate its emissions in the interest of its energy security and sustainable development, India will take further voluntary and nationally appropriate actions for addressing climate change strictly in accordance with the priorities and objectives laid down under the National Action Plan for Climate Change.

Copenhagen Conference, December 2009

15th Conference of the Parties (CoP 15) to the UNFCCC was held in Copenhagen from December 7-18, 2009, with a view to reach agreed outcomes on the negotiations. The Copenhagen conference was a culmination of a two year process that began in Bali in December 2007. The negotiations have proceeded in two parallel tracks since Bali—one relating to the long term cooperative action of the Parties under the Bali Action Plan—known as LCA track and the other relating to the commitment of the Annex I Parties for the second commitment period under the Kyoto Protocol—known as the KP track.

At the Copenhagen Conference, the talks in the two tracks were to be concluded and outcomes to be reached. India participated in the negotiations constructively with a view to contribute to outcomes in accordance with the principles and provisions of the Convention, Kyoto Protocol and the Bali Action Plan.

However, differences among Parties on several critical issues, particularly those relating to mitigation and finance for climate change persisted, despite some movement on issues relating to e.g. technology, adaptation and Reducing Deforestation and Degradation in Developing Countries (REDD plus). As a result, the talks at Copenhagen could not be concluded and it was decided that the negotiations in two-tracks will continue till CoP 16 scheduled at Mexico from Nov 29-Dec 10, 2010.

At the Copenhagen conference, an attempt was also made by the Danish Prime Minister i.e. the President of the Conference of Parties (CoP), to forge a consensus on outstanding issues through informal consultations amongst a select group of countries including India and present it to the parties in the form of a 'Copenhagen Accord'. However, there was no consensus and the 'Accord' could not be adopted. In the absence of adoption under the multilateral process, the Accord was only taken 'note of' by the parties.

India's Actions on Climate Change

India, being vulnerable to adverse effects of climate change, is very conscious of its global responsibilities towards climate as also the need to minimize adverse effects of climate change on its large population. Although India's total CO_2 emissions are about 4% of total global CO_2 emissions, India is committed to contribute to climate protection by de-coupling the growth of its emissions from the rising economic development. Even with 8-9% GDP growth every year for the next decade or two, India's per capita emissions is likely to be well below developed country averages. India's energy intensity of production has been falling with improvements in energy efficiency, autonomous technological changes and economical use of energy. India's climate modeling studies show that its per capita emissions will be around 2-2.5 tonnes of carbon dioxide equivalent by 2020 and around 3-3.5 tonnes of carbon dioxide equivalent by 2030, as compared to around 1-1.2 tonnes presently. Prime Minister has already stated that India will never allow its per capita emissions to exceed that of the developed countries. Accordingly, India has announced that, it will endeavour to reduce 20 to 25 per cent by 2020 in comparison to the 2005 level. This will be achieved through actions in specific sectors with necessary provision of financial and technological resources including domestic and international support.

While engaging constructively with the international community on the issue, India has pursued a strong domestic agenda for addressing climate change. India recognizes that a strategy for addressing climate change has to be based on the strategy of sustainable development. This is reflected in the major programmes addressing climate variability. Current Government expenditure in India on adaptation to climate variability exceeds 2.6 per cent of the GDP, with agriculture, water resources, health and sanitation, forests, coastal zone infrastructure and extreme events, being specific areas of concern and action.

National Action Plan on Climate Change

In pursuance of its voluntary actions to address climate change related concerns, India released its National Action Plan on Climate Change (NAPCC) on 30th June 2008. The National Action Plan advocates a strategy that promotes, firstly, the adaptation to Climate Change and secondly, further enhancement of the ecological sustainability of India's development path.

The National Action Plan stresses that maintaining a high growth rate is essential for increasing living standards of the vast majority of people of India and reducing their vulnerability of the impacts of climate change. Accordingly, the Action Plan identifies measures that promote the sustainable development while also yielding co-benefits for addressing climate change.

Eight National Missions e.g. National Solar Mission, National Mission on Enhanced Energy Efficiency, National

Mission on Sustainable Habitat, National Water Mission, National Mission for sustaining the Himalayan Ecosystem, National Mission for a Green India, National Mission for Sustainable Agriculture and National Mission on Strategic knowledge for Climate Change form the core of the National Action Plan and represent multi-pronged, long term and integrated strategies for achieving key goals in the context of climate change. Besides the 8 Missions, the NAPCC also outlines 24 Initiatives aimed at promoting technologies and actions in the sectors pertaining to energy generation, transport, renewable, disaster management and capacity building that will have substantial benefits in terms of addressing climate change, when integrated with the development plans of the Ministries.

The National Missions are to be institutionalized by the respective Ministries. The Prime Minister's Council on Climate Change, set up in June, 2007 monitors the preparation of and approves the national missions, while the Ministry of Environment & Forests coordinates the implementation of the Action Plan and other climate change related actions in India. Documents in respect of the national missions as prepared by the nodal Ministries are at various stages of adoption and approval.

It is notable that India's Five Year plans outline a strategy for sustainable growth resulting in low carbon sustainable development. 11th Five Year Plan includes an indicative target of increasing energy efficiency by 20% by 2016-17. The National Mission on Enhanced Energy Efficiency implemented by the Ministry of Power through the Bureau of Energy Efficiency seeks to pursue this goal.

NAPCC will guide India's further actions in regard to low carbon growth strategy. Based on the exercises for Mid-Term Appraisal in the 11th Five Year Plan that indicates that the emission intensity has declined by 17.6 per cent between 1990 and 2005, the Planning Commission has concluded that a 20 to 25 per cent reduction in emission intensity between 2005 and 2020 is possible.

This will require that necessary actions in specific sectors are undertaken to reduce emission intensity and corresponding emission reduction outcomes with necessary provisions of financial and technological resources. These could include specific performance targets in industry, energy, transport, agriculture, buildings and forestry for the year 2020 & 2030. These could be institutionalized through either legislative or executive action under the NAPCC and the Five Year Plan documents. Actions may also be taken to enhance such domestic actions in line with specific domestic targets as outlined in 11th and subsequent five-year plans with domestic and international resources as available.

State Level Action Plans on Climate Change

The Prime Minister in his address to the Ministers of Environment and Forests from various states on 18th August 2009 had called upon all state governments to prepare State level Action Plans on Climate Change consistent with the strategy outlined in the NAPCC. The state level plans will enable communities and ecosystems to adapt to climate change effectively and help achieve the objective of the NAPCC. Accordingly, a programme for preparation of state level plans has been initiated.

Some of the States have already responded and initiated positive action. The Government of Himachal Pradesh has drawn up a programme and sought technical assistance and funding from the World Bank for the projected activities. The Government of Delhi has prepared an Action Plan outlining the activities which was launched in November 2009. The Government of Karnataka has initiated activities and proposed a technical assistance programme with the World Bank for this purpose. Kerala Government has constituted a steering committee to oversee the preparation of an Action Plan. Gujarat has taken proactive steps to set up a dedicated department for climate change and prepare its action plan.

India's International Obligations

As a part of its international obligations under the UNFCCC, India prepares periodically the National

Communication (NATCOM) that gives an inventory of the greenhouse gases (GHG) emissions in India, and assesses the vulnerability and impacts and makes appropriate recommendations regarding social, economic and technological measures for addressing climate change. Preparation of NATCOM is an exercise based on an extensive network of research and scientific institutions in India and draws upon expertise and excellence from different institutions. 131 research teams collaborated to prepare India's first NATCOM and present it in 2004. India's Second National Communications (NATCOM-II) which will put together an even more detailed assessment of national GHG inventories and of the vulnerabilities faced by the key sectors in India is under preparation. This was expected to be available by late 2010 and will be presented to the UNFCCC in 2011. Systemic improvements to enhance the scope and transparency of India's national communications are also being considered with a view to better inform the various relevant stakeholders of the actions and initiatives that India is taking on climate change.

Clean Development Mechanism

India has participated effectively in the Clean Development Mechanism (CDM) which is designed to help developed countries in meeting their emission reduction targets while contributing to sustainable development in developing countries through purchase of Certified Emission Reduction Certificates (CERS) from developing countries by the developed countries businesses and governments. India's CDM potential represents a significant component of the global CDM market.

The Government of India has set up the National CDM Authority in December 2003 with its office in the Ministry of Environment & Forests. The National CDM Authority evaluates and recommends CDM projects for host country approval. At the end of 2009, India had a profile of 1551 approved host country projects in the sectors of energy efficiency, fuel switching, industrial processes, municipal solid waste and renewable energy. Out of these, 478 projects (against total number of 2011 globally registered projects) are registered by the CDM Executive Board and have the potential of generating 74.22 mm CERs out of total 366.17 mm registered CERs. If all the approved projects get registered, the projects can attract an overall inflow of approximately US$ 6.27 billion by the year 2012 at a conservative price of the US$10 per CER.

CDM is an important subject of negotiations under Kyoto Protocol. India is of the view that CDM has helped the developing countries enhance their sustainable development and should be further strengthened in the 2nd commitment period of the Protocol from 2013.

Institutional Mechanism for Addressing Climate Change

The Government of India has set up an elaborate institutional mechanism to consider and address issues relating to climate change. A Council chaired by the Prime Minister called Prime Minister's Council on Climate Change was constituted in June 2007 to coordinate national action for assessment, adaptation and mitigation of climate change. The Council provides the overall guidance to climate change related actions taken by various Ministries in the Government and other agencies. The Ministry of Environment & Forests is the national focal point for UNFCCC and coordinates various activities relating to the NAPCC and other climate change related policies and actions.

An expert committee set up under the chairmanship of the Principal Scientific Adviser to Government of India has studied (2008) the impact of anthropogenic climate change on India and has come out with its first set of findings and the research agenda that the ministries need to follow and implement in order to address India's vulnerability to anthropogenic climate change impacts.

With the pro-active measure pursued by governments in the domestic and International fronts, it is hoped that climate change issues will be addressed significantly and seriously in future years. Increasing awareness about Climate change and concentrated action of the central and State governments will help fulfill the global goal of climate stabilization (Rashmi and Satapathy, 2010).

Evaluation of Some Contributing Factors

Given the fact that human civilization and industrialization have amplified the emission of 'Green House Gases' (GHG), the question is whether they really are the main causal factors accelerating climate change. GHGs constitute Carbon Dioxide (CO_2), Methane (CH_4), Nitrous Oxide (NO_2), Hydrofluorocarbons (HFCs), Perflurocarbons (PFCs) and Sulpurhexafluride (SF_6). In addition to these, water vapor is considered important, which absorbs the heat radiations from sun and traps such radiations in the atmosphere making the earth warmer. Emission of GHGs beyond certain limits makes earth's atmosphere hotter and can induce climate change. The extent of GHGs in the atmosphere increased phenomenally from 280ppm (1750) to 379ppm in 2005 (IPCC-AR4). The available global data on CO_2 since 1970 indicates that the annual emission has increased by about 80% from 21 to 38 gigatons, which represents 77% of the total anthropogenic emission. The global increase in CO_2 concentration is primarily due to increase in fossil fuel use, land-use change, changes in agricultural activities, industrial development and loss of forests. CO_2 originates from burning of fossil fuel (56.6%), deforestation and decay of biomass (17.3%), agriculture etc. As per the estimates of United Nations Development Programme, the total emission of CO_2 in India is 1,342 Mt in 2004 which is 4.6 per cent of the world total. The CO_2 emission is growing at the rate of 6.9 per cent and the per capita emission is 1.2 tonnes which is 17 times lower than that of USA and 8 times lower than that of European countries (HDR 2007/2008).

The energy sector is the major producer of CO_2 in India. Our energy needs are met from coal (53%), which is abundant, locally available and cheap when compared to alternative fuels. As per the data published by Central Electricity Authority, CO_2 emission in the power sector is continuously increasing at the annual rate of 4.43 per cent in all parts of the country. Compared to global consumption of coal for energy production (about 40 per cent), the use of coal for energy production in India is high. It is therefore, important to maintain statistics on CO_2 emission by sources. Interestingly, about 14 per cent of the world production of coal is consumed by USA, out of which 37 per cent is used for electricity generation.

The global atmospheric concentration of methane has increased from pre-industrial value of about 715ppb to 17874ppb in 2005 (IPCC-AR4). Methane is generated from the activities like agriculture, biomass burning, coal mining and handling, flaring of natural gas, waste disposal, land-use pattern, forestry and shifting cultivation practice. In India, methane emission in the year 1994 was 18,583 Gg., out of which 78% came from agriculture, 16% from energy production and 6% from waste disposal. The measure of methane emission due to various activities needs to be estimated for analyzing temporal changes in its concentration in atmosphere.

There is considerable reduction in the forest cover in the past few years due to encroachment and land use change, economic development activities like construction of roads, canals and power stations. However, there is a slight improvement in the forest cover as per the 2007 assessment as reported by the State of Forest Report-2009. Forests are the major source of carbon sequestration and the womb of the biodiversity, which acts as the main artery of sustainability of environment and the ecosystem. National Action Plan on Climate Change (NAPCC) estimates that 68 to 77% of the forest areas in the country are likely to experience change in forest types by the end of the 21st century. Since the enactment of Forest Conservation Act, 1980, a huge portion of forestland has been diverted for non-forest use. The reported figure for the year 1981 is 1331 hectares whereas the cumulative figure till 2004 is 9,54,839 Ha.

Economic development and urbanization are positively correlated. As per the United Nations Human Settlements Programme (UNHSP) figures, the global urbanization has increased from 2% in 1800 to 47% in 2000. As reported by TERI (2007), the daily generation of waste in Delhi alone is 5922 Tonnes, out of which 54.42% are compostable and 15.52%

recyclables. Wastes pollute water and atmosphere and degrade land. If left untreated, they ferment and generate bio-gas, which contains 65-70% of methane. The heat trapping capacity of methane is 34 times higher than that of CO_2. The present data is insufficient to gauge the amount of recycling that happens at the source level and the amount of methane and other pollutants emitted by solid waste.

Issues Concerning Impact Assessment

The resilience of the ecosystem is likely to be disturbed in the future due to abrupt climate change, which could appear in the form of floods, drought, wildfires, ocean acidification etc, inducing further loss of biodiversity and jeopardizing the earth's latent capacity to mitigation and regeneration. The rise in temperature, change in precipitation patterns, sea level rise, melting of snow cover and mountain glaciers, coastal erosion and occurrence of health hazards and disaster events are perceived as the visible impacts of climate change.

In India, an increase of about 0.40C in the surface air temperature has been observed in the past century. A trend of warming is visible along the west coast, central India, interior peninsula and the North-Eastern India, but some cooling trends are also visible in the North-West India and parts of South-India (NAPCC-2008). India Meteorological Department (IMD) is the nodal agency to provide and analyse long-term series of temperature data.

Indian monsoon rains are the backbone of Indian economy as most of our agricultural activities; river flows and replenishment of ground water source depend on monsoon rains. Rainfall data are collected by the IMD in respect of the meteorological subdivisions of the country on a day-to-day basis. A significantly long series of rainfall data is, therefore, available to analyze patterns of change in distribution, intensity and duration of rainfall. About 10 to 12% increase in monsoon rains are reported to have taken place along the west coast, northern Andhra Pradesh and north-western India during the last century. A decrease of about 6 to 8% has been observed over eastern Madhya Pradesh, north-eastern India and some parts of Gujarat and Kerala (NAPCC-2008).

The ice and snow deposits on the Himalayan ranges are the lifelines of northern India. They provide a perennial supply of water though many rivers, which cater to the livelihood, drinking water, and water for industry and irrigation. The available data on snowfall in the Himalayan ranges shows a recession of snow cover in some parts of the Himalayan ranges. The river systems of the Brahmaputra, the Ganges and the Indus draw water directly from melting of the Himalayan glaciers. The National Remote Sensing Agency (NRSA) and Snow and Avalanche Studies Establishment (SASE) are responsible for collection and supply of data on cry sphere.

India is one of the species-rich countries in the world and about 6% of the world's biodiversity is reported from India. The existing data does not provide any insight into the loss of biodiversity in the country which happened over the years due to rapid economic growth, urbanization and land-use change. The NAPCC also emphasizes on the need for 'creation of biodiversity registers' (at national, district and local levels) for documenting genetic diversity and the associated traditional knowledge. Zoological Survey of India, Botanical Survey of India, Forest Survey of India and the State Forest Departments are responsible for collection and supply of data related to biodiversity.

IPCC has estimated a sea level rise of 1 to 2mm per year globally. In India, a study conducted by Unnikrishanan and Shankar also showed a trend of 1.06 to 1.75 mm rise of sea level per year. No official data is however, available in India to empirically check the authenticity of these estimated figures. Due to sea level rise, the fresh water sources near the coastal areas will suffer from salt intrusion and inundation of coastal areas, where a large section of the population is highly dependent on the sea for livelihood activities.

India is predominantly an agrarian economy, as 52% of the population directly depends on agriculture either as farmers or agricultural labourers out of which 76% resides in villages. Climate change will have a direct impact on the livelihood of these people. Food production in India is sensitive to climate change effects on temperature and monsoon rainfall. Rise in temperature is likely to have a direct impact on the Rabi crops as every 10C rise in temperature will reduce wheat production by 4 to 5 Million Tonnes. Every small change in temperature and rainfall has significant effect on the quality and quantity of production of fruits, vegetables, tea, coffee, basmati rice and aromatic and medicinal plants. It is predicted that a loss of 10 to 40% in production of food grains may occur by 2100 due to climate change (NAPCC). Time series data on area, production and yield of major crops, season-wise and State-wise and for all-India are available from Department of Agriculture & Cooperation, Ministry of Agriculture. However, the production figures are required to be analyzed with reference to the climate change data over time.

Populations in coastal regions are vulnerable to natural disasters like cyclones, floods, droughts, soil and land erosion. These phenomena may accentuate due to climate change leading to irreparable loss or damage to sown areas. About 40 million hectares of land is flood prone, including rive-deltas on three sides of the country stretching over 6000 Km of coastal belt, affecting about 30 million people on an average each year. National Disaster Management Authority (NDMA) is responsible for the collection and compilation of the disaster data. State governments are also going to engage their system to compile data on disasters at district levels.

Roles of different government agencies as envisaged in the NAPCC are highly compartmentalized. As a result, the data related to different constituents of Climate Change are resident in different domain-specific systems under the control and administration of independent agencies. The inter-connectivity of these data systems under an over-arching system for management and technical knowledge-mix is largely missing. The atmosphere is one single entity, but what goes into it emanates from various sources. Measuring the net effect of the factors is therefore, a cross-cutting issue, which requires cross-pollination of domain-knowledge elements in every possible way they may fertilize to meaningfully signify reasons of change and their quantitative measures. Is Indian Network of Climate Change Assessment (INCCA) an answer to this? We think it should be able to provide adequate space to knowledge integration and data blending (Chakrabarti and Kumar, 2010).

Population and Poverty

Poverty stimulates population growth. Direct poverty alleviation is essential; business as usual on poverty alleviation is irresponsible. MacNeill[51] states it plainly: "...reducing rates of population growth ..." is an essential condition to achieve sustainability. This is as important, if not more so, in industrial countries as it is in developing countries. Industrial countries over consume per capita, consequently over pollute, and so are responsible for by far the largest share of our approach to the limits. The richest 20% of the world consumes over 70% of the world's commercial energy. Twenty-five nations already have essentially stable population size, so it is not utopian to expect others to follow.

Developing countries contribute to exceeding limits because they are so populous today (77% of the world's total) and because their populations are increasing far faster than their economies can provide for them (90% of world population growth). Real incomes are declining in some areas. If left unchecked, it may be halfway through the 21st century before the number of births will fall back even to current high levels. Developing countries' population growth alone would account for a 75% increase in their commercial energy consumption by 2025, even if per capita consumption remained at current inadequate levels[52]. These countries need so much scale growth that this can only be freed up by the transition to sustainability in industrial countries.

The poor must be given the chance, must be assisted, and will justifiably demand to reach at least minimally acceptable material living standards by access to the remaining natural resource base. When industrial nations switch from input growth to qualitative development, more resources and environmental functions will be available for the South's needed growth. It is in the interests of developing countries and the world commons not to follow the fossil fuel model. It is in the interest of industrial countries to subsidize alternatives. This view is repeated by Dr. Qu Wenhu of the Chinese Academy of Sciences, who says: "...if 'needs' include one automobile for each of a billion Chinese, then is impossible...." Developing populations account for only 17% of total commercial energy use now, but unchecked this will almost double by 2020[53].

Merely meeting unmet demand for family planning would help enormously. Educating young females and providing them with credit for productive purposes and employment opportunities are probably the next most effective measures. A full 25% of U.S. births and a much larger number of developing country births are to unmarried or teenage mothers who provide less child care. Many of these births are unwanted, which also tends to result in less care. Certainly, international development agencies should assist high population growth countries to reduce to world averages as an urgent first step, instead of trying only to increase infrastructure without population measures.

Beyond Brundtland

To the extent that the economic subsystem both has become large relative to the global ecosystem on which it depends and is exceeding the regenerative and assimilative capacities of sources and sinks, the growth called for by the Brundtland report will dangerously exacerbate surpassing the limits outlined above. Opinions differ. MacNeill[54] claims "a minimum of 3% annual per capita income growth is needed to reach sustainability during the first part of the next century," and this would require higher growth in national income, given population trends. Hueting[55] disagrees, concluding that for sustainability "...what we need least is an increase in national income." Sustainability will be achieved only to the extent quantitative throughput growth stabilizes and is replaced by qualitative development, holding inputs constant or even reducing them. Remembering that the scale of the economy is population times per capita resource use, both per capita resource use and population must decline.

Brundtland is excellent on three of the four necessary conditions for sustainability: first, producing more with less (e.g., conservation, efficiency, technological improvements, and recycling); second, reducing the population explosion; and third, redistribution from over consumers to the poor. Brundtland was probably being politically astute in leaving fuzzy the fourth necessary condition. This is the transition from input growth and growth in the scale of the economy over to qualitative development, holding the scale of the economy consistent with the regenerative and assimilative capacities of global life-support systems. In several places the Brundtland report hints at this. Qualitatively improved assets replace depreciated assets, and births replace deaths, so that stocks of wealth and people are continually renewed and even improved[56]. A developing economy is one that is getting better, not necessarily bigger, so that the well-being of the (stable) population improves. An economy growing in throughput is only getting bigger, exceeding limits, and damaging the self-repairing capacity of the planet.

The poor need an irreducible minimum of basics: food, clothing, and shelter. These basics require throughput growth for poor countries with compensating reductions in such growth in rich countries. Apart from colonial resource draw-downs, industrial country growth historically has increased markets for developing countries' raw materials, hence presumably benefiting poor countries. But it is industrial country growth that has to contract to free up ecological room for the minimum growth needed in poor country economies. Tinbergen and Hueting[57] put it plainest: "...no further production growth in rich countries... ." All approaches to sustainability must internalize this constraint if the crucial goals of poverty alleviation and halting damage to global life-support systems are to be approached.

Toward Sustainability

As economies change from agrarian through industrial to more service-oriented, throughput growth may change to growth that is less damaging to sources and sinks (for example, coal and steel to fiber optics and electronics). We must shift rapidly to production which is less throughput-intensive. We must accelerate technical improvements in resource productivity; Brundtland's "producing more with less." Presumably this is what the Brundtland Commission and subsequent follow-up authors[58] label "growth, but of a different kind." Vigorous promotion of this trend will indeed help the transition to sustainability and is probably essential. It is also largely true that conservation and efficiency improvements and recycling can be made profitable the instant environmental externalities (e.g., carbon dioxide emissions) are internalized.

But this approach, while necessary, will be insufficient for four reasons[59]. Because of the inescapable laws of thermodynamics, all material growth consumes resources and produces wastes, even Brundtland's unspecified new type of growth. First, to the extent we have reached limits to the ecosystem's regenerative and assimilative capacities, throughput growth exceeding such limits will not herald sustainability. Second, the size of the service sector relative to the production of goods has limits. Third, even many services are fairly throughput-intensive, such as tourism, higher education, and health care. And fourth, and highly significant, is that less throughput-intensive growth is "hi-tech"; hence the one place where there has to be more growth—tiny, impoverished, developing-country economies—is less likely to be able to afford Brundtland's "new" growth.

Environmental Social Responsibility

The natural environment and the corporate manufacturing functions are becoming inextricably linked. Profitability, productivity and environmental consciousness are increasingly viewed as integral goals of manufacturing organizations. Yet, like any other policies, strategies or programmes, risk is involved and sometimes the win/win situations may not arise (Walley and Whitehead, 1994). The manufacturing function will be central and critical to an organization's role in the eccentric (Shrivastava, 1995), eco-efficient (Schmidheiny, 1992), and/or eco-effective (McDonough & Braungart, 1998) organization of the next industrial revolution.

Issues of Environmental Social Responsibility

Organizational Strategy and the Environment: There has been significant progress recently in the development of management and organization theory as it applies to the natural environment. These developments include literature related to business and society research, where the specific social dimension is the natural environment. A major portion of the philosophical content of these concepts includes "stakeholder" theory, which incorporates environmental concerns as part of stakeholder concerns (Starik, 1995); natural recourses based view (Hart, 1995), and eccentric management (Shrivastava, 1995). These theories help to explain and guide the organization's practice with relation to the natural environment. There is a clear linkage between impacts on organizational development and strategy and impact on manufacturing strategy.

Manufacturing Strategy and the Environment: The discussion on a general manufacturing strategy considers both product and process categories. The perspective will be more general than the traditional volume/variety matrix and production process comparisons (Hayes and Wheelwright, 1979). In addition, a "practices" section is included to incorporate some of the more organizational and philosophical elements of manufacturing strategy. Within these categories a "technological" dimension is integrated with manufacturing strategy, since manufacturing is a function that is very technology driven. Initially, some issues related to technology, manufacturing and the environment are presented. Technological influences and the relationship to manufacturing strategy process, manufacturing process developments from an environmental perspective can be linked to issues of reduction, reuse, recycling and remanufacturing. Reduction from a process perspective will require integration of ideas for waste minimization. Reduction is easy to introduce for organizations that have strategic quality initiatives. Recycling, remanufacturing, and reuse, are all differing levels of the general term, recycling. Wastewater closed-loop production processes are being increasingly adopted by industry, primarily due to the ease of incorporating such systems and their accrued benefits.

Product: Product strategy within a manufacturing function is the most closely associated with Design for the Environment (DfE) and Life-Cycle Analysis (LCA) issues. Product and materials flexibility will be necessary for both product development and materials substitution. This capability should be adopted not only for environmental reasons, but competitive reasons as well, as product life-cycle will continue to decrease and product customization increases. DfE and LCA influence an organization's "product" stewardship philosophy. Product stewardship is the minimization of the product's harmful effects on the environment in every stage of its product life-cycle, from design and development to manufacturing, distribution, use and disposal (Hickle and Stitzhal, 2003).

Practice: From a policy perspective, the expertise and knowledge of the organization relied on manufacturing personnel to realize and "buy-in" and the idea of evaluating products and processes based on environmental characteristics. Similar to Total Quality Management (TQM) initiatives where empowerment makes everyone responsible for equality in a manufacturing setting, organizations need to mature environmental responsibilities to the level of pervasiveness. Integrating environmental management knowledge into every day workforce practice will require similar efforts as diffusing equality management responsibility. This is the role of Total Quality Environmental Management (TQEM). TQEM has become increasingly used in pollution prevention and other environmental management strategies (Sarkis, 1998; Pojasek, 2000).

Another environmentally based influence of concern to organizational manufacturing practices is ISO 14000 certification. ISO 14000 certification (or any other technology, programme, etc.), alone, does not guarantee a successful environmentally benign system. In one study of three organizations, Kitazawa and Sarkis (1998), found that environmental management systems (two of which were ISO 14000 certified) to be successful at waste minimization and source reduction, required significant employee support. That is, along with environmental management systems, employee practices, training, support, was necessary for successful implementation of source reduction programmes. Just-In-Time (JIT) manufacturing practices will also have implications for environmental management and sustainability within organizations. Many aspects of JIT are environmentally sound. For example, a major tenet of JIT and TQM is the minimization of waste (reduction and prevention) (Klassen, 2000).

Other Manufacturing Strategy Related Issues

Control and Measurement Systems: One of the central production control systems in a manufacturing setting is manufacturing resources planning and requirements planning systems (MRPII, MRP). These systems will require integration of a number of environmental characteristics, especially in a remanufacturing environment. The research, and practice, in this area have been quite limited (Guide, et al., 1996). One such issue is the integration of reverse bills of material that will aid in managing inventory disassembly of products. The planning and forecasting for material flows into a system will also be an issue. The diversity of "Suppliers" in this type of environment is greater since it is heavily dependent on the variety of customers. Another reason for the uncertainty is due to the immature reverse logistics channels in most manufacturing industries. Completing master scheduling plans for materials that organizations have little control over is also a concern (Guide, et al., 1996).

Location and Facility Decisions: Location and expansion decisions for manufacturing facilities are also impacted by environmental issues. The location/expansion of plants may be limited by the permitting process, which only allows facilities' waste generation capacity (into air, water) up to a certain level. Facility development has to take into consideration new developments, practices and technology. For example, for the design of a new facility in a developing country, Intel corporation designers considered possible improvements in chemical, water, and energy use of possible future technology. Flexible facility design is critical to the cradle-to-grave mentality of product stewardship (Denton, 1998).

Customer and Supplier Relationships: Manufacturing process inputs and outputs play a role in how effectively manufacturing can become green. Managing these inputs and outputs are central to supply chain management (EPA, 2000). The supply chain, of which manufacturing is the central component, for an organization includes relationships with other organizations, primarily as suppliers or customers. Closing the "external" loop with manufacturing will require the efforts of the partners. The manufacturing organizations will be heavily reliant on customers as suppliers of used materials and products. These practices cover a broad set of industries from ceramics and abrasives where Norton Company has a programme to recycle grinding wheel stubs, to electronic equipment such as computers and copiers, such as Xerox and Hewlett Packard.

In addition, customer-supplier relationships will involve joint projects and designs of processes and products, requiring participation with internal design teams from both these groups. Sharing and integrating environmental ideas and concerns organizational boundaries will greatly enhance the abilities of the manufacturing function to remain green.

Numerous examples appear in which multiple multi-organizational relationship benefit from environmentally conscious partners. For example, DuPont has developed a partnership with Ford Motor in which DuPont's payments are based on the number of cars that are painted. This creates an incentive for the two companies to use paint as efficiently as possible (Denton, 1998).

Interventional Relationships: Interventional relationships with manufacturing are now described, especially those relationships that will influence corporate environmental issues. Included in this set of organizational functions are marketing, accounting/finance, human resources and information systems. Engineering is another function which could be viewed as separate from manufacturing.

Marketing, Manufacturing and the Environment: Green marketing will be greatly influenced by the manufacturing capabilities of most organizations. Organizations will make appeals to green consumers concerning the environmental soundness of their products. This green marketing will include process capabilities and product characteristics.

Another dimension of marketing and services associated with demanufacturing and disassembly from a marketing (and profitability) perspective is evidenced by Digital's (now Compaq) materials recovery facilities (Sarkis et al., 1998). These facilities began as cost centres to help defuse and manage the costs associated with the end of life for Digital electronic equipment. Eventually, marketing viewed this as another capability of the "services" that can be offered by Digital. To be effectively marketed as a green company, an image is not enough; "practicing what you preach" is critical (Ottman & Terry, 1998). Environmentally conscious manufacturing is central to the practice.

Accounting, Finance, Manufacturing and the Environment: Accounting and finance's major relationships to manufacturing include cost management, performance measurement, and capital budgeting. Each of these areas will necessarily have to be adjusted to include environmental concerns and impacts within the manufacturing function. Manufacturing practices will change when environmental influences (whether proactive or reactive) put more pressure on the function. Accounting and finance practices need to be willing to change. Costing products and activities within the manufacturing function is already a tricky proposition with the debate focusing on traditional versus activity based costing approaches. Categorizing and estimating costs based on environmental factors will make the problem more complex.

Human Resources, Manufacturing and the Environment: Total quality initiatives, source reduction, introduction of new technologies are all part of integrating and improving the eco-efficiency of organizations. The success or failure of these programmes and initiatives begins with upper management. The implementation and execution progress rests with the lower level employees of the organization. Training and expertise for evaluation environmental issues within a manufacturing plant are difficult. Similar in context to quality, the roles of shop floor personnel do not include responsibility for the measurement and management of environmental issues. The environmental management of organizational processes and practices has traditionally been relegated to the specialized staff personnel, with technical skills required to manage these activities. Empowerment, within the environmental management context, implies that workers will have to become more capable at evaluating the environmental ramifications of their equipment's operations.

Manufacturing Information Systems: Information systems permeate every function within the organizations. It is expected that enterprise wide systems will be commonplace. Accounting systems need to incorporate environmental factors so that accurate costing of products and costs can be properly allocated across systems and products. From a control perspective, traditional manufacturing control system (e.g. MRP and ERP) will require adaptation. An important environmental management factor for consideration is that information systems will be required to trace and help in the planning and control of mass balances of environmentally sensitive products. This tracing may be required for either regulatory or competitive reasons. These systems will also be critical from a life-cycle analysis situation where information on process inputs and outputs will be needed to make more accurate evaluations of product/material environmental impacts.[60]

The Fragmentation of Economics and the Natural Sciences

Before tackling the difficult questions raised in the previous sections, let us first analyze why they are such difficult questions in the first place. A large part of the problem lies in the way we have organized our intellectual activities. The problems outlined above are global, long term, and they involve many academic disciplines and especially the connections between disciplines. The academic disciplines are today very isolated from each other and this contributes to the difficulty of addressing the questions posed above. But it was not always so.

Until roughly the beginning of the 20th century, economics and the other sciences were relatively well integrated. There were relatively few scientists then and one could argue that they had to talk across disciplines just to have someone to talk to. But then there was a shift in worldview. Newtonian physics became the dominant academic paradigm. Its view of the world as linear, separable, mechanical subsystems that could be easily aggregated to yield the behavior of the whole system encouraged the fragmentation of science into separate disciplines. There was also the size problem. As academia and the total body of knowledge grew, it became increasingly difficult to deal with it as a whole. For convenience it had to be ever more finely subdivided.

Ecology emerged as a science only in the mid-20th century around the ideas of holism and system integration. It departed from the Newtonian physics model to develop a worldview that is adapted to deal with complex living systems. It is evolutionary and nonlinear and acknowledges the inability to scale by simple aggregation[61]. "Ecology" in this sense is becoming the dominant scientific paradigm and it is an inherently interdisciplinary, "systems" perspective. Ecological economics represents an attempt to recast economics in this different scientific paradigm, to reintegrate the many academic threads that are needed to weave the whole cloth of sustainability.

References and Notes

1. Goodland, R., H.E. Daly, and S. El Serafy (1992), Population, Technology, and Lifestyle Washington, DC: Island Press. ISBN: 1559631996

2. Daly, H. E. and J. Cobb (1989), *For the Common Good: Redirecting the Economy Towards Community, the Environment, and a Sustainable Future*. Boston: Beacon Press. ISBN: 0807047023

—Cobb, C. W., J. B. Cobb, Jr., et al. (1994), *The Green National Product*. Boston: University Press of America. ISBN: 0819193216—Max-Neef, M. 1995. Economic growth and the quality of life: A threshold hypothesis. *Ecological Economics* 15:115–118.

3. Feshbach, M. and A. Friendly, Jr. (1992), *Ecocide in the USSR: Health and Nature under Siege*. New York: Basic Books. ISBN: 0465017819
4. Gore, A. (1992), *Earth in the Balance: Ecology and the Human Spirit*. New York: Houghton Mifflin Co. ISBN: 0395578213
5. Brown, L.R. (1997), *State of the World*. Washington, DC: Worldwatch Institute (annual). ISBN: 039331569X
6. Tinbergen, J. and R. Hueting (1991), GNP and Market Prices: Wrong Signals for Sustainable Economic Development that Disguise Environmental Destruction. In Robert Goodland, Herman Daly, and S. El Serafy (eds.), *Population, technology, and lifestyle: The transition to sustainability*, pp. 52–62. Washington, DC: Island Press. ISBN: 1559631996

   —Ehrlich, P. and A. Ehrlich (1990), *The Population Explosion*. New York: Simon and Schuster. ISBN: 0671689843
7. WCED (1987), Our Common Future. World Commission on Environment and Development (The Brundtland Report). Oxford: Oxford University Press. ISBN: 019282080X
8. Meadows, D.H., D.L. Meadows, and J. Randers (1992), *Beyond the Limits: Confronting Global Collapse, Envisioning a Sustainable Future*. Post Mills, VT: Chelsea Green. ISBN: 0930031628
9. Vitousek, P.M., et al. (1986), Human Appropriation of the Products of Photosynthesis. *Bioscience* 34(6):368–37.
10. Daly, H.E. (1991a), Sustainable Development: From Conceptual Theory Towards Operational Principles. *Population and Development Review* 16: supplement.—Daly, H. E. 1991b. *Steady-state economics* (2nd ed.). Washington, DC: Island Press. ISBN: 155963071X
11. Arrhenius, E. and T.W. Waltz (1990), The Greenhouse Effect: Implications for Economic Development. Discussion Paper 78. Washington DC: The World Bank. ISBN: 082131520X
12. Pimentel, D., et al. (1987), World Agriculture and Soil Erosion. *BioScience* 37(4):277–283.

13. Kendall, H.W. and D. Pimentel (1994), Constraints on the Expansion of the Global Food Supply. *Ambio* 23:198–216.

14. Goodland, R. (1991), Tropical Deforestation: Solutions, Ethics and Religion. *Environment Department Working Paper* 43. Washington, DC: The World Bank.

15. India's Total CO_2 emissions are 1,342 million tonnes, fourth largest in the world after US (6,045), China (5,007) and Russia (1,524). India's per capita emissions are 1.2 tonnes, well below the US (20.6) and the world average of 4.5 tonnes.

16. This is the total primary commercial energy supply to the economy and includes energy sources such as coal, diesel, petrol, kerosene, LPG, naphtha, coke, natural gas, hydroelectricity, nuclear power and renewables. It excludes non-commercial energy sources such as fire-wood, dung and other biomass used for cooking.

17. *'Integrated Energy Policy Report'*, Planning Commission, Government of India, August 2006.

18. This is just one of the several possible scenarios. The purpose of this article is to assess the potential of carbon-free technologies in powering India's growth.

19. On a life cycle basis, CO_2 emissions of wind energy are estimated at 7-120 grams per kwh, solar PV (13-730), nuclear (2-59), hydropower (2-48), natural gas (389-511) and coal (790-1182).

20. Normally 2000-3000 jatropha trees are planted per hectare. The average seed yield is 1 to 2.5 kg per tree and seeds contain about 30 per cent oil. This translates to an oil yield of about 1 to 1.5 tonnes per hectare.

21. Present ethanol production is about 2 billion litres, out of which just about 5 per cent is available for blending with petrol. Drip irrigation and fertigation and increase sugarcane yield to almost 150 tonnes per hectare.

22. Coal gasification produces a combustible gas which is burnt in the gas turbine. Gasification is amenable for CO_2 capture because it is captured pre-combustion.

23. If one hectare of land is planted with a biofuel producing crop, it produces about 1.5 tonnes of oil, equivalent to 17,500 kwh energy per annum. If solar PV panels are installed on the land, the expected energy output is about 1,000,000 kwh per annum

assuming solar radiation of 5 kwh/m2, 10 per cent efficiency and 200 days of sunshine.

24. Bharadwaj, A. (2007), Carbon Counting, *Economic and Political Weekly*, December 15.
25. It was the first ever meeting of the 157 parties to the Kyoto Protocol (CoP/MoP 1). At the same time, it was the opening of the 11th conference of the 189 Parties to the UNFCCC.
26. The Marrakech Accords comprise rules and operational details to meet emission reduction target. The accords gave in place all three market-based mechanisms-joint implementation (JI), emission trading and clean development mechanism (CDM). These mechanisms are embodied in the Kyoto Protocol pursuant to Articles 6, 17 and 12 respectively. All the three mechanisms allow Annex I parties to achieve their Article 3.1 emission reduction commitments of greenhouse gases. Under JI trading will take place between one Annex I party and another. Under emission trading, trading will take place only between those industrialised countries which have obligations to reduce greenhouses up to 5.2 per cent (during the first commitment period 2008-2012) below what it was in 1990. Under CDM, the investors (public/private) from the developed countries will invest in greenhouse gas mitigation projects, which will generate Certified Emission Reduction Units (CERUs). The CERUs with the investors from the developed country parties may be used by them to meet a part of their obligations. In this article, emission reduction "units" and "credits" have been interchangeably used, though generation of credits through trading under JI and emission trading is known as Emission Reduction Units (ERUs) and Assigned Amount Units (AAUs), respectively. These credits may also be used by the Annex I countries to meet their greenhouse gas emission reduction commitments under Article 3.1
27. 37 International Legal Material (ILM) 22 (1998), p.35
28. *Ibid*, p.33. The Annex I parties have to individually or jointly reduce their emissions of six greenhouse gases mentioned in Annex A of the protocol (carbon dioxide, methane, hydrofluorocarbon, nitrous oxide, sulphur hexafluoride and perfluorocarbon) by at least 5 per cent below 1990 levels in the commitment period 2008-12.
29. See Bruce Yandle and Stuart Buck, 'Boot-leggers, Baptists, and the Global Warming Battle', *Harvard Environmental Law Review*, Vol.26 No.1, (1992), pp.194-95.

30. 31 ILM-849 (1992), p.854. Article 3(1) of the climate change convention says that the parties should protect the climate system for the benefit of present and future generations of humankind on the basis of equity and in accordance with their common but differentiated responsibilities and respective capabilities. Accordingly, the developed country parties should take the lead in combating climate change and adverse effects thereof.

31. Emily Richman, Emission Trading and the Development Critique: Exposing the Threat to Developing Countries, *New York University Journal of International Law and Politics*, Vol.36, No.1, 2003, p.170.

32. New represents new sources of fund and additional represents what is more than the existing flow of aid under Official Development Assistance given by the Organisation of Economic Corporation and Development countries to developing countries.

33. The Global Environment Facility 1991 is a trust fund, which is jointly operated by the International Bank for Reconstruction and Development, United Nations Development Programme, and United Nations Environment Programme. It provides an agreed to incremental cost in six focal areas - climate change, biological diversity, ozone layer depletion, international waters, persistent organic pollutant and land degradation-to a developing country party. The agreed incremental cost means the cost, covering both investment operation as well as cost of transfer of technology, which has been agreed between a developing country party and the GEF for meeting the obligations of an MEA to achieve "global environmental benefits."

34. The designated operational entity is either a domestic legal entity or an international organization accredited and designated, on a provisional basis until confirmed by the executive board. It has two functions: (1) It validates and subsequently requests registration of a proposed CDM project activity which will be considered valid after eight weeks if no request for review was made; (2) It verifies emission reduction of a registered CDM project activity certifies as appropriate and requests the board to issue CERUs accordingly. The entity verifies it on the basis of on-site inspections, as appropriate that comprise, inter alia, a review of performance records, interviews with project participants and local stakeholders, collection of measurements, observation of established practices and testing of the accuracy of monitoring equipment.

35. The Clean Development Mechanism executive board supervises the CDM, under the authority and guidance of the CoP/MoP and is fully accountable to the CoP/MoP. The board consists of 10 members and 10 alternates. They are drawn from all constituencies of Parties and they act in their personal capacities. The board issues the CERUs to participants involved in a CDM project.

36. See *op.cit.*, No.6, p.854, Article 2.

37. The building of adaptive capacity may be defined as the ability of a system to adapt to climate change, to moderate potential damages, to take advantage of opportunities or to cope with the consequences.

38. See *op.cit.*, No.3, p.38. This is consistent with Article 12.8 of the Kyoto Protocol. The decision to charge 2 per cent levy on the implementation of CDM projects was taken at the Marrakech CoP meeting in 2001.

39. The GEF council functions as an independent board of directors, with primary responsibility for developing, adopting, and evaluating GEF programmes. The council consists of 32 members (16 members from developing countries, 14 from developed countries, and two from countries with transitional economies), which meet twice each year for three days.

40. Joyeeta Gupta, *The Climate Change Convention and Developing Countries: From Conflict to Consensus*? (Dordrecht/Boston/London: Kluwer Academic Publishers, 1997), pp.106-07.

41. The idea to charge a levy on the other two mechanisms, 'Joint Implementation' and 'Emission Trading' was given by the Tata Energy Research Institute. The paper titled 'Vulnerability and Adaptation to Climate Change: Concepts, Issues, Assessment Methods' prepared by Santiago Olmos for the climate change knowledge network incorporates the idea (available at *www. cckn.net.*).

42. See *op.cit.*, No.6, p.858.

43. Article 11(1) of the UNFCCC provides that the financial mechanism has to function under the guidance of and be accountable to the conference of parties, which takes decision on its policies, programme priorities and eligibility criteria to this convention.

44. Roda Verheyen, 'Adaptation to the Impacts of Anthropogenic Climate Change-The International Legal Framework', Review of European Community and International Environmental Law, Vol.11, No.2, 2002, p.138.

45. *Op cit.* No.7, p.855, Article 4(1) (b) calls on all parties, in accordance with the common but differentiated responsibilities, to formulate, implement, publish and regularly update national and where appropriate, regional programmes containing measures to mitigate climate change by addressing anthropogenic emissions by sources and removals by sinks of all greenhouse gases not controlled by the Montreal Protocol, and measures to facilitate adequate adaptation to climate change.

46. At the time of GEF's inception in 1991, there were four areas-climate change, biological diversity, ozone layer depletion and international waters. In 2002, two more areas persistent organic pollutant and land degradation-were assigned for funding from GEF.

47. *Op cit,* No 3, p.35. Article 5(1) says that each party included in Annex I should have in place, no later than one year prior to the start of the first commitment period, national system for the estimation of anthropogenic emissions by sources and removals by sinks of all greenhouse gases not controlled by the Montreal Protocol.

48. *Ibid.* Under Article 7, Annex I parties have to incorporate in its annual inventory of anthropogenic emissions by sources and removals by sinks of greenhouse gases not controlled by the Montreal Protocol. The guidelines for the preparation of national inventory are to be decided by the conference of parties.

49. *Op cit,* No.3, Article 12(2) of the Kyoto protocol provides that the purpose of clean development mechanism is to assist parties not included in Annex I, i.e. developing countries in achieving sustainable development and contributing to the ultimate objective of the convention.

50. Sadat, A. (2007), Some Unanswered Questions in the Climate Change Regime, *Economic and Political Weekly,* April 28, pp. 1496-1500.

51. MacNeill, J. (1989), Strategies for Sustainable Development. *Scientific American* 261(3):154–165.

52. OTA 1991. *Energy in Developing Countries.* Washington, DC: U.S. Congress, Office of Technology Assessment. ISBN: 0160272041

53. OTA (1991), *Energy in Developing Countries*. Washington, DC: U.S. Congress, Office of Technology Assessment. ISBN: 0160272041

54. MacNeill, J. (1989), Strategies for Sustainable Development. *Scientific American* 261(3):154–165.

55. Hueting, R. (1990), The Brundtland Report: A Matter of Conflicting Goals. *Ecological Economics* 2(2):109–118.

56. Daly, H.E. (1990), Toward Some Operational Principles of Sustainable Development. *Ecological Economics* 2:1–6.

57. Tinbergen, J. and R. Hueting (1991), GNP and Market Prices: Wrong Signals for Sustainable Economic Development that disguise environmental destruction. In Robert Goodland, Herman Daly, and S. El Serafy (eds.), *Population, technology, and lifestyle: The transition to sustainability*, pp. 52–62. Washington, DC: IslandPress. ISBN: 1559631996

58. e.g., MacNeill, J. (1989), Strategies for Sustainable Development. *Scientific American* 261(3):154–165.

59. Goodland, R. (1995), The Concept of Environmental Sustainability. *Annals of Ecology & Systematics* 26:1–24.

60. Bhayani, S.J. (2009), Environmental Social Responsibility: A Comparative Analysis of Perceptions of Indian Managers, Journal of Accounting and Finance, April-September, Vol. 23, No. 2. pp. 15-33.

61. Costanza, R., L. Wainger, C. Folke, and K.-G. Mäler (1993), Modeling Complex Ecological Economic Systems: Toward an Evolutionary, Dynamic Understanding of Humans and Nature. *BioScience* 43(8): 545–555.

3

Problems of Environmental Economics: Competition for Growth

A complementary way of characterizing ecological economics is to list the basic problems and questions it addresses. We see three basic problems: allocation, distribution and scale. Neoclassical economics deals extensively with allocation, secondarily with distribution, and not at all with scale. Ecological economics deals with all these, and accepts much of neoclassical theory regarding allocation. Our emphasis on the scale question is made necessary by its neglect in standard economics. Inclusion of scale is the biggest difference between ecological economics and neoclassical economics.

Allocation refers to the relative division of the resource flow among alternative product uses—how much goes to production of cars, to shoes, to plows, to teapots, and so on. A good allocation is one that is efficient, that is, that allocates resources among product end-uses in conformity with individual preferences as weighted by the ability of the individual to pay. The policy instrument that brings about an efficient allocation is relative prices determined by supply and demand in competitive markets.

Distribution refers to the relative division of the resource flow, as embodied in final goods and services, among alternative people. How much goes to you, to me, to others, to future generations. A good distribution is one that is just or fair, or at least one in which the degree of inequality is limited within some acceptable range. The policy instrument for bringing about a more just distribution is transfers, such as taxes and welfare payments.

Scale refers to the physical volume of the throughput, the flow of matter–energy from the environment as low-entropy raw materials and back to the environment as high-entropy wastes. It may be thought of as the product of population time's per capita resource use. It is measured in absolute physical units, but its significance is relative to the natural capacities of the ecosystem to regenerate the inputs and absorb the waste outputs on a sustainable basis. Perhaps the best index of scale of throughput is real GNP. Although measured in value units (P x Q, where P is price and Q is quantity), real GNP is an index of change in Q. National income accountants go to great lengths to remove the influence of changes in price, both relative prices and the price level. For some purposes the scale of throughput might better be measured in terms of embodied energy.[7] The economy is viewed as an open subsystem of the larger, but finite, closed, and non growing ecosystem. Its scale is significant relative to the fixed size of the ecosystem. A good scale is one that is at least sustainable, that does not erode environmental carrying capacity over time. In other words, future environmental carrying capacity should not be discounted as done in present value calculations. An optimal scale is at least sustainable, but beyond that it is a scale at which we have not yet sacrificed ecosystem services that are at present worth more at the margin than the production benefits derived from the growth in the scale of resource use.

Scale in this context is not to be confused with the concept of "economies of scale," which refers to the way efficiency changes with the scale or size of production within a firm or industry. Here we are using scale to refer to the overall scale or size of the total macro-economy and throughput.

Priority of Problems

The problems of efficient allocation, fair distribution, and sustainable scale are highly interrelated but distinct; they are most effectively solved in a particular priority order, and they are best solved with independent policy instruments[8]. There are an infinite number of efficient allocations, but only one for each distribution and scale. A locative efficiency does not guarantee sustainability[9]. It is clear that scale should not be determined by prices, but by a social decision reflecting ecological limits. Distribution should not be determined by prices, but by a social decision reflecting a just distribution of assets. Subject to these social decisions, individualistic trading in the market is then able to allocate the scarce rights efficiently.

Distribution and scale involve relationships with the poor, future generations, and other species that are fundamentally social in nature rather than individual. *Homo economics,* as the self-contained atom of methodological individualism or as the pure social being of collectivist theory, is a severe abstraction. Our concrete experience is that of "persons in community." We are individual persons, but our very individual identity is defined by the quality of our social relations. Our relations are not just external, they are also internal—that is, the nature of the related entities (ourselves in this case) changes when relations among them change. We are related not only by a nexus of individual willingness-to-pay for different things, but also by relations of trusteeship for the poor, future generations, and other species. The attempt to abstract from these concrete relations of trusteeship and reduce everything to a question of individual willingness-to-pay is a distortion of our concrete experience as persons in community—an example of what A. N. Whitehead called "the fallacy of misplaced concreteness"[10].

The prices that measure the opportunity costs of reallocation are unrelated to measures of the opportunity costs of redistribution or of a change in scale. Any trade-off among the three goals (e.g., an improvement in distribution in exchange for a worsening in scale or allocation, or more unequal distribution in exchange for sharper incentives seen as instrumental to more efficient allocation), involves an ethical judgment about the quality of our social relations rather than a willingness-to-pay calculation. The contrary view, that this choice among basic social goals and the quality of social relations that help to define us as persons should be made on the basis of individual willingness-to-pay, just as the trade-off between chewing gum and shoelaces is made, seems to be dominant in economics today, and is part of the retrograde modern reduction of all ethical choice to the level of personal tastes weighted by income.

It is instructive to consider the historical attempt of the scholastic economists to subsume distribution under allocation (or more likely they were subsuming allocation under distribution – at any rate they did not make the distinction). This was the famous "just price" doctrine of the Middle Ages which has been totally rejected in economic theory, although it stubbornly survives in the politics of minimum wages, farm price supports, water and electric power subsidies, etc. However, we do not as a general rule try to internalize the external cost of distributive injustice into market prices. We reject the attempt to correct market prices for their unwanted effects on income distribution. Economists nowadays keep allocation and distribution quite separate and argue for letting prices serve only efficiency, while serving justice with the separate policy of transfers. This follows Tinbergen's dictum of equality of policy goals and instruments: one instrument for each policy. The point is that just as we cannot subsume distribution under allocation, neither can we subsume scale under allocation.

It seems clear, then, that we need to address the problems in the following order: first, establish the ecological limits of sustainable scale and establish policies that assure that the throughput of the economy stays within these limits. Second, establish a fair and just distribution of resources using systems of property rights and transfers. These property rights systems can cover the full spectrum from individual to government ownership, but intermediate systems of common ownership and systems for dividing the ownership of resources into ownership of particular services need much more attention[11]. Third, once the scale and distribution problems are solved, market-based mechanisms can be used to allocate resources efficiently. This involves extending the existing market to internalize the many environmental goods and services that are currently outside the market. Policy instruments to achieve the three goals of sustainable scale, fair distribution, and efficient allocation are discussed in detail. First we delve a little more deeply into the scale and distribution problems.

From Empty-World Economics to Full-World Economics

Ecological economics argues that the evolution of the human economy has passed from an era in which human-made capital was the limiting factor in economic development to an era in which remaining natural capital has become the limiting factor. Economic logic tells us that we should maximize the productivity of the scarcest (limiting) factor, as well as try to increase its supply. This means that economic policy should be designed to increase the productivity of natural capital and its total amount, rather than to increase the productivity of human-made capital and its accumulation, as was appropriate in the past when it was the limiting factor. It remains to give some reasons for believing this "new era" thesis, and to consider some of the far-reaching policy changes that it would entail, both for development in general and for particular institutions.

Reasons the Turning Point Has Not Been Noticed

Why has this transformation from a world relatively empty of human beings and human-made capital to a world relatively full of these not been noticed by economists? If such a fundamental change in the pattern of scarcity is real, as we think it is, then how could it be overlooked by economists whose job is to pay attention to the pattern of scarcity? Some economists, including *Boulding*[12] and *Georgescu-Roegen*[13] have indeed signaled the change, but their voices have been largely unheeded.

One reason is the deceptive acceleration of exponential growth. With a constant rate of growth the world will go from half full to totally full in one doubling period—the same amount of time that it took to go from 1% full to 2% full. Of course the doubling time it has shortened, compounding the deceptive acceleration. If we return to the example of the per cent appropriation by human beings of the net product of land-based photosynthesis as an index of how full the world is of humans and their furniture, then we can say that it is 40% full because we use, directly and indirectly, about 40% of the net primary product of land-based photosynthesis[14]. Taking 40 years as the doubling time of the human scale (i.e., population time's per capita resource use) and calculating backwards, we go from the present 40% to only 10% full in just two doubling times or 80 years, which is about an average U.S. lifetime. Also, "full" here is taken as 100% human appropriation of the net product of photosynthesis which is ecologically unlikely and socially undesirable (only the most recalcitrant species would remain wild; all others would be managed for human benefit). In other words, effective fullness occurs at less than 100% human preemption of net photosynthetic product, and there is much evidence that long-run human carrying capacity is reached at less than the existing 40%. The world has rapidly gone from relatively empty (10% full) to relatively full (40% full). Although 40% is less than half full, it makes sense to consider it as relative fullness because it is only one doubling time away from 80%, a figure which represents excessive fullness. This change has been faster than the speed with which fundamental economic paradigms shift.

According to physicist Max Planck, a new scientific paradigm triumphs not by convincing the majority of its opponents, but because its opponents eventually die. There has not yet been time for the empty-world economists to die, and meanwhile they have been cloning themselves faster than they are dying by maintaining tight control over their guild. The disciplinary structure of knowledge in modern economics is far tighter than that of the turn-of-the-century physics that was Planck's model. Full-world economics is not yet accepted as academically legitimate, but it is beginning to be seen as a challenge. This book, based on full-world economics, challenges the empty-world economics prevailing today.

Complementarity vs. Substitutability

A major reason for failing to note the major change in the pattern of scarcity is that in order to speak of a limiting factor, the factors must be thought of as complementary. If factors are good substitutes, then a shortage of one does not significantly limit the productivity of the other. A standard assumption of neoclassical economics has been that factors of production are highly substitutable. Although other models of production have considered factors as not at all substitutable (e.g., the total complementarity of the Leontief model), the substitutability assumption has dominated. Consequently, the very idea of a limiting factor was pushed into the background. If factors are substitutes rather than complements, then there can be no limiting factor and hence no new era based on a change of the limiting role from one factor to another. It is therefore important to be very clear on the issue of complementarity versus substitutability.

The productivity of human-made capital is more and more limited by the decreasing supply of complementary natural capital. Of course in the past when the scale of the human presence in the biosphere was low, human-made capital played the limiting role. The switch from human-made to natural capital as the limiting factor is thus a function of the increasing scale and impact of the human presence. Natural capital is the stock that yields the flow of natural resources—the forest that yields the flow of cut timber; the petroleum deposits that yield the flow of pumped crude oil; the fish populations in the sea that yield the flow of caught fish. The complementary nature of natural and human-made capital is made obvious by asking: what good is a saw-mill without a forest? Is a refinery without petroleum deposits? Is a fishing boat without populations of fish? Beyond some point in the accumulation of human-made capital it is clear that the limiting factor on production will be remaining natural capital. For example, the limiting factor determining the fish catch is the reproductive capacity of fish populations, not the number of fishing boats; for gasoline the limiting factor is petroleum deposits, not refinery capacity; and for many types of wood it is remaining forests, not sawmill capacity. Costa Rica and Peninsular Malaysia, for example, now must import logs to keep their saw mills employed. One country can accumulate human-made capital and deplete natural capital to a greater extent only if another country does it to a lesser extent—for example, Costa Rica must import logs from somewhere. The demands of complementarily between human-made and natural capital can be evaded within a nation only if they are respected between nations.

Of course multiplying specific examples of complementarily between natural and human-made capital will never suffice to prove the general case. But the examples given above at least serve to add concreteness to the more general arguments for the complementarily hypothesis given later.

Because of the complementary relation between human-made and natural capital, the very accumulation of human-made capital puts pressure on natural capital stocks to supply an increasing flow of natural resources. When that flow reaches a size that can no longer be maintained, there is a big temptation to supply the annual flow unsustainably by liquidation of natural capital stocks, thus postponing the collapse in the value of the complementary human-made capital. Indeed in the era of empty-world economics natural resources and natural capital were considered free goods (except for extraction or harvest costs). Consequently, the value of human-made capital was under no threat from scarcity of a complementary factor. In the era of full-world economics, this threat is real and is met by liquidating stocks of natural capital to temporarily keep up the flows of natural resources that support the value of human-made capital. Hence the problem is sustainability.

Policy Implications of the Turning Point

In this new full-world era, investment must shift from human-made capital accumulation toward natural capital preservation and restoration. Also, technology should be aimed at increasing the productivity of natural capital more than human-made capital. If these two things do not happen then we will be behaving uneconomically, in the most orthodox sense of the word. That is, the emphasis should shift from technologies that increase the productivity of labor and human-made capital to those that increase the productivity of natural capital. This would occur by market forces if the price of natural capital were to rise as it became scarcer. What keeps the price from rising? In most cases natural capital is un-owned and consequently non-marketed. Therefore it has no explicit price and is exploited as if its price was zero. Even where prices exist on natural capital, the market tends to be myopic and excessively discounts the costs of future scarcity, especially when under the influence of economists who teach that accumulating capital is a near-perfect substitute for depleting natural resources!

Natural capital productivity is increased by: (1) increasing the flow (net growth) of natural resources per unit of natural stock (limited by biological growth rates); (2) increasing product output per unit of resource input (limited by mass balance); and especially by (3) increasing the end-use efficiency with which the resulting product yields services to the final user (limited by technology). We have already argued that complementarily severely limits what we should expect from (2) and complex ecological interrelations and the law of conservation of matter–energy limits the increase from (1). Therefore the ecological economics focus should be mainly on (3).

The above factors limit productivity from the supply side. From the demand side, tastes may limit the economic productivity of natural capital in a way more stringent than the limit of biological productivity. For example, game ranching and fruit and nut gathering in a natural tropical forest may, in terms of biomass, be more productive than cattle ranching. But undeveloped tastes for game meat and tropical fruit may make this use less profitable than the biologically less productive use of cattle ranching. In this case a change in tastes can increase the biological productivity with which the land is used.

Since human-made capital is owned by the capitalist we can expect that it will be maintained with an interest to increasing its productivity. Labor power, which is a stock that yields the useful services of labor, can be treated in the same way as human-made capital. Labor power is human-made and owned by the laborer who has an interest in maintaining it and enhancing its productivity. But non-marketed natural capital (the water cycle, the ozone layer, the atmosphere, etc.) is not subject to ownership, and no self-interested social class can be relied upon to protect it from overexploitation.

If the thesis argued above were accepted by development economists, what policy implications would follow? The role of economic development banks in the new era would be increasingly to make investments that replenish the stock and that increase the productivity of natural capital. In the past, development investments have largely aimed at increasing the stock and productivity of human-made capital. Instead of investing mainly in sawmills, fishing boats, and refineries, development should now focus on reforestation, restocking of fish populations, and renewable substitutes for dwindling reserves of petroleum. The latter should include investment in energy efficiency, since it is impossible to restock petroleum deposits. Since natural capacity to absorb wastes is also vital, resource investments that preserve that capacity (e.g., pollution reduction) also increase in priority. For marketed natural capital this will not represent a revolutionary change. For non-marketed natural capital it will be more difficult, but even here economic development can focus on complementary public goods such as education, legal systems, public infrastructure, and population prudence. Investments in limiting the rate of growth of the human population are of the greatest importance in managing a world that has become relatively full. Like human-made capital, human-made labor power is also complementary with natural resources and its growth can increase demand for natural resources beyond the capacity of natural capital to supply sustainably.

The clearest policy implication of the full-world thesis is that the level of per capita resource use of the rich countries cannot be generalized to the poor, given the current world population. Present total resource use levels are already unsustainable, and multiplying them by a factor of 5 to 10 as envisaged in the Brundtland Report, albeit with considerable qualification, is ecologically impossible. As a policy of growth becomes less possible, the importance of redistribution and population prudence as measures to combat poverty increases correspondingly. In a full world both human numbers and per capita resource use must be constrained. Poor countries cannot cut per capita resource use; indeed they must increase it to reach a sufficiency, so their focus must be mainly on population control. Rich countries can cut both, and for those that have already reached demographic equilibrium the focus would be more on limiting per capita consumption to make resources available for transfer to help bring the poor up to sufficiency. Investments in the areas of population control and redistribution therefore increase in priority for development.

Investing in natural capital (non-marketed) is essentially an infrastructure investment on a grand scale and in the most fundamental sense of infrastructure—that is, the biophysical infrastructure of the entire human niche, not just the within-niche public investments that support the productivity of the private investments. Rather, we are now talking about investments in biophysical infrastructure ("infra-infrastructure") to maintain the productivity of all previous economic investments in human-made capital, be they public or private, by investing in rebuilding the remaining natural capital stocks that have come to be limiting. Since our ability actually to re-create natural capital is very limited, such investments will have to be indirect—that is, they must conserve the remaining natural capital and encourage its natural growth by reducing our level of current exploitation. Investments in waiting (e.g., fallow) have been respectable and accepted since Alfred Marshall in 1890. This includes investing in projects that relieve the pressure on these natural capital stocks by expanding cultivated natural capital (plantation forests to relieve pressure on natural forests), and by increasing end-use efficiency of products.

The difficulty with infrastructure investments is that their productivity shows up in the enhanced return on other investments, and is therefore difficult both to calculate and to collect for loan repayment. Also, in the present context these ecological infrastructure investments are defensive and restorative in nature—that is, they will protect existing rates of return from falling more rapidly than otherwise, rather than raising their rate of return to a higher level. This circumstance will dampen the political enthusiasm for such investments but will not alter the economic logic favoring them. Past high rates of return to human-made capital were possible only with unsustainable rates of use of natural resources and consequent (uncounted) liquidation of natural capital. We are now learning to deduct natural capital liquidation from our measure of national income[15]. The new era of sustainable development will not permit natural capital liquidation to count as an income, and will consequently require that we become accustomed to lower rates of return on human-made capital—rates on the order of magnitude of the biological growth rates of natural capital, since that will be the limiting factor.

Once investments in natural capital have resulted in equilibrium stocks that are maintained but not expanded (yielding a constant total resource flow), then all further increases in economic welfare would have to come from increases in pure efficiency resulting from improvements in technology and clarification of priorities. Certainly investments are made in increasing biological growth rates, and the advent of genetic engineering may add greatly to this thrust. However, experience to date (e.g., the green revolution) indicates that higher biological yield rates usually require the sacrifice of some other useful quality (disease resistance, flavor, strength of stalk). In any case, the law of conservation of matter–energy cannot be evaded by genetics: more food from a plant or animal implies either more inputs or less matter–energy going to the non-food structures and functions of the organism[16]. To carry the arguments for infrastructure investments into the area of biophysical/environmental infrastructure or natural capital replenishment will require new thinking by development economists. Since much natural capital is not only public but also globally public in nature, the United Nations seems to be the appropriate agency for a leadership role.

Consider some specific cases of biosphere infrastructure investments and the difficulties they present.

(1) A largely deforested country will need reforestation to keep the complementary human-made capital of sawmills (carpentry, cabinetry skills, etc.) from losing their value. Of course the deforested country could for a time resort to importing logs. To protect the human-made capital of dams from silting up the reservoirs behind them, the water catchment areas feeding the lakes must be reforested or original forests must be protected to prevent erosion and sedimentation. Agricultural investments depending on irrigation can become worthless without forested water catchment areas that recharge aquifers.

(2) At a global level enormous stocks of human-made capital and natural capital are threatened by depletion of the ozone layer, although the exact consequences are too uncertain to be predicted.

(3) The greenhouse effect is a threat to the value of all coastally located and climatically dependent capital (such as agriculture), be it human-made (port cities, wharves, beach resorts) or natural (estuarine breeding grounds for fish and shrimp). And if the natural capital of fish populations diminishes due to loss of breeding grounds, then the value of the human-made capital of fishing boats and canneries will also be diminished in value, as will the labor power (specialized human capital) devoted to fishing, canning, and so on.

We have begun to adjust national accounts for the liquidation of natural capital, but have not yet recognized that the value of complementary human-made capital must also be written down as the natural capital that it was designed to exploit disappears. Eventually the market will automatically lower the valuation of fishing boats as fish disappear, so perhaps no accounting adjustments are called for. But ex ante policy adjustments aimed at avoiding the ex post writing down of complementary human-made capital, whether by market or accountant, is certainly overdue.

Initial Policy Response to the Historical Turning Point

Although there is as yet no indication of the degree to which development economists would agree with the fundamental thesis argued here, three UN agencies (World Bank, UNEP, and UNDP) have nevertheless embarked on a project, however exploratory and modest, of biosphere infrastructure investment known as the Global Environmental Facility. The Facility provides concessional funding for programs investing in the preservation or enhancement of four classes of biosphere infrastructure or non-marketed natural capital. These are: protection of the ozone layer, reduction of greenhouse gas emissions, protection of international water resources, and protection of biodiversity. If the thesis argued here is correct, then investrnents of this type should eventually become very important in development economics. It would seem that the "new era" thesis merits serious discussion, especially since it appears that our practical policy response to the reality of the new era has already outrun our theoretical understanding of it. We need a much deeper understanding of natural capital and the ecosystem services it provides. The current status of this understanding is discussed below.

Ecosystems, Biodiversity, and Ecological Services

An *ecosystem* consists of plants, animals, and microorganisms that live in biological communities and that interact with each other, with the physical and chemical environment, with adjacent ecosystems and with the atmosphere. The structure and functioning of an ecosystem is sustained by synergistic feedbacks between organisms and their environment. For example, the physical environment puts constraints on the growth and development of biological subsystems that, in turn, modify their physical environment.

Solar energy is the driving force of ecosystems, enabling the cyclic use of materials and compounds required for system organization and maintenance. Ecosystems capture solar energy through photosynthesis by plants. This is necessary for the conversion, cycling, and transfer to other systems of materials and critical chemicals that affect growth and production, i.e., biogeochemical cycling. Energy flow and biogeochemical cycling set an upper limit on the quantity and number of organisms, and on the number of tropic levels that can exist in an ecosystem[17].

Holling[18] has described ecosystem behavior as the dynamic sequential interaction between four basic system functions: exploitation, conservation, release, and reorganization. The first two are similar to traditional ecological succession. *Exploitation* is represented by those ecosystem processes that are responsible for rapid colonization of disturbed ecosystems during which organisms capture easily accessible resources. *Conservation* occurs when the slow resource accumulation builds and stores increasingly complex structures. Connectedness and stability increase during the slow sequence from exploitation to conservation and a "capital" of biomass is slowly accumulated. *Release* or *creative destruction* takes place when the conservation phase has built elaborate and tightly bound structures that have become "over-connected," so that a rapid change is triggered. The system has become brittle. The stored capital is then suddenly released and the tight organization is lost. The abrupt destruction is created internally but caused by an external disturbance such as fire, disease, or grazing pressure. This process of change both destroys and releases opportunity for the fourth stage, *reorganization,* during which released materials are mobilized to become available for the next exploitative phase.

The stability and productivity of the system is determined by the slow exploitation and conservation sequence. *Resilience,* the system's capacity to recover after disturbance or its capacity to absorb stress, is determined by the effectiveness of the last two system functions. The self-organizing ability of the system, or more particularly the resilience of that self-organization, determines its capacity to respond to the stresses and shocks imposed by predation or pollution from external sources.

Some natural disturbances, such as fire, wind, and herbivores, are an inherent part of the internal dynamics of ecosystems and in many cases set the timing of succession cycles[19]. Natural perturbations are parts of ecosystem development and evolution and seem to be crucial for ecosystem resilience and integrity. If they are not allowed to enter the ecosystem, it will become even more brittle and thereby even larger perturbations will occur, with the risk of massive and widespread destruction. For example, small fires in a forest ecosystem release nutrients stored in the trees and support a spurt of new growth without destroying all the old growth. Subsystems in the forest are affected, but the forest remains. If small fires are blocked from a forest ecosystem, forest biomass will build up to high levels, and when the fire does come it will wipe out the whole forest. Such events may flip the system to a totally new state that will not generate the same level of ecological functions and services as before[20]. These sorts of flips may occur in many ecosystems. For example, savanna ecosystems[21], coral reef systems[22], and shallow lakes[23] all can exhibit this kind of behavior. The flip from one state to another is often induced by human activity; for example, cattle ranching in savanna systems can lead to completely different grass species assemblages; nutrient enrichment and physical disturbance around coral reefs can lead to replacement with algae-dominated systems; and nutrient additions can lead to *eutrophication* of lakes.

Natural ecosystems, including human-dominated systems, have been called "complex adaptive systems." Because these systems are evolutionary rather than mechanistic, they exhibit a limited degree of predictability. Understanding the problems and constraints these evolutionary dynamics pose for ecosystems is a key component in managing them *sustainably*[24].

Biodiversity and Ecosystems

Species diversity appears to have two major roles in the self-organization of large-scale ecosystems. First, it provides the units through which energy and materials flow, giving the system its functional properties. There is some experimental evidence[25] that species diversity increases the productivity of ecosystems by utilizing more of the possible pathways for energy flow and nutrient cycling. Second, diversity provides the ecosystem with the resilience to respond to unpredictable surprises[26].

"Keystone process" species are those that control the system during the exploitation and conservation phases. The species that keep the system resilient in the sense of absorbing perturbation are those that are important in the release and reorganization phases. The latter group can be thought of as a form of ecosystem "insurance"[27]. The insurance aspect includes the reservoirs of genetic material necessary for the evolution of microbial, plant, animal, and human life. Genes preserve information about what works and what worked in the past. Genes thereby constrain the self-organization process to those options that have a higher probability of success. They are the record of successful self-organization[28]. Günther and *Folke*[29] distinguish between working and latent information in terms of the function of genes. Similarly, the organisms or groups of organisms that are controlling the ecosystem during the exploitation and conservation phases could be looked upon as working information; those with the ability to take over the system during the release and reorganization phases, that is, those who keep the system resilient, as latent information. Both are part of functional diversity.

Hence, it is the number of organisms involved in the structuring set of processes during the different stages of ecosystem development, and at different spatial and temporal scales that determines functional diversity. This number is not necessarily the same as the number of all organisms in the system[30]. Therefore, it is not simply the diversity of species that is important; it is how that diversity is organized into a coherent whole system. The degree of organization of a system is contained in the network of interactions between the component parts[31], and it is this organization, along with system resilience and productivity (or vigor), which jointly determine the overall health of the system[32].

Ecosystems and Ecological Services

Ecological systems play a fundamental role in supporting life on earth at all hierarchical scales. They form the life-support system without which economic activity would not be possible. They are essential in global material cycles such as the carbon and water cycles. Ecosystems produce renewable resources and ecological services. For example, a fish in the sea is produced by several other "ecological sectors" in the food web of the sea. The fish is a part of the ecological system in which it is produced, and the interactions that produce and sustain the fish are inherently complex.

Ecological services are those ecosystem functions that are currently perceived to support and protect human activities or affect human well-being[33]. They include maintenance of the composition of the atmosphere, amelioration and stability of climate, flood controls and drinking water supply, waste assimilation, recycling of nutrients, generation of soils, pollination of crops, provision of food, maintenance of species and a vast genetic library, and also maintenance of the scenery of the landscape, recreational sites, aesthetic and amenity values[34]. Biodiversity at genetic, species, population, and ecosystem levels all contribute in maintaining these functions and services. Cairns and Pratt[35] argue that if a society was highly environmentally literate, it would probably accept the assertion that most, if not all, ecosystem functions are, in the long term, beneficial to society.

Ecosystem services are seldom reflected in resource prices or taken into account by existing institutions in industrial societies. Many current societies employ social norms and rules, which: (1) bank on future technological fixes and assume that it is possible to find technical substitutes for the loss of ecosystem goods and services; (2) use narrow indicators of welfare; and (3) employ worldviews that alienate people from their dependence on healthy ecosystems. But as the scale of human activity continues to increase, environmental damage begins to occur not only in local ecosystems, but regionally and globally as well. Humanity now faces a novel situation of jointly determined ecological and economic systems. This means that as economies grow relative to their life-supporting ecosystems, the dynamics of both become more tightly connected. In addition, the joint system dynamics can become increasingly discontinuous the closer the economic systems get to the carrying capacity of ecosystems[36].

The support capacity of ecosystems in producing renewable resources and ecological services has only recently begun to receive attention, despite the fact that this "factor of production" has always been a prerequisite for economic development. In the long run a healthy economy can only exist in symbiosis with a healthy ecology. The two are so interdependent that isolating them for academic purposes has led to distortions and poor management.

Defining and Predicting Sustainability in Ecological Terms

Defining sustainability is actually quite easy: "a sustainable system is one which survives or persists"[37]. Biologically, this means avoiding extinction and living to survive and reproduce. Economically, it means avoiding major disruptions and collapses, hedging against instabilities and discontinuities. Sustainability, at its base, always concerns with temporality and, in particular, longevity.

The problem with the above definition is that, like "fitness" in evolutionary biology, determinations can only be made *after the fact*. An organism alive right now is fit to the extent that its progeny survive and contribute to the gene pool of future generations. The assessment of fitness today must wait until tomorrow. The assessment of sustainability must also wait until after the fact.

What often pass as definitions of sustainability are therefore usually predictions of actions taken today that one hopes will lead to sustainability. For example, keeping harvest rates of a resource system below rates of natural renewal should, one could argue, lead to a sustainable extraction system—but that is a prediction, not a definition. It is, in fact, the foundation of MSY-theory (maximum sustainable yield), for many years the basis for management of exploited wildlife and fisheries populations[38]. As learned in these fields, a system can only be known to be sustainable after there has been time to observe if the prediction holds true. Usually there is so much uncertainty in estimating natural rates of renewal, and observing and regulating harvest rates, that a simple prediction such as this, as Ludwig, Hilborn, and Walters[39] correctly observe, is always highly suspect, especially if it is erroneously thought of as a definition.

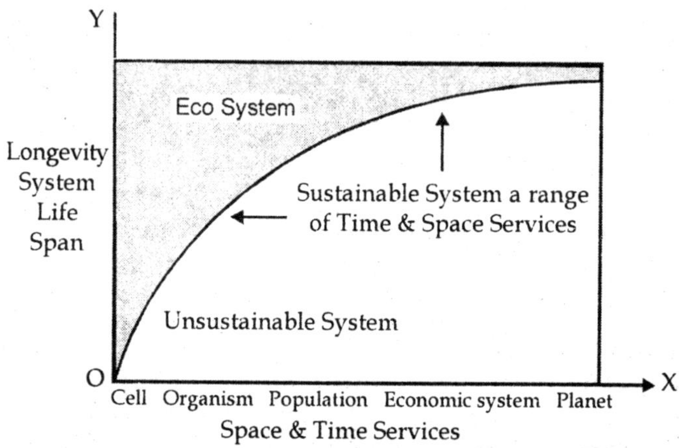

Source: Costanza and Patten 1995[1]

Figure 1: Sustainability as Scale (time and space) Dependent Concepts

The second problem is that when one says a system has achieved sustainability, one does not mean an infinite life span, but rather a life span that is consistent with its time and space scale. Figure 1 indicates this relationship by plotting a hypothetical curve of system life expectancy on the y-axis versus time and space scale on the x-axis.

We expect a cell in an organism to have a relatively short life span, the organism to have a longer life span, the species to have an even longer life span, and the planet to have a longer life span. But no system (even the universe itself in the extreme case) is expected to have an infinite life span. A sustainable system in this context is thus one that attains its full expected life span.

Individual humans are sustainable in this context if they achieve their "normal" maximum life span. At the population level, average life expectancy is often used as an indicator of health and well-being of the population, but the population itself is expected to have a much longer life span than any individual, and would not be considered to be sustainable if it were to crash prematurely, even if all the individuals in the population were living out their full "sustainable" life spans.

Since ecosystems experience succession as a result of changing climatic conditions and internal developments, they have a limited (albeit fairly long) life span. The key is differentiating between changes due to normal life span limits and changes that cut short the life span of the system. Things that cut short the life span of humans are obviously contributors to poor health. Cancer, AIDS, and a host of other ailments do just this. Human-induced *eutrophication* in aquatic ecosystems causes a radical change in the nature of the system (ending the life span of the more oligotrophic system while beginning the life span of a more eutrophic system). We would have to call this process "unsustainable" using the above definitions since the life span of the first system was cut "unnaturally" short. It may have gone eutrophic eventually, but the anthropogenic stress caused this transition to occur "too soon."

More formally, this aspect of sustainability can be thought of in terms of the longevity of the system and its component parts:

- A system is sustainable if and only if it persists in nominal behavioral states as long as or longer than its expected natural longevity or existence time; and
- Neither component- nor system-level sustainability, as assessed by the longevity criterion, confers sustainability to the other level.

Within this context, one can begin to see the subtle balance between longevity and evolutionary adaptation across a range of scales that is necessary for overall sustainability. Evolution cannot occur unless there is limited longevity of the component parts so that new alternatives can be selected. And this longevity has to be increasing hierarchically with scale as shown schematically in Figure 1. Larger systems can attain longer life spans because their component parts have shorter life spans and can adapt to changing conditions. Systems with an improper balance of longevity across scales can become either "brittle" when their parts last too long and they cannot adapt fast enough[40] or "unsustainable" when their parts do not last long enough and the higher level system's longevity is cut unnecessarily short.

Ecosystems as Sustainable Systems

Ecological systems are our best current models of sustainable systems. Better understanding of ecological systems and how they function and maintain themselves can thus yield insights into designing and managing sustainable economic systems. For example, in mature ecosystems all waste and by-products are recycled and used somewhere in the system or are fully dissipated. This implies that a characteristic of sustainable economic systems should be a similar "closing the cycle" by finding productive uses and recycling currently discarded material, rather than simply storing it, diluting it, or changing its state, and allowing it to disrupt other existing ecosystems and economic systems that cannot effectively use it.

Ecosystems have had countless eons of trial and error to evolve these closed loops of recycling of organic matter, nutrients, and other materials. A general characteristic of closing the loops and building organized non-polluting natural systems is that the process can take a significant amount of time. The connections, or feedback mechanisms, in the system must evolve and there are characteristics of systems that enhance and retard evolutionary change. Humans have the special ability to perceive this process and potentially to enhance and accelerate it. The economic system should reinvent the decomposer function of ecological systems.

The first by-product, or pollutant, of the activity of one part of the system that had a disruptive effect on another part of the system was probably oxygen, an unintentional by-product of photosynthesis that was very disruptive to anaerobic respiration. There was so much of this "pollution" that the earth's atmosphere eventually became saturated with it, and new species evolved that could use this by-product as a productive input in aerobic respiration. The current biosphere represents a balance between these processes that have evolved over millions of years to ensure that the formerly unintentional by-product is now an absolutely integral component process in the system.

Eutrophication and toxic stress are two current forms of by-products that result from the inability of the affected systems to evolve fast enough to convert the "pollution" into useful products and processes. Eutrophication is the introduction of high levels of nutrients into formerly lower nutrient systems. The species of primary producers (and the assemblages of animals that depend on them) that were adapted to the lower nutrient conditions are outcompeted by faster growing species adapted to the higher nutrient conditions. But the shift in nutrient regime is so sudden that only the primary producers are changed, and the result is a disorganized collection of species with much internal disruption (i.e., plankton blooms, fish kills), which can rightly be called pollution. The introduction of high levels of nutrients into a system not adapted to them because's pollution (called eutrophication in this case), whereas the introduction of the same nutrients into a system that is adapted to them (i.e., marshes and swamps) would be a positive input. We can minimize the effects of such by-products by finding the places in the ecosystem where they represent a positive input and placing them there. In many cases, what we think of as waste are resources in the wrong place.

Toxic chemicals represent a form of pollution because there are *no* existing natural systems that have ever experienced them and so there are no existing systems to which they represent a positive input. The places where toxic chemicals can most readily find a productive use are probably in other industrial processes, not in natural ecosystems. The solution in this case is to encourage the evolution of industrial processes that can use toxic wastes as productive inputs or to encourage alternative production processes that do not produce the wastes in the first place.

Substitutability vs. Complementarity of Natural, Human, and Manufactured Capital

The upshot of these considerations is that natural capital (natural resources) and human-made capital are complements rather than substitutes. The neoclassical assumption of near perfect substitutability between natural resources and human-made capital is a serious distortion of reality, the excuse of "analytical convenience" notwithstanding. To see how serious this is, just imagine that in fact human-made capital was indeed a perfect substitute for natural resources. Then it would also be the case that natural resources would be a perfect substitute for human-made capital. Yet if that were so, then we would have had no reason whatsoever to accumulate human-made capital since we were already endowed by nature with a perfect substitute! Historically, of course, we did accumulate human-made capital long before natural capital was depleted, precisely because we needed human-made capital to make effective use of the natural capital (complementarity!). It is amazing that the substitutability dogma should be held with such tenacity in the face of such an easy *reductio ad absurdum*. Add to that the fact that capital itself requires natural resources for its production—i.e., the substitute itself requires the very input being substituted for—and it is quite clear that human-made capital and natural resources are fundamentally complements, not substitutes. Substitutability of capital for resources is limited to reducing waste of materials in process, for example, collecting sawdust and using a press (capital) to make particleboard. And no amount of substitution of capital for resources can ever reduce the mass of material resource inputs below the mass of the outputs, given the law of conservation of matter–energy.

Substitutability of capital for resources in aggregate production functions reflects largely a change in the total product mix from resource-intensive to different capital-intensive products. It is an artifact of product aggregation, not factor substitution (i.e., along a given product is quant). It is important to emphasize that it is this latter meaning of substitution that is under attack here—producing a given physical product with fewer natural resources and more capital. No one denies that it is possible to produce a different product or a different product mix with fewer resources. Indeed new products may be designed to provide the same or better service while using fewer resources, and sometimes less labor and less capital as well. This is technical improvement, not substitution of capital for resources. Light bulbs that give more lumens per watt represent technical progress, qualitative improvement in the state of the art, not the substitution of a quantity of capital for a quantity of natural resource in the production of a given quantity of a product.

It may be that economists are speaking loosely and metaphorically when they claim that capital is a near perfect substitute for natural resources. Perhaps they are counting as "capital" all improvements in knowledge, technology, managerial skill, and so on—in short anything that would increase the efficiency with which resources are used. If this is the usage, then "capital" and resources would by definition be substitutes in the same sense that more efficient use of a resource is a substitute for using more of the resource. But to define capital as efficiency would make a mockery of the neoclassical theory of production, where efficiency is a ratio of output to input, and capital is a quantity of input.

The productivity of human-made capital is more and more limited by the decreasing supply of complementary natural capital. Of course in the past when the scale of the human presence in the biosphere was low, human-made capital played the limiting role. The switch from human-made to natural capital as the limiting factor is thus a function of the increasing scale of the human presence.

Growth vs. Development

Improvement in human welfare can come about by pushing more matter–energy through the economy, or by squeezing more human want satisfaction out of each unit of matter–energy that passes through. These two processes are so different in their effect on the environment that we must stop conflating them. Better to refer to throughput increase as growth, and efficiency increase as development[41]. Growth is destructive of natural capital and beyond some point will cost us more than it is worth—that is, sacrificed natural capital will be worth more than the extra man-made capital whose production necessitated the sacrifice. At this point growth has become anti-economic, impoverishing rather than enriching. Development, or qualitative improvement, is not at the expense of natural capital. There are clear economic limits to growth, but not to development. This is not to assert that there are no limits to development, only that they are not as clear as the limits to growth, and consequently there is room for a wide range of opinion on how far we can go in increasing human welfare without increasing resource throughput. How far can development substitute for growth? This is the relevant question, not how far can human-made capital substitute for natural capital, the answer to which, as we have seen, is "hardly at all."

Some people believe that there are truly enormous possibilities for development without growth. Energy efficiency, they argue, can be vastly increased[42]. Likewise for the efficiency of water is used. Other materials are not so clear. Others[43] believe that the bond between growth and energy use is not so loose. This issue arises in the Brundtland Commission's Report[44] where on the one hand there is a recognition that the scale of the human economy is already unsustainable in the sense that it requires the consumption of natural capital, and yet on the other hand there is a call for further economic expansion by a factor of 5 to 10 in order to improve the lot of the poor without having to appeal too much to the "politically impossible" alternatives of serious population control and redistribution wealth. The big question is: how much of this called for expansion can come from development, and how much must come from growth? This question is not addressed by the Commission. But statements from the secretary of the WCED, Jim MacNeil[45] that "The link between growth and its impact on the environment has also been severed", and "the maxim for sustainable development is not 'limits to growth'; it is "the growth of limits," indicate that WCED expects the lion's share of that factor of 5 to 10 to come from development, not growth. They confusingly use the word "growth" to refer to both cases, saying that future growth must be qualitatively very different from past growth. When things are qualitatively different it is best to call them by different names, hence our distinction between growth and development. Our own view is that WCED is too optimistic—that a factor of 5 to 10 increase cannot come from development alone, and that if it comes mainly from growth it will be devastatingly unsustainable. Therefore the welfare of the poor and indeed of the rich as well, depends much more on population control, consumption control, and redistribution than on the technical fix of a 5- to 10-fold increase in total factor productivity.

We acknowledge, however, that there is a vast uncertainty on this critical issue of the scope for economic development from increasing efficiency. We have therefore devised a policy that should be sustainable regardless of who is right in this debate. We save its full description for the final section. For now we mention only the basic logic: protect the pessimists against their worst fears and encourage the optimists to pursue their dreams by the same policy; namely, limit throughput. First some general principles are of sustainable development.

More on Complementarity vs. Substitutability

The main issue is the relation between natural capital, which yields a flow of natural resources and services that enter the process of production, and the human-made capital that serves as an agent in the process for transforming the resource inflow into a product outflow. Is the flow of natural resources (and the stock of natural capital that yields that flow) substitutable by human-made capital? Clearly one resource can substitute for another—we can transform aluminum instead of copper into electric wire. We can also substitute labor for capital, or capital for labor, to a significant degree even though the characteristic of complementarity is also important. For example, we can have fewer carpenters and more power saws, or fewer power saws and more carpenters and still build the same house. In other words one resource can substitute for another, albeit imperfectly, because both play the same qualitative role in production: both are raw materials undergoing transformation into a product. Likewise capital and labor are substitutable to a significant degree because both play the role of agent of transformation of resource inputs into product outputs. However, when we come to substitution across the roles of transforming agent and material undergoing transformation (efficient cause and material cause), the possibilities of substitution become very limited and the characteristic of complementarity is dominant. For example, we cannot make the same house with half the lumber no matter how many extra power saws or carpenters we try to substitute. Of course we might substitute brick for lumber, but then we face the analogous limitation—we cannot substitute masons and trowels for bricks.

More on Natural Capital

Thinking of the natural environment as "natural capital" is in some ways unsatisfactory, but useful within limits. We may define capital broadly as a stock of something that yields a flow of useful goods or services. Traditionally capital was defined as produced means of production, which we call here human-made capital, as distinct from natural capital which, though not made by man, is nevertheless functionally a stock that yields a flow of useful goods and services. We can distinguish renewable from nonrenewable natural capital, and marketed from non-marketed natural capital, giving four cross-categories. Pricing natural capital, especially nonmarketable natural capital, is so far an intractable problem, but one that need not be faced here. All that need be recognized for the argument at hand is that natural capital consists of physical stocks that are complementary to human-made capital. We have learned to use the concept of human capital (i.e., skills, education, etc.) which departs even more fundamentally from the standard definition of capital. Human capital cannot be bought and sold, although it can be rented. Although it can be accumulated it cannot be inherited without effort by bequest as can ordinary human-made capital, but must be re-learned anew by each generation. Natural capital, however, is more like traditional human-made capital in that it can be bequeathed. Overall the concept of natural capital is less a departure from the traditional definition of capital than is the commonly used notion of human capital.

There is a large subcategory of marketed natural capital that is intermediate between natural and human-made, which we might refer to as "cultivated natural capital." This consists of such things as plantation forests, herds of livestock, agricultural crops, fish bred in ponds, and so on. Cultivated natural capital supplies the raw material input complementary to human-made capital, but does not provide the wide range of natural ecological services characteristic of natural capital proper (e.g., eucalyptus plantations supply timber to the sawmill, and may even reduce erosion, but do not provide a wildlife habitat or conserve biodiversity). Investment in the cultivated natural capital of a plantation forest, however, is useful not only for the lumber, but as a way of easing the pressure of lumber interests on the remaining true natural capital of natural forests.

Marketed natural capital can, subject to the important social corrections for common property and myopic discounting, be left to the market. Non-marketed natural capital, both renewable and nonrenewable, will be the most troublesome category. Remaining natural forests should in many cases be treated as non-marketed natural capital, and only replanted areas treated as marketed natural capital. In neoclassical terms, the external benefits of remaining natural forests might be considered "infinite" thus removing them from market competition with other (inferior) uses. Most neoclassical economists, however, have a strong aversion to any imputation of an "infinite" or prohibitive price to anything.

Sustainability and Maintaining Natural Capital

Solutions to the problems of sustainability will only be robust and effective if they are fair and equitable. Philosopher

John Rawls[46] has argued that policies that represent an overlapping consensus of the interest groups involved in a problem will most likely be fair, effective, and resilient. The normal political process tends to accentuate conflict, and majority voting often sidetracks efforts to find overlapping consensus. The policies resulting from majority voting often are unfair to the minority and are not resilient since the minority spends all of its time fighting the decision and trying to build a new majority to overthrow the previous majority. In addition, interest groups important to global, long-run decisions (like future generations and other species) are given little if any representation in the process.

There is, however, a growing, global, overlapping consensus that attempts to acknowledge the interests of future generations and other species. The consensus is that the appropriate long-term social goal is sustainability[47]. Consensus on exactly what is meant by sustainability is still emerging[48], but we interpret this as healthy disagreement over the means, not the ends. The goal is a system that will survive indefinitely and in good shape, and one can only be sure one has achieved that goal in retrospect. In prospect, there is disagreement over which current policies will achieve the goal and, as discussed above, we need to be especially cognizant of the inherent uncertainty of our ability to predict the future. The "precautionary principle" is beginning to achieve a degree of consensus as the basic approach to uncertainty[49]. For this reason the focus should be on policies that are aimed at assuring sustainability over as wide a range of future conditions as possible.

For example, a sustainable system is one with "sustainable income," defined in a Hicksian sense as the amount of consumption that can be sustained indefinitely without degrading capital stocks, including "natural capital" stocks[50]. Since "capital" is traditionally defined as produced (manufactured) means of production, the term "natural capital" needs explanation. It is based on a more functional definition of capital as "a stock that yields a flow of valuable goods or services into the future." What is functionally important is the relation of a stock yielding a flow; whether the stock is manufactured or natural is in this view a distinction between kinds of capital and not a defining characteristic of capital itself. For example, a stock or population of trees or fish provides a flow or annual yield of new trees or fish (along with other services), a flow which can be sustainable year after year. The sustainable flow is "natural income," the stock that yields the sustainable flow is "natural capital." Natural capital may also provide services like recycling waste materials or water catchment and erosion control, which are also counted as natural income. Since the flow of services from ecosystems requires that they function essentially as whole systems, the structure and biodiversity of the ecosystem is a critical component in natural capital.

To achieve sustainability, we must therefore incorporate natural capital, and the ecosystem goods and services that it provides, into our economic and social accounting as well as our systems of social choice. In estimating these values, we must consider how much of our ecological life support systems we can afford to lose. To what extent can we substitute manufactured for natural capital, and how much of our natural capital is irreplaceable? For example, could we replace the radiation screening services of the ozone layer if it were destroyed?

Daly[51] has developed three basic criteria for the maintenance of natural capital and ecological sustainability:

1. For renewable resources, the rate of harvest should not exceed the rate of regeneration (sustainable yield);
2. The rates of waste generation from projects should not exceed the assimilative capacity of the environment (sustainable waste disposal); and
3. For nonrenewable resources the depletion of the nonrenewable resources should require comparable development of renewable substitutes for that resource.

Population and Carrying Capacity

A primary question is: Are there limits to the carrying capacity of the earth system for human populations? Ecological economics gives an unequivocal yes. Where doubt sets in is on the precise number of people that can be supported, about the standard of living of the population, and about the way in which food production will reach the limit imposed by the carrying capacity. These issues must be the priority research topics for the next decades.

Various estimates of global carrying capacity of the earth for people have appeared in the literature ranging from 7.5 billion[52] to 12 billion[53], 40 billion[54], and 50 billion[55]. However, many authors are skeptical about the criteria—amount of food, or kilocalories—used as a basis for these estimates. "For humans, a physical definition of needs may be irrelevant. Human needs and aspirations are culturally determined: they can and do grow so as to encompass an increasing amount of 'goods,' well beyond what is necessary for mere survival"[56]. For a long and careful, if somewhat inconclusive, discussion of the population issue see Cohen[57].

Cultural evolution has a profound effect on human impacts on the environment. By changing the learned behavior of humans and incorporating tools and artifacts, it allows individual human resource requirements and their impacts on their resident ecosystems to vary over several orders of magnitude. Thus it does not make sense to talk about the "carrying capacity" of humans in the same way as the "carrying capacity" of other species[58] since, in terms of their carrying capacity, humans are many subspecies. Each subspecies would have to be culturally defined to determine levels of resource use and carrying capacity. For example, the global carrying capacity for *Homo americanus* would be much lower than the carrying capacity for *Homo indus*, because each American consumes much more than each Indian does. And the speed of cultural adaptation makes thinking of species (which are inherently slow changing) misleading anyway. *Homo americanus* could change its resource consumption patterns drastically in only a few years, while *Homo sapiens* remain relatively unchanged. We think it best to follow the lead of Daly[59] in this and speak of the product of population and per capita resource use as the total impact of the human population. It is this total impact that the earth has a capacity to carry, and it is up to society to decide how to divide it between numbers of people and per capita resource use. This complicates population policy enormously, since one cannot simply state a maximum population, but rather must state a maximum number of impact units. How many impact units the earth can sustain and how to distribute these impact units over the population is a dicey problem indeed, but that must be the focus of research in this area.

Many case studies indicate that "there is no linear relation between growing population and density, and such pressures towards land degradation and desertification"[60]. In fact, one study found that land degradation can occur under rising pressure of population on resources (PPR), under declining PPR, and without PPR[61]. Therefore, the scientific agenda must look toward more complex, systemic models where the effects of population pressures can be analyzed in their relationships with other factors. This would allow us to differentiate population as a "proximate" cause of environmental degradation from the concatenation of effects of population with other factors as the "ultimate" cause of such degradation.

Research can begin by exploring methods for more precisely estimating the total impact of population time's per capita resource use. For example, the "Ehrlich identity" (Pollution/Area = People/Area x Economic Production/ People x Pollution/Economic Production) can be operationalized as (CO_2 Emissions/Km = Population/Km x GNP/ Population x CO_2 Emissions/GNP). Thus no single factor dominates the changing patterns of total impact across time. These points to the need for local studies of causal relations among specific combinations of populations, consumption, and production, noting that these local studies need to aim for a general theory that will account for the great variety of local experience.

Another research priority is to look at the effect adding a new person has on resources, according to consumption levels and the effect that efficiency has on rising levels of consumption. Decreasing energy consumption in developed countries could dramatically decrease CO_2 emissions globally. It is only under a scenario of severe constraints on emissions in the developed countries that population growth in less developed ones play a major global role in emissions growth. If energy efficiency could be improved in the latter as well as the former, then population increase would play a much smaller role.

Research priority should also look at situations where demand (either subsistence or commercial) becomes large relative to the maximum sustainable yield of the resource, where the regenerative capacity of the resource is relatively low, or where the incentives and restraints facing the exploiters of the resource are such as to induce them to value present gains much more highly than future gains.

Some authors single out a high rate of population growth as a root cause of environmental degradation and overload of the planet's carrying capacity. Consequently, the policy instrument is obviously population control. Ehrlich and his colleagues maintain "There is no time to be lost in moving toward population shrinkage as rapidly as is humanly possible"[62]. But, as Ehrlich himself fully recognizes, the policy of focusing solely on population control is known to be insufficient. It has repeatedly been shown that it is not easily achieved in and of itself, and that in addition important social and economic transformations must accompany it, such as the reduction of poverty. Even in those cases where population growth has been relatively successfully controlled, as in China, the welfare of the people has not necessarily improved and the environment is not necessarily exposed to lower rates of hazard.

The opposite position is taken by those who see high rates of population growth as stimulating economic development through inducing technological and organizational changes[63] or as a phenomenon that can be solved through technological change[64].

Such positions, however, ignore the dangers of environmental depletion implicit in unchecked economic growth: consumption increases, and rapidly growing populations can put a very real burden upon the resources of the earth and bring about social and political strife for control of such resources. This position also assumes that technological creativity will have the same outcomes in the future as in the past, and in the South as in the North, a questionable assumption. In particular, it assumes that new technology solves old problems without creating new ones that may be even worse. Finally, it heavily discounts the importance of the loss of biodiversity—a loss that is irreversible and whose human consequences are as yet unknown.

According to a World Bank study of 64 countries, when the income of the poor rises by 1%, general fertility rates drop by 3%[65]. In contrast, other authors state that "population is not a relevant variable" in terms of resource depletion and stress that resource consumption, particularly overconsumption by the affluent, is the key factor[66]. OECD countries represent only 16% of the world's population and 24% of land areas, but their economies account for about 72% of the world gross product, 78% of road vehicles, and 50% of global energy use. They generate about 76% of world trade, 73% of chemical products exports, and 73% of forest product imports[67]. The main policy instrument in this case, in the short term, is reducing consumption, and this can be most easily achieved in those areas where consumption per capita is highest.

Thus a new framework should expand the definitions of issues: focus not only on population size, density, rate of increase, age distribution, and sex ratios, but also on access to resources, livelihoods, social dimensions of gender, and structures of power. New models have to be explored in which population control is not simply a question of family planning but of economic, ecological, social, and political planning; in which the wasteful use of resources is not simply a question of finding new substitutes but of reshaping affluent lifestyles; and in which sustainability is seen not only as a global aggregate process but also as one having to do with sustainable livelihoods for a majority of local peoples.

Measuring Welfare and Well-Being

Getting a better handle on how to measure the well-being and health of both ecological and economic systems, and the welfare of humans within them, is critical. This section looks at the conventional macroeconomic measures of welfare (GNP and related measures) with an eye toward how to improve them to better reflect natural capital and sustainability.

The GNP and Its Political Importance

Economists want the market to perform well. They are deeply convinced that when the market performs well, people in general benefit. Most of their research is geared accordingly in one way or another to understanding what makes the market function well.

Although many of their theories about healthy market functioning are deductive, economists are also interested in measurement of market success, both in particular sectors of the market and for the market as a whole. The single most important measure in most countries is the gross national product. Most economists view growth in GNP, or GNP per capita, as a sign of a healthy market, which means for them a healthy economy.

With respect to some aspects of economic teaching, such as opposition to government intervention in the labor market, economists are regularly overruled by the public, acting through its elected representatives. But with respect to growth as measured by GNP, there has been no major public dissent. All political parties are committed to economic growth, and that means an increased GNP. When alarm is expressed about the difficulty of stimulating adequate growth today, the meaning is that the policies adopted have not sufficiently increased the GNP. The general public also accepts this view of economic health and is more likely to keep a party in power when it believes the economy—and that means chiefly the GNP—is growing.

Other countries also measure their national products. Although complete standardization has not been attained and difficulties in inter-country comparisons are recognized, the

GNP measurements are also used by international financial agencies to measure the comparative success of development programs. Both the World Bank and the International Monetary Fund shape their policies by this indicator. Successful economic development means that the rate of increase of per capita GNP is satisfactory.

Humanitarians also often cite GNP figures. Their object is to arouse sympathy for people whose income is very low. They usually imply that the countries with high per capita GNP should find means of transferring some of their wealth to countries with low per capita GNP. In short, GNP as the standard measure of economic success is widely accepted by economists, politicians, financiers, humanitarians, and the general public. It is enormously important. This merits closer examination.

All groups assume that GNP measures something of importance to the economy and most assume that this is closely bound up with human welfare. It is recognized, of course, that human welfare has dimensions other than the economic one. But it is rightly held that the economic element in welfare is very important, and that the stronger the economy the greater the contribution to human welfare. It is also often thought that the economy is the major area of welfare subject to political influence. In any case, there is little consensus on any other measure, so that none of the others that have been proposed exert even a remotely comparable influence on public policy.

The tendency to forget that the GNP measures only some aspects of welfare and to treat it as a general index of national well-being is, of course, a typical instance of the fallacy of misplaced concreteness, as devastatingly shown by Daly and Cobb[68]. It is obvious and need not detain us. It can be countered by giving increasing visibility to social indicators, such as the Physical Quality of Life Index, which measures literacy, infant mortality, and life expectancy at age one. Indicators of ecological health should also be developed and publicized[69]. Although not stated in the form of statistical indexes, Lester Brown's annual *State of the World*[70] volumes and the annual *Vital Signs*[71] scorecards help in this regard.

The assumption that economic welfare as measured by GNP can simply be added to other elements of welfare reflects the reductionist view of reality generally. The whole is found by putting together the parts into which it was divided for study. That assumes that the parts are in fact unchanged by their abstraction from the whole, which is clearly not true. Hence the first question to ask is whether growth in the economy as measured by GNP actually contributes to the total well-being of people.

Until recently this question was hardly raised, and even today it is not taken seriously in most economic and political circles. Nevertheless, the question is now before the world. There is a mounting chorus of critics who point out how high the cost of growth of GNP has been in psychological, sociological, and ecological terms[72]. The relation of GNP to total human welfare requires further discussion.

But there is also a question about the relation of GNP to economic welfare itself. This question is familiar to economists. Indeed, no knowledgeable economist supposes that the GNP is a perfect measure of welfare. Most recognize both that the market activity that GNP measures has social costs, which it ignores, and that it counts positively market activity devoted to countering these same social costs. Obviously GNP overstates welfare! There are other weaknesses that make it vulnerable to ridicule, but there is a widespread assumption that these are minor weaknesses and that what the GNP measures comes close enough to economic welfare that it can be used without further ado in a whole range of practical contexts.

When economists or political leaders forget that what is measured by GNP is quite distinct from economic welfare, and when they then draw conclusions from the GNP about economic welfare, the fallacy of misplaced concreteness appears again. Although economists quickly acknowledge this, they also quickly deny its importance. Our task will be to examine more closely the discussion of GNP and economic welfare to determine whether this wide consensus among economists is justified or whether the fallacy, in this instance, is more important than they suppose. We will discuss three moves away from GNP. First we consider a move toward a conceptually more correct concept of income (Hicksian income). The issue here is not to measure economic welfare at all, but simply to do a better job of measuring income. Of course there is a relation between income and welfare, and a better measure of income is likely to be a better index of welfare also, but Hicksian income does not directly address the relation to economic welfare in general. The second move away from GNP is toward a measure of economic welfare, component by component. The third is a move toward a more comprehensive measure of total human welfare, in which economic welfare is only one component.

GNP: Concepts and Measurement

The definition of GNP has remained fairly consistent over the years. This is one of its appeals. There is a long historical record. Sherman[73] defines GNP as follows:

> The gross national product (GNP) may be calculated in two different ways, corresponding to the money flow from households to business or the equal money flow from business to households. In the first way, we examine the aggregate money demand for all products. This is the flow of money spending on consumer goods, investment goods, government expenditure, and net export spending.

The second way is to add up the money paid out by businesses for all of its costs of production. Most of these costs of production constitute flows of money income to households. These incomes include wages paid for services of labor, rent for the use of land, interest for the use of borrowed capital, and profit for capital invested[74].

The text notes that depreciation and excise taxes must be added to the second way. When this is done, the first and second ways must attain identical results. Equality between the spending and income streams is guaranteed by the residual nature of profit. Any difference between the two streams appears as either profit or loss, which when added to the income stream guarantees the equality of the two flows.

Sherman goes on to show that by subtracting depreciation from GNP one arrives at net national product: by subtracting retained corporate profits, corporate income taxes, and contributions for social insurance and adding government transfer payments at net interest paid by government, one arrives at personal income; and by subtracting personal income taxes from this, one arrives at disposable personal income.

If Sherman were asked directly whether GNP is a measure of economic welfare, we are not sure what he would answer. But that he regards it as such for practical purposes and communicates this regard to his readers there can be no doubt. After having cautioned that each industry's contribution to the national product is only the value added rather than the total value of its output, Sherman[75] writes:

> A second qualification is necessary if we wish to measure accurately the year-to-year improvement in *national welfare*.... We must always deflate the changes in the money value of the national product by the price changes to find the real amount of change in the national product.
>
> Lastly, we may not be interested in the total national product but in the national product per person of the population.... Therefore, if we wish to measure the improvement in individual welfare, we must always deflate the increase in our total national product by the increase in our population.

One would expect from this textbook account that the actual measure of the GNP in the National Income Accounts was a straight measure of market activity only. There are those who would find this limitation beneficial in their work[76]. However, this has never been the case.

The reason that GNP has never been based on market activity alone is that this would distort the actual economic situation drastically. From the beginning of the accounts, two major additions to market activity have been the food and fuel produced and consumed by farm families and the rental value of owner-occupied dwellings. The reasons for including, these are obvious. Consider a scenario: suppose someone lives in a home he rents from someone else while owning a house elsewhere that he rents out to another party. Both rentals constitute market activity. If, he then moves into his own home, market activity is reduced, and if only market activity is counted then the GNP is reduced. Yet intuitively, no one feels that the economy has been damaged. (Also imputed have been the value of food and clothing provided to the military as well as banking services rendered to depositors without payment[77].)

Our point is that from the beginning there has been a tension in the consideration of what it is that GNP measures. The tension is visible in the textbook accounts. On the one hand the emphasis is on market activity. On the other hand, there is a concern to make judgments about improvement in welfare. The GNP has emphasized the market but has made modest adjustments in the direction of welfare by imputing a rental value for owner-occupied housing. But the same logic that justifies the inclusion of these items would justify the inclusion of many others. Accordingly, many proposals have been advanced to impute additional values in computing the GNP. Thus far, none have been adopted. As Otto Eckstein comments,

> NIPA (National Income and Product Accounts) has many purposes; to gauge economic performance, compare economic welfare over time and across countries, measure the mix of resources used between private and public sectors and between consumption and investment, and to identify the functional distribution of income and of the tax burden. Inevitably, these purposes clash and the accounts must be a compromise[78].

A compromise cannot be completely satisfactory to anyone. Our concern, however, is not whether as a result of the compromise comparisons of "economic welfare over time and across countries" are slightly warped, but whether the GNP, which remains primarily a measure of market activity, is in general a useful measure of economic welfare at all. Might it not be better to have a measure of market activity that would work well for the more technical purposes to which the GNP is put and which made no adjustments whatever in the direction of measuring welfare? Then the question of how much correlation there is between increasing market activity and the economic welfare of the people could be asked more clearly and neutrally.

There is a second respect in which the GNP fails to be a pure measure of market activity. At some points it also concerns itself with wealth; specifically, capital. This is apparent where depreciation is included as a part of the cost of doing business. This operates in a rather odd way. The greater the depreciation of capital assets of business is in a given year, the greater the GNP (all other things being equal). The decline in the value of a factory and its equipment increases the GNP. That this decline is not a contribution to economic welfare is recognized by the deletion of this figure in calculating the net national product and the national income. But we must remember that it is GNP rather than these other figures that functions in most comparative studies of economic welfare.

These comments indicate that although depreciation of capital assets does enter into GNP figures, it does so in a way that is opposite to its relation to national wealth. Some of the figures in the GNP do indicate a positive relation to the increase in national wealth; others are neutral in this respect and some, as we have seen, are negative. It is possible to ask whether measures of national wealth might not correlate more highly with national economic welfare than does either market activity or GNP. In fact, one great economist, Irving Fisher, argued strongly that this is the case[79]. In Fisher's view nearly all consumer goods are classed as capital or as wealth, and their consumption represents depreciation. For Fisher, welfare is the service (the psychic sense of want satisfaction) rendered by this capital, and for the most part would have to be imputed. For example, the value of the annual service of your overcoat is what it would cost you to rent it, which is the same imputation as with owner-occupied houses only more difficult since we have no rental markets for overcoats. But the logic is the same. It is at least essential that no one suppose that GNP measures national wealth or has any necessary correlation with its increase or decrease.

None of these comments are intended to imply that the National Income and Product Accounts of the U.S. government or similar accounts in other countries are of no use. Our concern here is with one particular use: namely, their use as a measure of economic welfare. Until we understand exactly what GNP does and does not measure, we cannot make reasonable judgments on these questions.

Like most of what happens in the world, the explanation of why the GNP measures what it does is historical rather than systematic. The Commerce Department began reporting statistics on the net product of the national economy in 1934. But it has been noted that it was the mobilization for World War II and the consequent demand for data relating to the economy as a whole that was primarily responsible for shaping the accounts. The central questions posed by the war were how much defense output could be produced and what impact defense production would have upon the economy as a whole[80].

Similar developments were occurring in other countries, and the United States compared its approach with those of the British and Canadians during 1944. The next year the League of Nations convened a meeting on national income accounting. So, by 1947, the United States was ready to publish its newly developed national accounting system. Although this was supplemented in various ways in later years and revised in 1958 and 1965, with respect to our concerns it has remained basically unchanged.

There have, however, been critical discussions of the National Income Accounts that raised questions relevant to our concerns. This was especially true of the 1971 Conference on Income and Wealth, which did concern itself with welfare questions. It became clear that:

> Many users considered that the present emphasis of the national income and product accounts on market transactions led to a perspective that was too narrow for the measurement of economic and social performance. It was cogently argued that additional information was required on non-market activity, on the services of consumer and government durables and intangible investment, and on environmental costs and benefits[81].

There was some discussion of the evaluation of leisure. But such considerations involved large imputation that would render the accounts less useful to "Those who used the national accounts for the analysis of economic activity in the short run, with a focus on inflation, the business cycle, and fiscal policy"[82]. For this reason the concerns of those interested in measuring long-term economic and social performance have not been dealt with in the accounts.

On the other hand, BEA (Bureau of Economic Analysis) has established a new program to develop measures of nonmarket activity within the framework of GNP accounts. In part this work is a response to the emphasis put on this topic at the 1971 Conference on Income and Wealth, but it also reflects the strong interest in environmental studies within the Department of Commerce. The federal government's concern with the measurement of the costs of pollution control and environmental damage has stimulated work in this area. BEA's current program, however, includes not only environmental questions but also (1) time spent in nonmarket work and leisure, (2) the services of consumer durables, and (3) the services of government capital. The close relationship to the national income accounting system in this work is stressed, but as yet it has not been formally integrated[83].

The tension we have noted between a measure of market activity and a measure of economic welfare is clearly being felt by those responsible for National Income Accounts. The problem seems to be insoluble as long as the effort is to have a single summary figure, such as GNP.

Richard Ruggles[84], whose historical account we have been following, concludes:

> There is no well-defined universe of nonmarket activities and imputations to be covered. The set of all possible imputations is unbounded. The only criterion that can be employed is whether the imputations are considered to be useful and necessary for the particular purpose at hand....
>
> For all these reasons, an explicit separation of market transactions from imputations in the national accounts would

> seem highly desirable.... It would be recognized, however, that imputations alone cannot meet the information needs for measuring economic and social performance.... No amount of imputation can convert a one-dimensional summary measure such as the GNP into an adequate or appropriate measure of social welfare.

From GNP to Hicksian Income and Sustainable Development

Not only is GNP a poor measure of welfare, it is also a poor measure of income. In subsequent sections we discuss the effort to move from GNP toward a measure of welfare. This is a very difficult task involving many controversial issues. In this section, the focus is on the less controversial issue of converting GNP into a better measure of income. Unlike welfare, the concept of income has a fairly clear theoretical definition, although there are big problems in making that definition operational. In measuring welfare one cannot avoid— to a large extent— implicitly defining the concept by one's very measure of it. With income, we have an explicit independent definition to which our measurements may to a greater or lesser degree correspond. With welfare, we have no such independent theoretical definition. It is therefore useful to keep these two departures from GNP quite separate.

The central criterion for defining the concept of income has been well stated by Sir John Hicks in *Value and Capital*[85]:

> The purpose of income calculations in practical affairs is to give people an indication of the amount which they can consume without impoverishing themselves. Following out this idea, it would seem that we ought to define a man's income as the maximum value which he can consume during a week, and still expect to be as well off at the end of the week as he was at the beginning. Thus when a person saves he plans to be better off in the future; when he lives beyond his income he plans to be worse off. Remembering that the practical purpose of income is to serve as a guide for prudent conduct, I think it is fairly clear that this is what the central meaning must be.

The same basic idea of income holds at the national level and for annual time periods. Income is not a precise theoretical concept but rather a practical rule-of-thumb guide to the maximum amount that can be consumed by a nation without eventual impoverishment. We all know that we cannot consume the entire GNP without eventually impoverishing ourselves, so we subtract depreciation to get net national product (NNP), which is usually taken as income in Hicks's sense. Note that the central defining characteristic of income is sustainability. The term "sustainable income" ought therefore to be considered a redundancy. The fact that it is not is a measure of how far we have strayed from the central meaning of income, and consequently of the need for correction.

But could we really consume even NNP year after year without impoverishing ourselves? No, we could not, for two reasons: first, because the production of NNP at the present scale requires supporting biophysical transformations (environmental extractions and insertions) that are not ecologically sustainable; and second, because NNP overestimates net product available for consumption by counting many defensive expenditures (expenditures necessary to defend ourselves from the unwanted side effects of production) as final products rather than as intermediate costs of production. Consequently, NNP increasingly fails as a guide to prudent conduct by nations.

For example, a developing country may obtain 6% of its GNP from timber exports. Perhaps 2% is based on sustained yield exploitation and the remaining 4% is based on deforestation. The maximum sustainable consumption has been overestimated by 4%, not even counting the loss of unpriced natural services of the forest. That may sound small, but in an economy whose conventional GNP was growing at 3%, a 4% reduction is the difference between growth and decline, which makes a very big qualitative difference in a nation's perception of itself and its policies, and indeed, of its leaders. The last difference is one reason for resistance to this change in income accounting. No politician wants to be known as the minister under whom the country went from growth to decline in one year! Yet there is an opportunity for someone to be known as the leader who finally introduced the income accounting system that saved the nation from eventual impoverishment.

Two adjustments to NNP are necessary to arrive at a good approximation to Hicksian income and a better guide to prudent behavior. One adjustment is a straightforward extension of the principle of depreciation to cover consumption of natural capital stocks depleted as a consequence of production. The other is to subtract (regrettably necessary) defensive expenditures made to defend ourselves from the unwanted side effects of growing aggregate production and consumption. Defensive expenditures are of the nature of intermediate goods; that is, they are costs of production rather than final products available for consumption. Defensive expenditures include policing, door locks, window bars, increased frequency of painting property to prevent damage from acid rain corrosion, and so on. To correct for having counted defensive expenditures in NNP, their magnitude must be estimated and subtracted in order to arrive at an estimate of sustainable consumption or true income.

To summarize, let us define our corrected income concept, Hicksian income (HI), as net national product (NNP) minus both defensive expenditures (DE) and depreciation of natural capital (DNC). Thus,

$$HI = NNP - DE - DNC.$$

No interference whatsoever with the current national accounts (or loss of historical continuity or comparability) is entailed in this suggestion. Two additional adjustment accounts are introduced, not for frivolous or trendy reasons, but simply to gain a better approximation to the central and well-established meaning of income. Since these two adjustment accounts are also relevant to our attempt to measure welfare, they will be discussed in that context and are not further considered here.

What deserves some mention in this context is the recent surge of interest in "sustainable growth" or "sustainable development" within development agencies and Third World countries following the publication of the Brundtland Report[86]. Although the two terms are used synonymously, we suggest a distinction. As discussed earlier, "growth" should refer to quantitative expansion in the scale of the physical dimensions of the economic system, whereas "development" should refer to the qualitative change of a physically no growing economic system in dynamic equilibrium with the environment. By this definition, the earth is not growing but is developing. Any physical subsystem of a finite and no growing earth must itself also eventually become no growing. Therefore growth will become unsustainable eventually and the term "sustainable growth" would then be self-contradictory. But sustainable development does not become self-contradictory. Now that these terms have become buzzwords among the development agencies, it is important to make this distinction and even more important to define sustainable development in operational terms. If we had defined development operationally as an increase in Hicksian income rather than as an increase in GNP, then sustainability would have been guaranteed, as we have seen.

The main operational implication of Hicksian income is to keep capital intact. Our problem is that the category of capital we have endeavored to maintain intact is only humanly created capital. The category "natural capital" is left out, as is human capital such as the skills, education, and health of workers. Indeed it is left out by definition as long as one defines capital as "(humanly) produced means of production." We suggest a functional definition of capital as a stock that yields a flow of goods or services. As we have discussed before, there are then two categories of capital: natural and human-made. Natural capital is the non-produced means of producing a flow of natural resources and services. Only human-made capital has been maintained intact, along with some natural capital stocks that are privately owned (herds of cattle, plantation forests).

Another approach that is relevant both to making GNP a better measure of income and to operationalizing the definition of sustainable development has been advanced by Salah El

Serafy[87]. El Serafy tackles the difficult issue of how to treat receipts from nonrenewable resources in defining income. Or, what comes to the same thing, how can a community avoid the absurdity of leaving its nonrenewable resources forever in the ground doing no one any good, yet not allow their exploitation to deflect the community from the path of sustainable development? He argues that receipts from a nonrenewable resource can be divided into an income and a capital component. The income component is that portion of the receipts that could be consumed annually in perpetuity on the assumption that the remainder of the receipts was invested in renewable assets. The return on the renewable assets and the amount invested each year are such that when the nonrenewable resource is exhausted, the new renewable assets will be yielding an amount equal to the income component of the receipts.

The basic logic underlying El Serafy's method is that the finite series of earnings from the resource, say a 10-year series of annual extraction leading to the extinction of the resource, has to be converted to an infinite series of true income such that the capitalized value of the two series are equal. From the annual earnings from sale, an income portion has to be identified, capable of being spent on consumption, the remainder, the capital element, being set aside year after year to be invested in order to create a perpetual stream of income that would sustain the same level of "true" income, both during the life of the resource as well as after the resource had been exhausted.

To make the separation into income and capital components, it turns out that one need know only the rate of discount (which must ultimately be related to the rate of growth of renewable resources and the rate of growth of factor productivity, although this relation is not discussed by El Serafy) and the life expectancy of the nonrenewable resource (total reserve stock divided by the annual extraction rate). Social choices or assumptions about these magnitudes will allow the calculation of the percentage of the nonrenewable resource receipts that should be counted as income. For example, if the life expectancy of a nonrenewable resource is 10 years and the discount rate is 5%, then it can be shown that 42% of current receipts are income and the remaining 58% is the capital content that must be reinvested. Alternatively, if the discount rates were 10% and the life expectancy remained at 10 years, the income component would be 65%. A discount rate of 10% and a life expectancy of 50 years would result in a 99% income component.

El Serafy's method is elegant and parsimonious in terms of its information requirements. The effect of rising costs of extraction can be taken into account as a reduction of reserves. The whole calculation can be redone on the assumption of rising relative price of resources, rather than the assumption of constant prices used for simplicity. As a correction of GNP, El Serafy's method is more radical than the subtraction of depletion of natural capital from NNP, because it would change the very calculation of GNP itself. Instead of keeping the present overestimate of Hicksian income and then subtracting an adjustment figure, El Serafy's method would avoid the overestimate from the beginning by calculating GNP differently. While this is logically neater, it is politically more difficult to convince national income accountants to do this because it sacrifices historical continuity in the way accounts are kept. But even if the estimation of a natural capital depreciation adjustment account were favored for this reason, El Serafy's method would still be useful in calculating natural resource depreciation, which would still be receipts in excess of the income component. assuming this amount was being consumed rather than invested.

If a development bank or agency takes sustainable development as its guiding principle, then, ideally, each of the projects it finances should be sustainable. Whenever this is not possible, as with the exploitation of a nonrenewable resource, there should be a complementary project that would ensure sustainability for the two taken together. The receipts from the nonrenewable extraction should be divided into an income and capital component as discussed above, with the capital component invested each year in the renewable complement (long-run replacement). Furthermore if projects or combinations of projects must be sustainable, then it is inappropriate to calculate the net benefits of a project or policy alternative by comparing it with an unsustainable option—that is, by using a discount rate that reflects rates of return on alternative uses of capital that are themselves unsustainable. For example, if a sustainably managed forest can yield 4% and is judged an uneconomic use of land on the basis of a 6% discount rate, which on closer inspection turns out to be based on unsustainable uses of resources, including perhaps the unsustainable clearing of that same forest, then clearly the decision simply boils down to sustainable versus unsustainable use. If we have already adopted a policy of sustainable development, then of course we choose the sustainable alternative, and the fact that it has a negative present value when calculated at a non-sustainable discount rate is simply irrelevant. The present value criterion itself is not irrelevant because we are still interested in efficiency—in choosing the best sustainable alternative. But the discount rate must then reflect only sustainable alternative uses of capital. The allocation rule for attaining a goal efficiently (maximize present value) cannot be allowed to subvert the very goal of sustainable development that it is supposed to be serving! Use of an unsustainable discount rate would do just that. We suspect that discount rates in excess of 5% often reflect unsustainable alternatives. At least one should be required to give, say, five concrete examples of sustainable projects that yield 10% before one uses that figure as a discount rate.

Given acceptance of the goal of sustainable development, there still remains the question of the level of community at which to seek this goal. International trade allows one country to draw on the ecological carrying capacity of another country and thus be unsustainable in isolation, even though sustainable as part of a larger trading bloc. The trade issue raises again the question of complementarity versus substitutability of natural and human-made capital. If we follow the path of strong sustainability then this complementarity must be respected either at the national or international level. A single country may substitute human-made for natural capital to a high degree if it can import the products of natural capital (the flow of natural resources and services) from other countries that have retained their natural capital to a greater degree. In other words, the demands of complementarity can be evaded at the national level, but only if they are respected at the international level. One country's ability to substitute human-made for natural capital to a high degree depends on some other country's making the opposite (complementary) choice.

One reason for the unanimity of support given to the phrase "sustainable development" is precisely that it has been left rather vague—development is not distinguished from growth in the Brundtland Report, nor is there any distinction between strong and weak sustainability. Politically this was wise on the part of the authors. They managed to put high on the international agenda a concept whose unstated implications were too radical for consensus at that time. But in so doing they have guaranteed eventual discussion of these radical implications. Consider, for example, two questions immediately raised by any attempt to operationalize the definition of sustainable development as development that "meets the needs of the present without compromising the ability of future generations to meet their own needs." First there is the question of distinguishing "needs" from extravagant luxuries or impossible desires. If "needs" includes an automobile for each of a billion Chinese, then sustainable development is impossible. The whole issue of sufficiency can no longer be avoided. Second, the question of not compromising "the ability of future generations to meet its own needs" requires an estimate of that ability. It may be estimated on the basis of either strong or weak sustainability, depending on assumptions about substitutability between natural and humanly created capital. This will force deeper discussion of the substitutability issue, which lies near the heart of present economic theory.

We are very grateful to the Brundtland Commission for its fine work on this critical issue and suspect that it was not unaware of the difficulties we have raised, but rather thought wisely not to try to go too far too fast. In legitimating the concept of sustainable development they have made it easier for others to press the issue further. We hope that economists and development agencies will not abandon the ideal of sustainable development when its radical implications are realized. However, we hope they will abandon the oxymoron "sustainable growth," which now functions as a thought-stopping slogan.

From GNP to a Measure of Economic Welfare

Without claiming to devise a comprehensive measure of social welfare, it may still be possible to develop a convincing measure of the positive contribution of the economy to social welfare. This was the goal of Nordhaus and Tobin[88] in their construction of a Measure of Economic Welfare (MEW). However, this goal was for them a means to another goal, namely, the demonstration that the consensus among economists is correct, and that the existing GNP correlates sufficiently well with economic welfare to make it unnecessary to use the instrument they devise! This is their clear conclusion despite their early statement that "maximization of GNP is not a proper objective of policy"[89]. We will ignore this puzzling contradiction and describe their careful work on a new indicator of the MEW—in which they "attempt to allow for the more obvious discrepancies between GNP and economic welfare"[90].

Nordhaus and Tobin begin with the GNP and make three types of adjustments: "Reclassification of GNP expenditures as consumption, investment, and intermediate; imputation for the services of consumer capital, for leisure, and for the product of household work; correction for some of the disamenities of urbanization"[91]. With the exception of environmental costs and benefits they covered all the questions raised in the 1971 Conference on Income and Wealth mentioned above. We will follow their argument in summary.

GNP is a measure of production, not consumption, whereas economic welfare is a matter of consumption. Hence, the first task is to separate consumption from investment and intermediate expenditures. This entails the deletion of depreciation, as is already accomplished in the NNP. Beyond this, Nordhaus and Tobin consider the effects of treating all durables as capital goods but find that this has little effect. More important is the result of allowing for government capital and reclassifying education and health expenditures as capital investments.

An especially interesting adjustment follows from the recognition that welfare correlates with per capita consumption rather than with gross consumption. To sustain per capita consumption for a population, some portion of the NNP must be reinvested. Nordhaus and Tobin[92] accordingly subtract from NNP for this purpose to gain a "sustainable" per capita consumption figure. We will quote only these sustainable MEW figures.

The authors also note that some expenditure is regrettable necessities rather than contributions to welfare. In this category they place the costs of commuting to work, police services, sanitation services, road maintenance, and national defense. The assumption is that when more people spend longer periods driving to work, the increase in the GNP does not mean that more human wants are satisfied, and so with the others. These figures are, accordingly, subtracted.

The second task is to make appropriate imputations for capital services, leisure, and nonmarket work. The latter two have a very large effect on the statistics, and there is no one indisputable method for valuing them. Nordhaus and Tobin propose three methods. The question is whether leisure and nonmarket activity are affected by technological progress. The authors prefer the measure that leaves the value of leisure unaffected by technical progress even though nonmarket productive activity is so affected. We will report only the statistics generated by this choice.

The third task is to consider urban disamenities. Nordhaus and Tobin recognize that there are negative "externalities" connected with economic growth and suggest that these are most apparent in urban life. "Some portion of the higher earnings of urban residents may be simply compensation for the disamenities of urban life and work. We now have before us the full range of adjustments made by Nordhaus and Tobin. One or another may appear inappropriate to some. For example, it may be argued that police protection is a contribution to welfare, and that it should not be deleted. The counterargument, however, is convincing if our purpose is to compare welfare over time. The increasing cost of police protection does not imply that we are less vulnerable to crime than we were in the past. Should the social situation change so that much less protection was needed, this should not be regarded as a reduction of economic welfare.

The real question is whether the list of regrettable necessities is sufficiently inclusive. As Nordhaus and Tobin[94] recognize, the line between final and instrumental outlays is very hard to draw. For example, the philosophical problems raised by the malleability of consumer wants are too deep to be resolved in economic accounting. Consumers are susceptible to efforts of producers. Maybe all our wants are just regrettable necessities; maybe productive activity does no better than to satisfy the wants which it generates; maybe our net welfare product is tautologically zero.

Having said this, they ignore the problem. The same problem has been briefly considered and dismissed by Denison and Jaszi, who believe that regrettable or defensive expenditures should be counted as final consumption, as is currently the case[95], All expenditures, they argue, are basically defensive: thus food expenditures are a defense against hunger, clothing and housing expenditures defend against the cold and rain, and so forth—and even expenditures on churches defend against the devil! Clever though this riposte may be, it misses the point: namely, that "defensive" means a defense against the unwanted side effects of other production, not a defense against normal baseline environmental conditions of cold, rain, and so on. It is not the case that "our net welfare product is tautologically zero"[96]. Defensive expenditures are only those that were "regrettably made necessary" by other acts of production and consequently should be counted as costs of that other production; that is to say, counted as intermediate rather than final goods.

We are now ready to consider the results of Nordhaus and Tobin's new MEW. What is of special interest to us is how it correlates with GNP, since the question of whether growth of GNP indicates improved economic welfare motivated the whole study. First, we will quote the conclusion of Nordhaus and Tobin[97], and then we will examine the figures on the basis of which they make their judgment: Although the numbers presented here are very tentative, they do suggest the following observations. First, MEW is quite different from conventional output measures. Some consumption items omitted from GNP are of substantial quantitative importance. Second, our preferred variant of per capita MEW has been growing more slowly than per capita NNP (1.1% for MEW as against 1.7% for NNP, at annual rates over the period (1929–1965). Yet MEW has been growing. The progress indicated by conventional national accounts is not just a myth that evaporates when a welfare-oriented measure is substituted[98].

When their findings are more carefully examined for time frames other than the full period from 1929–1965, the relatively close association between growth of per capita GNP and MEW disappears[99]. For example, between 1945 and 1947, per capita GNP fell about 15% (from $2,528 to $2,142) while per capita sustainable MEW rose by over 16% (from $5,098 to $5,934). Of course, this is the period of demobilization after World War II, so no conclusions should be drawn from this short-term negative relationship. Yet the presumption that the growth of GNP could be used as a reasonable proxy for MEW growth does not find confirmation in other periods either. From 1935 to 1945, per capita GNP rose almost 90% (from $1,332 to $2,528), while per capita sustainable MEW rose only about 13% (from $4,504 to $5,098). More significantly, during the postwar period 1947–1965, when neither depression nor war nor recovery had a major impact on growth rates, per capita GNP rose about six times as fast as per capita sustainable MEW[100] (per capita GNP grew by 48% or about 2.2% per year, while per capita sustainable MEW grew by 7.5% or about 0.4% per year).

Moreover, if we assume, as Nordhaus and Tobin[101] did in one of their options, that the productivity of housework has not increased at the same rate as the productivity of market activities, then per capita sustainable MEW actually registers a decline of 2% during the period 1947–1965. Alternatively, we might consider the growth of per capita sustainable MEW in the absence of any imputation for leisure or household production because, as Nordhaus and Tobin admit, "Imputation of the consumption value of leisure and nonmarket work presents severe conceptual and statistical problems. Since the magnitudes are large, differences in resolution of these problems make big differences in overall MEW estimates"[102]. If that imputation is omitted, per capita sustainable MEW grows by 2% from 1947 to 1965. In any case, whether the appropriate figure for the change during that period in per capita sustainable MEW is 7.5%, 2%, or -2%, each of these results suggest that in fact "the progress indicated by conventional national accounts is ... just a myth that evaporates when a welfare-oriented measure is substituted"[103]. With their own figures, Nordhaus and Tobin have shed doubt on the thesis that national income accounts serve as a good proxy measure of economic welfare.

Nordhaus reflected again on the significance of his work with Tobin five years later. His interpretation of the results was unchanged: "Although GNP and other national income aggregates are imperfect measures of the economic standard of living, the broad picture of secular progress that they convey remains after correction for their most obvious deficiencies"[104].

He had still failed to remark upon the lack of similarity between the growth of MEW and GNP during the last 18 years of the period that he and Tobin had reviewed.

The Index of Sustainable Economic Welfare

We have shown that the national product, whether gross or net, is not identical with true national income and that subtracting indirect business taxes from NNP, as is done in the National Income Accounts to arrive at "national income," still does not give us a true measure of national income. True income is sustainable, and to calculate this Hicksian income would require a quite different approach.

We have also shown that there is a marked difference between what the GNP measures and economic welfare, and that the latter has been growing much more slowly than the former as measured by the two proposals that have been made for judging the U.S. economy. A defender of the continuing use of GNP as a guide to policy could argue that, even so, economic welfare has advanced along with GNP. If any advance in the welfare measure is truly a gain, it is still desirable to increase GNP. The recognition that it takes a great deal of increase in GNP to achieve a small improvement in real economic welfare could be used to argue that ever greater efforts are needed for the increase of GNP.

To counter such a claim two points need to be made. First, there are social and ecological indicators that seem to be adversely affected by growth of GNP. Not all of these are dealt with in any of the welfare measures. This is especially true of many of the pervasive externalities.

Second, the major reason that the welfare measures show some growth as GNP grows is that they incorporate the largest element of the GNP as part of their own statistics. That is private consumption. These welfare measures assume that the more goods and services that are consumed by the public, the better. For example, excessive consumption of tobacco, alcohol, and fatty foods are all counted positively. Few suppose that these actually add to welfare, but the task of sorting out approved and disapproved expenses would be formidable indeed. Furthermore, economists generally regard any effort to make such distinctions as elitism of a sort they reject. However a person spending money in the market is assumed to be in the interest of satisfying that person's wants and no further consideration of value is possible. We are not arguing against the necessity of assuming for these statistical purposes that consumption in general must be positively appraised. But we do think it well to point out that it is this inability or unwillingness to make judgments of this sort that allows welfare measures to advance even a little as GNP advances a lot. The small advance in welfare held to accompany the larger advance in GNP might well disappear if the most questionable items were deleted from the private consumption column.

This survey does not suffice to establish a way of measuring economic welfare. Closer examination of decisions that must be made in any such index shows how large the arbitrary element is. Any measure would abstract from many features of actual economic welfare and its use would lead to ignoring the degree of abstraction involved. The very existence of a measure invites the fallacy of misplaced concreteness. But whether a new measure should be devised and used, or whether measured welfare is a will-o'-the-wisp that should be abandoned, the results make clear that GNP does not come close enough to measuring economic welfare to warrant its continued use for that purpose. To use it as if it were a significant indicator of economic well-being—much worse of well-being in general—is an egregious instance of the fallacy of misplaced concreteness.

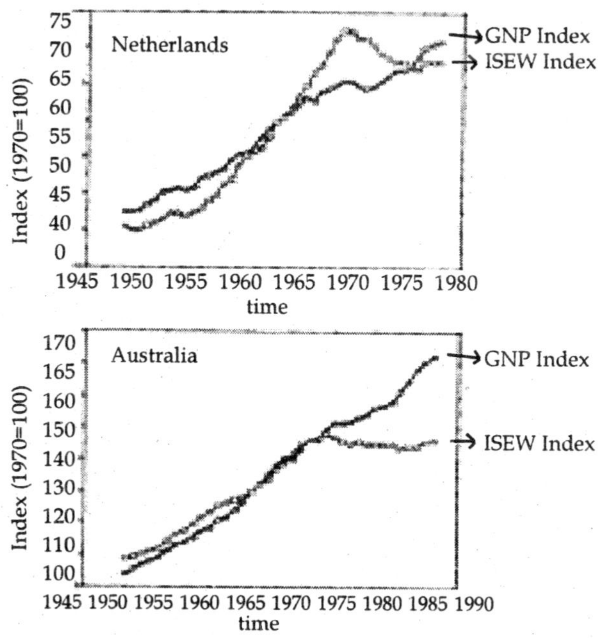

Figure 2: Comparisons of Indices of GNP Per Capita and ISEW Per Capita for Five OECD Countries (*Source:* Max-Neef 1995[21])

In an effort to address these issues (while remaining mindful of the pitfalls) Daly and Cobb[105] developed an Index of Sustainable Economic Welfare (ISEW). The ISEW takes the MEW of Nordhaus and Tobin and the Economic Aspects of Welfare (EAW) of Zoltas[106] as starting points, but incorporates the sustainability issues that EAW ignores and the environmental issues that MEW ignores. Rather than revising and bringing up to date the existing measures, they decided to create a new one that includes some of the elements not dealt with by any of the three indices already discussed, as well as fresh ways of treating topics that were included in them. To summarize these changes, ISEW:

- Factors in income distribution on the assumption that an additional dollar's worth of income adds more to the welfare of a poor family than a rich one.

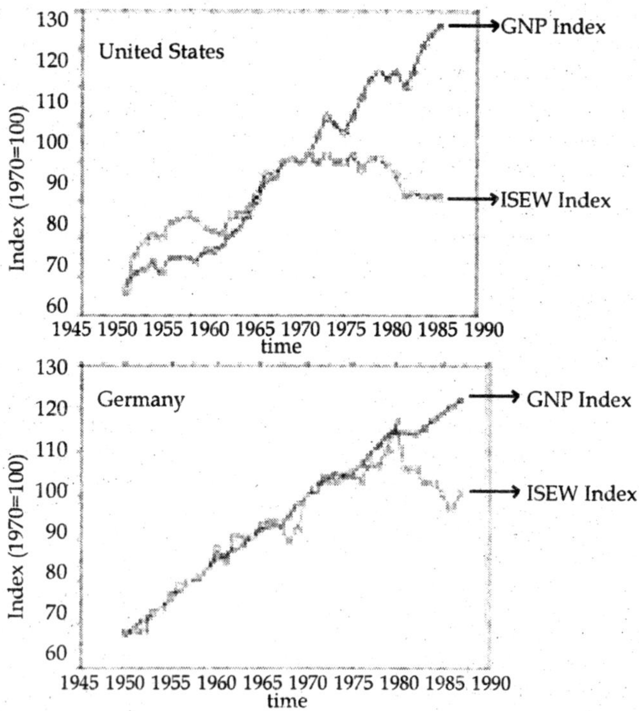

Figure 2 a: Comparisons of Indices of GNP Per Capita and ISEW Per Capita for Five OECD Countries. (*Source*: Max-Neef 1995[3])

- Considerably alters what Nordhaus and Tobin[107] did in the calculation of changes in net capital stock. Specifically, it includes only changes in the stock of fixed reproducible capital and excludes land and human capital in this calculation.
- Updates Zoltas's[108] estimates using more recent data for air and water pollution and adds an estimate of noise pollution.
- Includes estimates of costs of the loss of wetlands and farmlands, depletion of nonrenewable resources, commuting, urbanization, auto accidents, advertising, and long-term environmental damage.

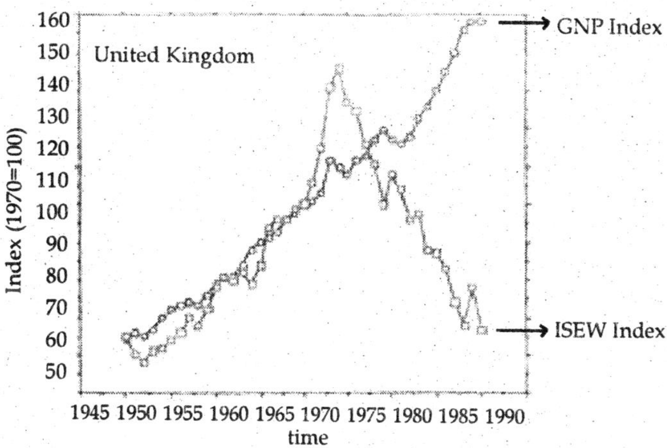

Figure 2 b: Comparisons of Indices of GNP Per Capita and ISEW Per Capita for Five OECD Countries. (*Source:* Max-Neef 1995[4])

- Omits any imputation of the value of leisure.
- Includes imputed values for the value of unpaid household labor.

Daly and Cobb[109] calculated ISEW for the U.S. economy from 1950 to 1986. Since then, ISEW has been updated for the U.S. and calculated for several other countries. These results are shown in Figure 3.2. While GNP per capita continued to rise over the entire interval for the countries shown, ISEW per capita paralleled GNP per capita during the initial period, but then leveled off and in some cases began to decline. When exactly this leveling occurred varies by country, but it has occurred in all the countries studied so far. Max-Neef[110] has postulated that this is evidence for the "threshold hypothesis," that economic growth increases welfare only until a threshold is reached where the costs of additional growth begin to outweigh the benefits. ISEW, by doing a better job of including both the costs and benefits of growth can clearly show when this threshold has been passed. In the U.S. it was around 1970. In the U.K. it was around 1975, and in the other cases (Germany, Netherlands, and Austria) around 1980. In the U.S. ISEW per capita continues to increase as GNP/capita increases until GNP per capita reaches about US$5,500 (in constant 1972 dollars per person), after which ISEW per capita declines with increasing GNP per capita. For the U.K. this relationship is very striking, with a very sharp peak at around £4700 (in constant 1985 pounds per person).

Toward a Measure of Total Human Welfare

While the ISEW goes a long way toward providing a better measure of economic welfare, it is certainly not a perfect measure of economic welfare and it falls far short of measuring total welfare. ISEW is still based on measuring how much is produced and consumed, with the tacit assumption that more consumption leads to more welfare. ISEW at least adjusts for the sustainability of this consumption, its negative impacts on natural capital, its distribution across income classes, and other reasonable adjustments. This is a huge improvement over GNP and one that tells a very different story about recent changes in aggregate economic welfare.

A completely different approach, however, would be to look directly at the actual well-being that is achieved—to separate the means (consumption) from the ends (well-being) without assuming that one is correlated with the other. Some authors have begun to look at the problem from this perspective. For example, Manfred Max-Neef[111] has developed a matrix of human needs and has attempted to address well-being from this alternative perspective. While human needs can be classified according to many criteria, Max-Neef organized them into two categories: existential and axiological, which he arranges as a matrix. He lists nine categories of axiological human needs which must be satisfied in order to achieve well-being: (1) subsistence, (2) protection, (3) affection, (4) understanding, (5) participation, (6) leisure, (7) creation, (8) identity, and (9) freedom. These are arrayed against the existential needs of (1) having, as in consuming; (2) being, as in being a passive part of without necessarily having; (3) doing, as in actively participating in the work process; and (4) relating, as in interacting in social and organizational structures. The key idea here is that humans do not have primary needs for the products of the economy. The economy is only a means to an end. The end is the satisfaction of primary human needs. Food and shelter are ways of satisfying the need for subsistence. Insurance systems are ways to meet the need for protection. Religion is a way to meet the need for identity. And so on. Max-Neef summarizes as:

> Having established a difference between the concepts of needs and satisfiers it is possible to state two postulates: first, fundamental human needs are finite, few and classifiable; second, fundamental human needs (such as those contained in the system proposed) are the same in all cultures and in all historical periods. What changes, both over time and through cultures, is the way or the means by which the needs are satisfied[112].

This is a very different conceptual framework from conventional economics, which assumes that human desires are infinite and that, all else being equal, more is always better. According to this alternative conceptual framework, we should be measuring how well basic human needs are being satisfied if we want to assess well-being, not how much we are consuming, since the two are not necessarily correlated.

Alternative Models of Wealth and Utility

We can summarize the foregoing discussion with reference to two alternative models of wealth and utility, based loosely on the ideas of Paul Ekins[113]. Figure 3 shows these relationships diagrammatically. Model 1 shows the conventional economic view of the process. The primary factors of land, labor, and capital combine in the economic process to produce goods and services (GNP) which is divided into consumption (which is the sole contributor to individual utility and welfare) and investment (which goes into

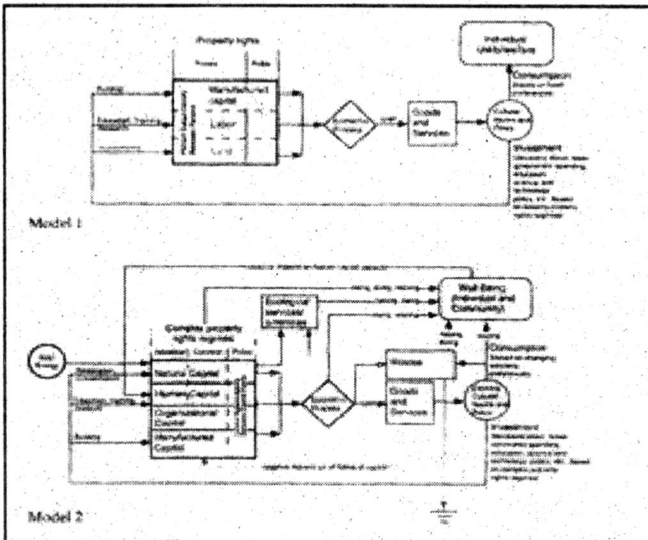

(*Source*: Ekins 1992[5])

Figure 3: Alternative Models of Economic Activity

maintaining and increasing the capital stocks). Preferences are fixed. In this model the primary factors are perfect substitutes for each other so land has been downplayed, and the lines between all the forms of capital are fuzzy. Property rights are usually simplified to either private or public and their distribution is usually taken as fixed and given.

Model 2 shows the alternative ecological economics view of the process. Notice that the key elements of the conventional view are still present, but more has been added and some priorities have changed. There is limited substitutability between the three basic forms of capital in this model: natural, human, and manufactured, and property rights regimes are complex and flexible, spanning the range from individual to common to public property. Natural capital captures solar energy and behaves as an autonomous complex system. Both economic goods and services and ecological services and amenities are produced and both contribute in different ways to satisfying basic human needs and creating both individual and community well-being. There is also waste production by the economic process which contributes negatively to well-being and has a negative impact on capital and ecological services. Preferences are adapting and changing but basic human needs are constant.

As Ekins[114] points out:

> It must be stressed that that the complexities and feedbacks of model 2 are not simply glosses on model 1's simpler portrayal of reality. They fundamentally alter the perceived nature of that reality and in ignoring them conventional analysis produce serious errors....

In the remaining sections we elaborate the various implications of these distinctions.

Valuation, Choice, and Uncertainty

While there may be no "right" way to value a forest or a river, there is a wrong way, which is to give it no value at all.

– Paul Hawken in the forward to Prugh et al.[115]

This section looks at the difficult and controversial issues of valuation, choice, and uncertainty. Conventional economic analysis usually assumes that individual human preferences are given and fixed, that the role of economics is to satisfy those preferences in the most efficient way possible, and that uncertainty can be handled in a fairly straightforward way by equating it to risk (uncertain events with known probabilities). As we will show, when one is concerned with sustainability, which is an inherently long-run problem, preferences cannot be considered to be fixed and given. Economics must then have a different and broader role, and we must acknowledge and deal with true uncertainty and indeterminacy, where probabilities are unknown and even the possibilities is often unknown.

Fixed Tastes and Preferences and Consumer Sovereignty

The conventional paradigm assumes tastes and preferences are fixed and given and that the economic problem consists of optimally satisfying those preferences. Tastes and preferences usually do not change rapidly and, in the short run (i.e., 1–4 yrs), this assumption makes sense. But preferences do change over longer time frames and in fact there is an entire industry (advertising) devoted to changing them. Sustainability is an inherently long-run problem, and in the long run it does not make sense to assume tastes and preferences are fixed. This is a very disturbing prospect for economists because it takes away the easy definition of what is "optimal." If tastes and preferences are fixed and given, then we can adopt a stance of "consumer sovereignty" and just give the people what they want. We do not have to know or care why they want what they want; we just have to satisfy their preferences as efficiently as possible. But if preferences are expected to change over time and under the influence of education, advertising, changing cultural assumptions, and so on, we need a different criterion for what is "optimal" and we have to figure out how preferences change, how they relate to this new criterion, and how they can or should be changed to satisfy the new criterion.

One alternative for this new criterion is sustainability itself or more completely, sustainable scale, fair distribution, and efficient allocation. This criterion implies a two-tiered decision process[116] of first coming to a social consensus on a sustainable scale and fair distribution and, second, using both the market and other institutions like education and advertising in order to implement these social decisions. This might be called "community sovereignty" as opposed to "consumer sovereignty." It makes most conventional economists very uncomfortable to stray from consumer sovereignty because it eliminates the tidy view of economics as simply optimally satisfying a fixed set of preferences and it opens a Pandora's Box of possibilities for manipulating preferences. If tastes and preferences can change, then who is going to decide how to change them? There is a real danger that a "totalitarian" government might be employed to manipulate preferences to conform to the desires of a select elite rather than the society as a whole.

Two points need to be kept in mind: (1) preferences are already manipulated every day; and (2) we can just as easily apply open democratic principles (as opposed to hidden or totalitarian principles) to the problem in deciding how to manipulate preferences. So the question becomes: do we want preferences to be manipulated unconsciously, either by a dictatorial government or by big business acting through advertising, or do we want to formulate them consciously based on social dialogue and consensus with a higher goal in mind? Ethics is the ordering and revising of our existing preferences in the light of a higher goal. Taking preferences as given would mean that the ethical problem has been solved once and for all. Either way, this is an issue that can no longer be avoided, or one which we believe can best be handled using open democratic principles and innovative thinking.

Valuation of Ecosystems and Preferences

The issue of valuation is inseparable from the choices and decisions we have to make about ecological systems. Some argue that valuation of ecosystems is either impossible or unwise. For example, some argue that we cannot place a value on such "intangibles" as human life, environmental aesthetics, or long-term ecological benefits. But, in fact, we do so every day. When we set construction standards for highways, bridges, and the like, we value human life—acknowledged or not—because spending more money on construction would save lives. Another often-made argument is that we should protect ecosystems for purely moral or aesthetic reasons, and we do not need valuations of ecosystems for this purpose. There are equally compelling moral arguments that may be in direct conflict with the moral argument to protect ecosystems. For example, the moral argument 'no one should go hungry". All we have done is to translate the valuation and decision problem into a new set of dimensions and a new language of discourse, one that in some senses makes the valuation and choice problem more difficult and less explicit.

So, while ecosystem valuation is certainly difficult, one choice we do not have is whether or not to do it. Rather, the decisions we make, as a society, about ecosystems imply valuations. We can choose to make these valuations explicit or not; we can undertake them using the best available ecological science and understanding or not; we can do them with an explicit acknowledgment of the huge uncertainties involved or not; but as long as we are forced to make choices we are doing valuation. The valuations are simply the relative weights we give to the various aspects of the decision problem.

We believe that society can make better choices about ecosystems if the valuation process is made as explicit and participatory as possible. This means taking advantage of the best information we can muster and making uncertainties about valuations explicit too. It also means developing new and better ways to make good decisions in the face of these uncertainties. Ultimately, it means stating explicitly our goals as a society, both in the short term and in the long term.

This leads back to the role of individual preferences in determining value. If individual preferences change (in response to education, advertising, peer pressure, etc.) then value cannot completely originate with preferences. We need to distinguish at least two kinds of value within this context: (1) short-term or current value based on current individual preferences; and (2) long-term or sustainable value based on the preferences needed to assure long-term sustainability (sustainable scale, fair distribution, and efficient allocation). Instead of being merely an expression of current individual preferences, sustainable value (at least in the mid to long term) becomes a system characteristic related to the item's evolutionary contribution to the survival of the linked ecological economic system. Current value is the expression of individual preferences in the short term and locally, while sustainable value is the expression of community preferences in the long term and globally.

Uncertainty, Science, and Environmental Policy

One of the primary reasons for the problems with current methods of environmental management is the issue of scientific uncertainty—not just its existence, but the radically different expectations and modes of operation that science and policy have developed to deal with it. If we are to solve this problem, we must understand and expose these differences about the nature of uncertainty and design better methods to incorporate it into the policy-making and management process.

To understand the scope of the problem, it is necessary to differentiate between *risk* (which is an event with a *known* probability, sometimes referred to as statistical uncertainty) and *true uncertainty* (which is an event with an *unknown* probability, sometimes referred to as indeterminacy). Every time you drive your car you run the *risk* of having an accident, because the probability of car accidents is known with very high certainty. We know the risk involved in driving because, unfortunately, there have been many car accidents on which to base the probabilities. These probabilities are known with enough certainty that they are used by insurance companies to set rates that will assure those companies of a certain profit. There is little uncertainty about the risk of car accidents. If you live near the disposal site of some newly synthesized toxic chemical you may be in danger as well, but no one knows to what extent. No one knows even the probability of your getting cancer or some other disease from this exposure, so there is true uncertainty. Most important environmental problems suffer from true uncertainty, not merely risk.

One can think of a continuum of uncertainty ranging from zero for certain information to intermediate levels for information with statistical uncertainty and known probabilities (risk) to high levels for information with true uncertainty or indeterminacy. Risk assessment has become the central guiding principle at the U.S. EPA[117] and other environmental management agencies, but true uncertainty has yet to be adequately incorporated into environmental protection strategy.

Science treats uncertainty as a given, a characteristic of all information that must be honestly acknowledged and communicated. Over the years scientists have developed increasingly sophisticated methods to measure and communicate uncertainty arising from various causes. It is important to note that the progress of science has, in general, uncovered more uncertainty rather that leading to the absolute precision that the lay public often mistakenly associates with "scientific" results. The scientific method can only set boundaries on the limits of our knowledge. It can define the edges of the envelope of what is known, but often this envelope is very large and the shape of its interior can be a complete mystery. Science can tell us the range of uncertainty about global warming and toxic chemicals, and maybe something about the relative probabilities of different outcomes, but in most important cases it cannot tell us which of the possible outcomes will occur with any degree of accuracy.

Our current approaches to environmental management and policy making, on the other hand, abhor uncertainty and gravitate to the edges of the scientific envelope. The reasons for this are clear. The goal of policy is making unambiguous, defensible decisions, often codified in the form of laws and regulations. While legislative language is often open to interpretation, regulations are much easier to write and enforce if they are stated in clear, black and white, absolutely certain terms. For most of criminal law this works reasonably well. Mr. Cain killed his brother or he didn't; the only question is whether there is enough evidence to demonstrate guilt beyond a reasonable doubt (i.e., with essentially zero uncertainty). Since the burden of proof is on the prosecution, it does little good to conclude that there was 80% chance that Mr. Cain killed his brother. But many scientific studies come to just these kinds of conclusions, because that is the nature of the phenomenon. Science defines the envelope while the policy process gravitates to its edges—generally the edge that best advances the policy maker's political agenda. We need to deal with the whole envelope and all its implications if we are to use science rationally to make policy.

The problem is most severe in the environmental area. Building on the legal traditions of criminal law, policy makers and environmental regulators desire absolute, certain information when designing environmental regulations. But much of environmental policy is based upon scientific studies of the likely health, safety and ecological consequences of human actions. Information gained from these studies is therefore only certain within their epistemological and methodological limits[118]. Particularly with the recent shift in environmental concerns from visible, known pollution to more subtle threats, like radon, regulators are confronted with decision making outside the limits of scientific certainty with increasing frequency[119].

Problems arise when regulators ask scientists for answers to unanswerable questions. For example, the law may mandate that the regulatory agency come up with safety standards for all known toxins when little or no information is available on the impacts of these chemicals. When trying to enforce the regulations after they are drafted, the problem of true uncertainty about the impacts remains. It is not possible to determine with any certainty if the local chemical company contributed to the death of some of the people in the vicinity of their toxic waste dump. One cannot prove the smoking/ lung cancer connection in any direct, causal way (i.e., in the courtroom sense), only as a statistical relationship. Global warming may or may not happen after all.

As they are currently set up, most environmental regulations, particularly in the United States, demand certainty, and when scientists are pressured to supply this nonexistent commodity there is not only frustration and poor communication but mixed messages in the media as well. Because of uncertainty, environmental issues can often be manipulated by political and economic interest groups. Uncertainty about global warming is perhaps the most visible current example of this effect.

The "precautionary principle" is one way the environmental regulatory community has begun to deal with the problem of true uncertainty. The principle states that rather than await certainty, regulators should act in anticipation of any potential environmental harm in order to prevent it. The precautionary principle is so frequently invoked in international environmental resolutions that it has come to be seen by some as a basic normative principle of international environmental law[120]. But the principle offers no guidance as to what precautionary measures should be taken. It "implies the commitment of resources now to safeguard against the potentially adverse future outcomes of some decision"[121], but does not tell us how many resources or which adverse future outcomes are most important.

This aspect of the "size of the stakes" is a primary determinant of how uncertainty is dealt with in the political arena. The situation can be summarized as shown in Figure 4, with uncertainty plotted against decision stakes. It is only the area near the origin with low uncertainty and low stakes that is the domain of "normal applied science." Higher uncertainty or higher stakes result in a much more politicized environment. Moderate values of either correspond to "applied engineering" or "professional consultancy," which allows a good measure of judgment and opinion to deal with risk. On the other hand, current methods are not in place to deal with high values of either stakes or uncertainty, which require a new approach; what might be called "post-normal" or "second-order science"[122]. This "new" science is really just the application of the essence of the scientific method to new territory. The scientific method does not, in its basic form, imply anything

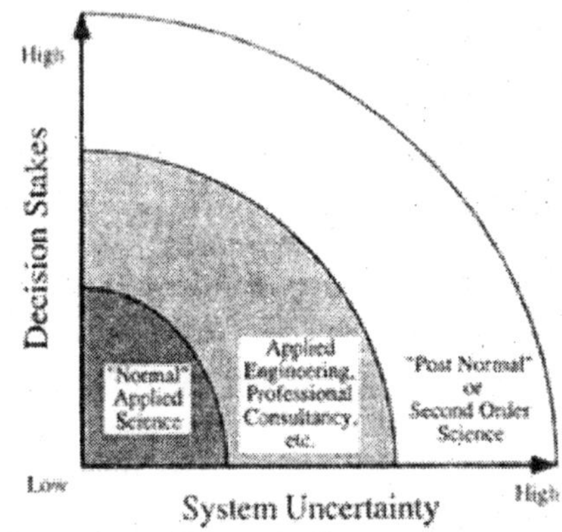

(*Source:* Funtowicz and Ravetz 1991[6])

Figure 4: Three Kinds of Science

about the precision of the results achieved. It *does* imply a forum of open and free inquiry without preconceived answers or agendas aimed at determining the envelope of our knowledge and the magnitude of our ignorance.

Implementing this view of science requires a new approach to environmental protection that acknowledges the existence of true uncertainty rather than denying it and that includes mechanisms to safeguard against its potentially harmful effects while at the same time encouraging development of lower impact technologies and the reduction of uncertainty about impacts. The precautionary principle sets the stage for this approach, but the real challenge is to develop scientific methods to determine the potential costs of uncertainty, and to adjust incentives so that the appropriate parties pay this cost of uncertainty and have appropriate incentives to reduce its detrimental effects. Without this adjustment, the full costs of environmental damage will continue to be left out of the accounting[123], and the hidden subsidies from society to those who profit from environmental degradation will continue to provide strong incentives to degrade the environment beyond sustainable levels.

Technological Optimism vs. Prudent Skepticism

Current economic policies are all based on the underlying assumption of continuing and unlimited material economic growth. This assumption allows problems of intergenerational, intra-generational, and interspecies equity and sustainability to be ignored (or at least postponed), since they are seen to be most easily solved by additional growth. Indeed, most conventional economists define "health" in an economy as a stable and high rate of growth. Energy, resource, and pollution limits to growth, according to these paradigms, will be eliminated as they arise by clever development and deployment of new technology. This line of thinking is often called "technological optimism."

An opposing line of thought (often called "technological skepticism") assumes that technology will not be able to circumvent fundamental energy and resource constraints and that eventually material economic growth will stop. It has usually been ecologists or other life scientists that take this point of view (notable exceptions among economists are J.S. Mill, *Georgescu-Roegen, Boulding,* and Daly), largely because they study natural systems that invariably *do* stop growing when they reach fundamental resource constraints. A healthy ecosystem is one that maintains a stable level. Unlimited growth eventually becomes cancerous, not healthy, under this view.

The technological optimists argue that human systems are fundamentally different from other natural systems because of human intelligence. History has shown that resource constraints can be circumvented by new ideas. Technological optimists claim that Malthus' dire predictions about population pressures have not come to pass and the "energy crisis" of the late 1970s is behind us.

The technological skeptics argue that many natural systems also have "intelligence" in that they can evolve new behaviors and organisms (including humans themselves). Humans are therefore a part of nature, not apart from it. Just because we have circumvented local and artificial resource constraints in the past does not mean we can circumvent the fundamental ones that we will eventually face. Malthus' predictions have not come to pass yet for the entire world, the pessimists would argue, but many parts of the world are in a Malthusian trap now, and other parts may well fall into it. Also those countries not in the Malthusian trap have avoided it precisely by heeding Malthus' advice to limit fertility.

This debate has gone on for many decades now. It was given an impulse by Barnett and Morse's[124] *Scarcity and Growth*, the publication of *The Limits to Growth* by Meadows et al.[125], and the Arab oil embargo in 1973. There have been thousands of studies on various aspects of our energy and resource future and different points of view have waxed and waned. But the bottom line is that there is still an enormous amount of uncertainty about the impacts of energy and resource constraints. In the next 20–30 years we may begin to hit real oil supply limits and CO_2 emission limits. Will fusion energy or solar energy or conservation or some as yet unthought-of of energy source step in to save the day and keep economies growing? The technological optimists say yes; the technological skeptics say no. Ultimately, no one knows. Both sides argue as if they were certain but the most insidious form of ignorance is misplaced certainty.

Whatever turns out to be the case, a more ecological approach to economics and a more economic approach to ecology will be beneficial in order to maintain our life-support

		Real State of the World	
		Opinion Right	**Skeptics Right**
Current Policy	**Technological Opinion Policy**	**High**	**Disaster**
	Technological Skeptic Policy	**Moderate**	**Sustainable**

Source: Authors

Figure 5: Payoff Matrix for Technological Optimism Vs. Skepticism

systems and the aesthetic qualities of the environment. But there are vast differences in the specific economic and environmental policies we should pursue today, depending on whether the technological optimists or pessimists are right.

We can cast this optimist/skeptic choice in a classic (and admittedly oversimplified) game theoretic format using the "payoff matrix" shown in Figure 3.6. Here the alternative policies that we can pursue today (technologically optimistic or skeptical) are listed on the left and the real states of the world are listed on the top. The intersections are labeled with the results of the combinations of policies and states of the world. For example, if we pursue the optimistic policy and the world really does turn out to conform to the optimistic assumptions then the payoffs would be high. This high potential payoff is very tempting and this strategy has paid off in the past. It is not surprising that so many would like to believe that the world conforms to the optimist's assumptions. If, however, we pursue the optimistic policy and the world turns out to conform more closely to the skeptical technological assumptions then the result would be "Disaster." The disaster would come because irreversible damage to ecosystems would have occurred and technological fixes would no longer be possible.

If we pursue the skeptical policy and the optimists are right then the results are only "Moderate." But if the pessimists are right and we have pursued the pessimistic policy then the results are within the framework of game theory; this simplified game has a fairly simple "optimal" strategy. Given that we only get to play this game once, and we therefore cannot assign probabilities to the various outcomes, and that society as a whole should be risk averse in this situation, then we should choose the policy that is the maximum of the minimum outcomes (i.e., the Maximum strategy in game theory jargon). In other words, we analyze each policy in turn, look for the worst thing (minimum) that could happen if we pursue that policy, and pick the policy with the largest (maximum) minimum. In the case stated above we should pursue the skeptical policy because the worst possible result under that policy ("Sustainable") is a preferable outcome to the worst outcome under the optimist policy ("Disaster").

In other words, given our high level of uncertainty about this issue, and the enormous size of the stakes, it is irrational to bank on technology's ability to remove resource constraints. If we guess wrong then the result is disastrous; there will be irreversible destruction of our resource base and civilization itself. We should at least for the time being assume that technology will not be able to remove resource constraints. If it does, we can be pleasantly surprised. If it does not, we are still left with a sustainable system. Ecological economics assumes this prudently skeptical stance on technical progress.

Social Traps

No complex system can be managed effectively without clear goals, and appropriate mechanisms for achieving them.

In managing the earth, we are faced with a nested hierarchy of goals that span a wide range of time and space scales. In any rational system of management, global ecological and economic health and sustainability should be "higher" goals than local, short-term national economic growth or private interests. Economic growth can only be supported as a policy goal in this context to the extent that it is consistent with long-term global sustainability.

Unfortunately, most of our current institutions and incentive structures deal only with relatively short-term, local goals and incentives[126]. This would not be a problem if the local and short-term goals and incentives simply added up to (or in other words were consistent with) appropriate behavior in the global long run, as many assume they do. Unfortunately, this goal and incentive consistency is frequently not the case. Individuals (or firms, or countries) pursuing their own private self-interests in the absence of mechanisms to account for community and global interests frequently run afoul of these larger goals and can often drive themselves to their own demise.

These goal and incentive inconsistencies have been characterized and generalized in many ways, beginning with Hardin's[127] classic paper on the tragedy of the commons (more accurately the tragedy of open-access resources) and continuing through more recent work on "social traps"[128]. Social traps occur when local, individual incentives that guide behavior are inconsistent with the overall goals of the system. Examples include cigarette and drug addiction, overuse of pesticides, economic boom and bust cycles, and a host of others. For example, overfishing in an open-access fishery is a social trap because by following the short-run economic road signs, fishermen are led to exploit the resource to the point of collapse.

Social traps are also amenable to experimental research to observe how individuals behave in trap-like situations and how to best avoid and escape from social traps[129]. The bottom line emerging from this research is that in cases where social traps exist the system is not inherently sustainable, and special steps must be taken to harmonize goals and incentives over the hierarchy of time and space scales involved. In economic jargon private costs and benefits must somehow be made to reflect social costs and benefits. Explicit, special steps must be taken to make the global and long-term goals incumbent on and consistent with the local and short-term goals and incentives.

This is in contrast to natural systems, which are forced to adopt a long-term perspective by the constraints of genetic evolution. This is not to say that individual species are immune to evolutionary traps set by adaptation to local conditions. But the system as a whole selects against these species in the long run. In natural systems, long-run "survival" generally equates to sustainability of the species as part of a larger ecosystem, and natural selection tends to find sustainable systems in the long run. Humans have broken the bonds of genetic evolution by the expanded use of learned behavior our large brain allows and by extending our physical capabilities with tools. The price we pay for this rapid adaptation is a misleading temporary partial isolation from long-term constraints and a susceptibility to social traps.

Another general result of social trap research is that the relative effectiveness of alternative corrective steps is not easy to predict from simple "rational" models of human behavior prevalent in conventional economic thinking. The experimental facts indicate the need to develop more realistic models of human behavior under uncertainty which acknowledge the complexity of most real-world decisions, and our species' limited information processing capabilities[130].

Escaping Social Traps

The elimination of social traps requires intervention: the modification of the reinforcement system. Indeed, it can be argued that the proper role of a democratic government is to eliminate social traps (no more and no less) while maintaining as much individual freedom as possible. Cross and Guyer[131] list four broad methods by which traps can be avoided or escaped from. These are education (about the long-term, distributed impacts); insurance; super ordinate authority (i.e., legal systems, government, religion); and converting the trap to a trade-off.

Education can be used to warn people of long-term impacts. Examples are the warning labels now required on cigarette packages and the warnings of environmentalists about future hazardous waste problems. People can ignore warnings, however, particularly if the path seems otherwise enticing. For example, warning labels on cigarette packages have had a partial but limited effect on the number of smokers.

The main problem with education as a general method of avoiding and escaping from traps is that it requires a significant time commitment on the part of individuals to learn the details of each situation. Our current society is so large and complex that we cannot expect even professionals, much less the general public, to know the details of all the extant traps. In addition, for education to be effective in avoiding traps involving many individuals, all the participants must be educated, and this is usually not possible.

Governments can, of course, forbid or regulate certain actions that have been deemed socially inappropriate (e.g., the smuggling of CFCs from developing countries into the U.S.).The problem with this direct, command-and-control approach is that it must be rigidly monitored and enforced, and the strong short-term incentive for individuals to try to ignore or avoid the regulations remains. A police force and legal system are very expensive to maintain, and increasing their chances of catching violators increases their costs exponentially (both the costs of maintaining a larger, better-equipped force and the cost of the loss of individual privacy and freedom).

Religion and social customs can be seen as much less expensive ways to avoid certain social traps. If a moral code of action and a belief in an ultimate payment for transgressions can be deeply instilled in a person, the probability of that person falling into the "sins" (traps) covered by the code will be greatly reduced, and with very little enforcement cost. On the other hand, using religion and social customs as means to avoid social traps is problematic because the moral code must be relatively static to allow beliefs learned early in life to remain in force later, and it requires a relatively homogeneous community of like-minded individuals to be truly effective. This system works well in culturally homogeneous societies that are changing very slowly. In modern, heterogeneous, rapidly changing societies, religion and social customs cannot handle all the newly evolving situations, or the conflict between radically different cultures and belief systems.

Many trap theorists believe that the most effective method for avoiding and escaping from social traps is to turn the trap into a trade-off. This method does not run counter to our normal tendency to follow the road signs; it merely corrects the signs' inaccuracies by adding compensatory positive or negative reinforcements. A simple example illustrates how effective this method can be. Playing slot machines is a social trap because the long-term costs and benefits are inconsistent with the short-term costs and benefits. People play the machines because they expect a large short-term jackpot, while the machines are in fact programmed to pay off, say, $0.80 on the dollar in the long term. People may "win" hundreds of dollars playing the slots (in the short run), but if they play long enough they will certainly lose $0.20 for every dollar played. To change this trap to a trade-off, one could simply reprogram the machines so that every time a dollar was put in $0.80 would come out. This way the short-term reinforcements ($0.80 on the dollar) are made consistent with the long-term reinforcements ($0.80 on the dollar), and only the dedicated aficionados of spinning wheels with fruit painted on them would continue to play. Requiring the true odds to be posted would also be helpful but not as effective.

In the context of social traps, the most effective way to make global and long-term goals consistent with local, private, short-term goals is to somehow modify the local, private, short-term incentives. These incentives are any combination of the reinforcements that are important at the local level, including economic, social, and cultural incentives. We must design the social and economic instruments and institutions to bridge the gulf between the present and future, between the private and social, between the local and global, between the ecological and economic parts of the system. Some instruments for accomplishing these goals are discussed in later sections.

The Dollar Auction Game

The "dollar auction game"[132] is a simple but enlightening model useful in showing the difference between local and global costs and benefits. This game is a social trap that was designed specifically to simulate the conflict escalation process. The dollar auction is just like a normal auction except that *both* the highest and the second-highest bidder have to pay the auctioneer their bid at the end of the game, but only the highest bidder gets the prize. You can try playing this game with a group or class. Simply offer a dollar bill for bid with the following rules: (1) both the highest bidder and the second-highest bidder pay; and (2) the minimum bid is $.05 over the current high bid (this just keeps the game moving).

This game usually results in some much unexpected behavior. Players in the dollar auction game frequently bid much more than $1 for a $1 prize—an irrational result that is the product of a series of "rational" decisions by the bidders. This happens because the structure of reinforcements in this game is a trap. Initially, it looks very appealing to bid $.05 on a $1 prize, but as the bidding escalates past $.50 it becomes clear that even though the winning bidder might make out, the auctioneer is now standing to make money on the auction (the two bids of more than $.50 minus the $1 prize). But the bidding usually does not stop at $.50, because the second-highest bidder (at say $.45) would lose his bid if he dropped out, and so usually rises to at least $.55. It continues under this logic up to the $1 level, where it is clear that even the highest bidder will lose money by bidding more than $1 for a $1 prize. Even when the bidding reaches the $1 point, it usually continues because of the structure of the incentives. For example, if player A had bid $1 and player B had the second-highest bid at $.95, player B reasons that if he drops out he loses $.95 while if he raises to $1.05 he only loses $.05 (assuming he wins the $1 prize). So he usually raises, and this pattern of "rational" escalation (beyond the point where the overall outcome is rational) continues quite often too well beyond the $1 point. Individual and group behavior in the dollar auction game has been extensively studied by Teger[133] who showed that almost all groups, from students to faculty to businessmen to clergy, are susceptible to being trapped in this game, and often bid as much as $5 or more for a $1 prize.

The dollar auction game can be converted to a trade-off by adding a "bidding tax" large enough to make dropping out rational in both the short run and the long run[134]. For example, if when player B was at $.95 he was told that it would now cost $2 to enter a bid of $1.05 (a $.95 bidding tax) he would reason that if he drops out he loses $.95 but if he raises he loses $1 even if he wins the prize! So the chances are increased that he would drop out and escape the trap. This method has proven to be effective in experiments using the dollar-auction game[135].

Trade and Community

During the 1980s, the international development, lending, and monetary agencies adopted the stance that development can best be achieved through opening up economies to international trade. During the 1990s, the North American Free Trade Agreement (NAFTA) and the Uruguay Round of the General Agreement on Tariffs and Trade were approved. These two agreements lowered tariffs and greatly facilitated the movement of financial capital between countries. The Uruguay Round established the World Trade Organization to monitor trade and adjudicate disputes. During this significant transformation in the international economic structure, economists took the position, based in the logic of exchange, that trade produced net benefits for both parties; hence freer trade was always better. Their position was consistent with 200 years of economic prescription. Environmentalists worried about national sovereignty with respect to environmental management, the likelihood that increased trade would lead to increased growth and environmental problems, and the difficulties of resolving environmental problems internationally. Labor unions in the industrialized nations were concerned that capital would move to the less developed nations both because wages were lower and environmental, health, and safety standards were lower. The economics profession had not considered how the expansion of trade relates to environmental management before the debate on international reorganization was well underway. Environmental economists took the position that trade can be good but that international environmental institutions would be needed to standardize regulations to keep nations from competing for industrial capital through lowering their environmental standards.

From the broader perspective of ecological economics, trading more goods across more national boundaries and freeing capital to move internationally raises many more issues than were acknowledged by conventional economists[136]. The issue of community in particular was never formally addressed. For 200 years, economists have used the logic of exchange to promote individual choice and disempowering communities. Ecological economists, on the other hand, acknowledge the role of communities in forming individual preferences, affecting human well-being, and facilitating environmental management. Each of these will be discussed in turn. First we consider whether the logic of exchange supports the general prescription of free trade.

Free Trade

The logic of exchange, Adam Smith's great discovery, has been used to promote free trade for two centuries. The logic is simply that *when two parties who are free to choose actually choose to enter into an exchange, it is because the exchange makes each party better off.* Based on this impeccable logic, economists have long intoned that governments should not restrict opportunities for people to make them better off through trade. Indeed, the political agenda of economics for 200 years to empower individuals and corporations and restrain governments and other forms of collective action has been bolstered, if not driven, by the logic of exchange. The logic is faultless under the assumption of informed, utility-maximizing parties and no effects beyond the two parties. Economists assume that the burden of proof as to whether any particular case does not meet the assumptions and is detrimental to society should be assumed by those who question free trade.

The political agenda of free trade for individuals and corporations, unfettered by taxes or other trade controls imposed through collective choice, however, does not logically follow from the logic of exchange. The problem, quite simply, is that the logic of exchange remains true regardless of how you define the parties entering into the exchange. It is true whether the parties are individuals, communities, bioregions, or nations. If it is true for nations, why should nations not be "free to choose" or be free to choose to affect the choices of individuals and corporations through taxes, quotas, or other controls? Economists have assumed that the parties should be individuals, in part because economics has followed the particular tradition in the social sciences that started with Hobbes and Locke assuming that societies are the sum of their individuals. But this is simply a convention in the dominant line of social science thought. Criteria beyond the logic of exchange are needed to determine which parties should be free to choose under different circumstances.

While economists and the majority of politicians today presume that the logic of exchange provides a sound basis for preferring individual choice over collective choice, the fundamental problem of political economy remains one of deciding when individuals, groups, communities, or the state should be entrusted with decision-making authority. This has been the central dilemma of social organization and politics for millennia; we have only been fooling ourselves for the past two centuries.

Had the atomistic premise of natural philosophy not been so readily translated to "individualism" in the dominant line of Western social thought, we might today presume that communities, bioregions, nations, or even spatially overlapping cultural groups should be free to choose. The difference between individual and community interest, of course, is intimately tied to the systemic character of environmental systems. Nature cannot readily be divided up and assigned to individuals. For this reason, collective management or collective limitations on individual choice are frequently appropriate. But the fact that the logic of exchange is indeterminate with respect to how we define the parties also tells us that commons institutions do not have to be justified on the grounds that individual behavior imposes costs on others. People may simply prefer to work together in common and share the fruits of their efforts in common. We do not need the failure of the logic of exchange to justify common activity since the logic of exchange is equally applicable to groups.

Community and Individual Well-Being

Economics is founded on self interest. But this self that interests us so much is in reality not an isolated atom, but is constituted by its relations in community with others – the very identity of the self is social rather than atomistic. If the very self is constituted by relations of community, then self-interest can no longer be atomistically self-contained or defined independently of the community interest. Some knowledge is individualistically diffuse and ephemeral, and while it is a great virtue of the market that it can tap that knowledge, other knowledge is quite public, universal, and fairly permanent: the laws of thermodynamics, for example, or the knowledge that murder and theft are wrong. To insist that everything is reducible to atomistic selfish individuals acting to maximize their gain on the basis of diffuse, piecemeal knowledge locked in their separate sealed heads is to treat an abstraction as more real than the concrete experience from which it has been abstracted.

Distribution and scale involve relationships with the poor, future generations, and other species that are more social than individual in nature. *Homo economicus*, whether the self-contained atom of methodological individualism or the pure social automaton of collectivist ideology, is in either case a severe abstraction. Our concrete experience is that of "persons in community." We are individual persons, but our very individual identity is defined by the quality of our social relations. Our relations to each other are not just external, they are also internal; that is, the nature of the related entities (ourselves in this case) changes when relations among them change. We are related not only by the external nexus of individual willingnesses-to-pay for different things, but also by relations of kinship, friendship, citizenship, and trusteeship for the poor, future generations, and for other species, not to mention our physical dependence on the same ecological life-support system, and our common heritage of language and culture. The attempt to abstract from all these relationships an atomistic *Homo economicus* whose identity is constituted only by individualistic willingness-to-pay, is a severe distortion of our concrete experience as persons in community, another example of Whitehead's "fallacy of misplaced concreteness"[137].

In ecological economics we consider maintenance of the capacity of the earth to support life as an objective, shared value that is constitutive of our identity as persons in community. We do not derive this fundamental value from subjective preferences of currently living individuals, weighted by their incomes.

Community, Environmental Management, and Sustainability

Some things can be conveyed better, at least initially, with a parable, a story selected or designed to illustrate a point. Imagine a society of near-subsistence farmers with rights to land. Parents can improve the quality of the land by planting trees. Trees also provide other goods and services at various stages of their lives. The parents might choose to reduce their consumption in their youth to invest in trees in order to have more consumption in their older age. When one's objective is to redistribute rewards over time for oneself, we think of the activity as an investment. One could also both invest in trees for oneself and accumulate them for transfer to one's children. Some of the returns from planting trees are enjoyed by the parents, while others go to their children. The extent to which current consumption is forgone and trees are planted to increase the parents' welfare or to meet the parents' "responsibility" to transfer assets to their children would be difficult to determine. Wealth, of course, does not simply accumulate linearly. Some parents choose to cut more wood for timber or firewood than grew during the period they enjoyed the land, transferring less to their children than they had themselves received from their own parents. Natural disasters and war set the process back periodically just as a string of good years might make greedy parents look like misers. And the total amount that can be accumulated at any given time is limited by the cultural knowledge, technologies, and the nature of cooperation in the society.

Responsibility is within quotation marks above to emphasize that this is a key piece of the story. The Iroquois of what is now the northeastern United States are said to have been conscious of seven generations when they made decisions affecting their future. Such a consciousness and whatever institutions maintained and implemented it are so different from modern consciousness and institutions that the very term "seven generations" symbolizes the un-sustainability, both environmentally and culturally, of modern life. A central argument of this book is that over centuries of believing that progress will take care of our progeny, modern peoples lost their sense of responsibility for their offspring and the institutions needed to assure appropriate transfers of assets. Let's consider the institutional aspects that complemented and maintained responsibility.

Protecting the well-being of future generations cannot be accomplished by individuals acting out of self-interest alone. It must be a common responsibility because one's great-great-grandchildren have seven sets of other great-great-grandparents in approximately one's own generation besides oneself and one's spouse. One never knows, however, who these other fourteen people are likely to be[138]. Furthermore, even if one could enter into an agreement with the other great-great-grandparents, there are numerous relatives in between who must carry out the agreement over time. Thus it is very difficult to assure the well-being of one's offspring beyond one's own immediate children unless the entire community throughout time is playing by a set of rules to achieve the desired outcome[139]. Patrilineal, matrilineal, and other rules of inheritance, the awarding of dowries, responsibilities to train youth, and diverse other practices and obligations can be interpreted as intergenerational commons institutions that have facilitated the transfer of assets to the next generation. The social concerns, consciousness, and institutions that promote individual responsibility are coevolved elements that are critical to the conservation of resources and their transfer to the next generation.

An additional element needs to be introduced into the parable. Indeed, economists would be very concerned if human-produced capital were not integral to the episode. Parents might save in order to acquire human-produced capital, for example, more saws, or perhaps a bigger or better type of saw with which they could more easily harvest their trees. The role of saws as capital is different from trees. Our stylized parents know that saws provide a return by reducing natural tree capital but not vice versa. Note that the existence of two types of assets, both trees and saws, considerably complicates the problem of collecting and processing information. It is the mix of trees and saws that is important. The next generation would not be very well off if it receives all trees and no saws and would be in dire straits indeed if it receives all saws and no trees. Assets need to be transferred from one generation to the next in the right proportions. Fortunately, in a small, relatively self-sufficient community, the proportion of trees and saws can be readily observed. Furthermore, members of the community can readily monitor the effects of their choices on their cumulative assets and adjust the mix accordingly.

To extend the parable, imagine that our once nearly isolated and relatively self-sufficient community becomes connected to a larger community by the clearing of trails and expansion of markets. While nothing else changes directly, the improvement in travel and introduction of markets open up new opportunities which, by exercising them, affect the community in a myriad of indirect ways. Some people, for example, might specialize by selling their trees and investing in the production of saws while others might invest more heavily in trees. As the community increasingly connects to markets, such decisions would be made in response to price signals from factor, commodity, and financial markets. The community institutions that had maintained a balance between trees and saws and heretofore sustained the community over time would fall into disuse and no longer is maintained.

The dynamics from here could be perverse. There may be an expanding market for saws precisely because, as communities were drawn into the market economy, people were choosing to cut trees, driving tree prices down, while the increased demand for saws would drive saw prices up, justifying greater investment in saws. If the market economy our community has joined has a way of assessing the overall mix of trees and saws within its area, informing everyone, and perhaps enforcing a proper mix, then disaster could be averted. Given the expanded area over which decisions are now interlinked, ultimately new intergenerational commons institutions will be needed to facilitate the appropriate transfer of assets over time. And yet the formation of commons institutions becomes more difficult the larger the community and now multiple smaller communities are combined into a larger community. One can imagine some efforts initially being made to establish commons institutions on a larger scale, but with the process of market expansion ongoing, such efforts are partially successful at best.

Eventually our community finds itself fully a part of modern society and a still globalizing economy. Though transfers of real assets in terms of land, housing, and factories from one generation to the next still constitute a significant portion of total transfers, parents are increasingly trying to meet their investment and intergenerational transfer objectives through financial claims to assets, through the education of their offspring and the cohorts they might marry, or through legislation at the state and national, and now even global, levels. In a complexly interconnected, globalizing economy with many types of interrelated assets such as we have today, comparable information on the mix of assets, let alone the complementarily of the mix, is much harder to assess.

Let's consider markets. Individual investors in financial markets only see interest rates, not the stocks of trees and saws, let alone the stocks of the myriad natural and human-produced capital supporting modern economies. But let's address the global issue first, the complexity issue second. Economists will argue that the value of a corporation's assets would decline if it cut all of its trees, but corporations can and do move on to other forests. Economic models assume good information. But who is keeping track of the whole picture? While most developed countries have fairly sophisticated monitoring institutions, even many of those nations do not make their data available to the public. Environmental monitoring in less developed countries is improving rapidly at the end of the twentieth century, but our increasing awareness of the importance of biodiversity, among other things, has increased the demand for monitoring far faster than the supply. But even if all investors individually realize they are investing in saws which are deforesting on net, they may continue to do so if there is not an enforcement institution. They have no alternative but to hope that the returns from an investment dependent on a rapidly depleting resource can be reinvested again in some other sector to the benefit of their children even if they can see that all in the further future are losing on net. This is the nature of a common pool problem unmatched by commons institutions.

The problem, however, is not simply one of monitoring and enforcement, but one of interpreting as well. With just trees and saws, contemplating the appropriate mix and deciding when there are too few of one or the other is relatively difficult. One must consider the age and species distribution of the trees as well as of the saws, the multiple uses of the trees, the likely future needs for tree services, and how these factors interact. Real economies, especially modern economies, depend on many more environmental resources and their services and the interactions greatly compound interpretation. Note that economic theory requires that decision makers be informed, not simply have access to great mounds of raw data. This means that global models of the physical interdependencies of the economy are necessary to produce the information required by economically rational investors as we go from relatively self-sufficient communities, where resource monitoring and assessment can be done informally, to global economies, where sophisticated monitoring and assessment systems are necessary.

With respect to trying to achieve our asset transfer objectives through education or the state, the situation is equally bleak. We have given little thought to which types of education complement trees or saws, or which substitute for them, let alone tried to affect the mix of education with the objective of sustainability in mind. Nor have we begun to analyze how modern institutions such as "pay-as-you-go" social security affect asset accumulation and transfers, let alone design new intergenerational commons institutions to facilitate appropriate individual behavior in a global economy.

The parable, of course, is highly stylized and too simple, but the point remains that people historically were closer to the resources they used and in a better position to monitor the overall set of assets on which they depended. Global agencies currently trying to oversee the whole picture with respect to resources and economic processes are very weak, short on conceptual justification, and an anathema to current market ideology. Ironically, the logic of markets in fact justifies information institutions at a minimum. The parable is about the interplay between community, environmental management, asset transfers, sustainability, and how they have been lost in the process of globalization.

Globalization, Transaction Costs, and Environmental Externalities

Economists have long argued that trade is good, more of it is even better, and governments should not intervene to constrain market transactions. Based on the logic of exchange, economists have provided strong justification for and generally favored the globalization of the world's economies through the expansion of the institution of the market.

At the same time, economists recognize that market exchanges entail transaction costs: the costs of perceiving a potential gain, contracting with other parties, and enforcing a contract. For individual goods traded in markets, transaction costs are relatively low and sufficiently overcome by the transactions to complete an exchange. To some extent in the markets for all goods, however, there are some benefits and costs associated with the exchange that are external to the transacting parties and fall on external parties. Where transaction costs are sufficiently low for the external parties, they can become internal parties and influence the exchange. The problem of market failure exists when these transaction costs are prohibitively high and those external parties experiencing benefits or costs from the exchange remain external and do not affect the exchange. Similarly, for commons institutions, it is the transaction costs of communicating and agreeing between individuals and enforcing agreements which ultimately determine whether commons institutions arise and are sustained for the management of environmental resources and the attainment of other collective goals.

While it is well recognized that high transaction costs prevent the success of commons institutions and the internalization of externalities, why there are transaction costs and what makes them change are rarely discussed by economists. Economists systematically address the symptom of externalities but do not ask from whence externalities come. Ironically the arguments for trade and the development of externalities are closely interrelated. Understanding transaction costs or the distances associated with trade identifies these connections.

The term "distance" helps us understand the interrelationships between trade and transactions costs[140]. Distance can be physical, social, or both. The subsistence community at the beginning of our parable could easily observe the effects of their interactions with nature, easily interpret the nature of problems, and easily communicate with each other and agree on a collective action. Their number, cultural homogeneity, geographic scope, and the relative character of the technologies they had available to them kept everything "close" and transaction costs low. The geographic expansion of exchange increases physical distance. With greater distance, it is more difficult for people to see the consequences of their actions. Those who see the consequences are in one place, those who can do something about it are in another, and the distance between them makes communicating and agreeing on a collective solution difficult.

Specialization, which goes along with increased trade, increases social distancing by reducing shared experiences and ways of seeing the world. The parable started with a world of generalist farmers and ended with a world of academics distanced by their disciplines, bankers with amazing international camaraderie, communications specialists who care little about the substance of their message, doctors and dentists with specialties of their own, engineers who think physics can and should be used to override ecological and sociological problems, and so on through the alphabet. Specialization not only makes communication difficult, specialization makes it difficult to perceive problems that defy specialties[141]. And as trade expands, existing national and cultural borders are crossed, further compounding the difficulties.

The likelihood that adequate intergenerational commons institutions evolve is a function of the size of the community. The difficulties of negotiating an agreement among individuals are a function, in part, of the number of connections between individuals. Two people have one connection, three people have three, four people have six, and five people have ten, thus increasing geometrically. To the extent that groups already exist and have appropriate communication hierarchies, then the costs of transacting individually can be lowered. But the appropriateness of a communication hierarchy depends on whether the groups' prior ordering of interests and knowledge to be communicated fits the new problem. In any case, the geographical expansion of trade increases the number of individuals in the area over which commons institutions are now needed, but, with a greater number of people, forming and maintaining commons are more difficult.

As trade expands, it creates new problems and challenges the communication systems of existing groups. Existing commons institutions become obsolete as the geographic scope of effects beyond the market that they managed expands beyond their existing boundaries. Thus, communities that have some autonomy, that are not constantly being challenged by strong external forces but rather are evolving largely through internal dynamics, are more likely to develop and sustain viable institutions to encourage individuals to transfer appropriate levels of assets. Such autonomy has not been a characteristic of the past few centuries of globalization. Thus there is good reason to be concerned that the rise of trade and geographic expansion of economic activity has broken down the institutions of many separate communities that facilitated asset transfer. This globalization has also worsened the conditions for new institutions to arise as the expanding number of people who must come to terms geometrically increases the cost of coming to a new agreement.

In summary, the increased material consumption of current generations attributed to the gains from trade may well have been facilitated by the breakdown of commons, which facilitated the transfer of assets to future generations and the absence of their replacement on a larger scale. While economists' promotion of exchange and specialization advances the markets for particular goods, it increases transaction costs and promotes the conditions for externalization of other goods through the failure of existing commons institutions and through a net increase in the externalization of environmental and other goods. Economics, by not using its own understanding of transaction costs more fully and acknowledging the problem of distancing, has unwittingly promoted two inextricably linked phenomena, both of which lead to more consumption in the present, but one of which results in less consumption in the future. There no doubt are gains from specialization and expansion of the market for the particular goods traded. At the same time, both specialization and geographic expansion increase the transaction costs for effects associated with exchange but prevented from being included in determining the exchange by the very same increased transaction costs.

The negotiations to "free" trade in North America were prolonged by the difficulties of making new international agreements to cover the expanded context of environmental and social problems. To the extent that externality-resolving institutions have not expanded in scope and adjusted as fast as have trading patterns, the gains from trade are less than expected, perhaps even negative, because the economy is working less efficiently than presumed. Equally important, however, is the absence of discussions concerning intergenerational equity and institutions to facilitate transfers of assets to future generations. The term "environmental externality" is now very much a part of the vocabulary of international discourse, though the international institutions designed to deal with externalities are far too weak[142]. The concepts of intergenerational commons and the transfer of assets to future generations are not even a part of trade negotiations.

Policy Implications

A country's external policies should complement its internal policies; that is, policies adopted with respect to foreigners should not contradict or undercut policies adopted with respect to the country's own citizens. Such contradictions would disrupt national community. We view international community as a federation—as a community of communities—not as one world cosmopolitan aggregation of individuals resulting from a "world without borders." National policies for national community are primary. The difficulty is that international free trade conflicts sharply with the basic national policies of: (a) getting prices right, (b) moving toward a more just distribution, (c) fostering community, (d) controlling the macro economy, and (e) keeping scale within ecological limits. Each conflict is discussed in turn.

Getting Prices Right: If one nation internalizes environmental and social costs to a high degree, following the dictates of adjustment, and then enters into free trade with a country that does not force its producers to internalize those costs, then the result will be that the firms in the second country will have lower prices and will drive the competing firms in the first country out of business. If the trading entities were nations rather than individual firms trading across national boundaries, then the cost-internalizing nation could limit its volume and composition of trade to an amount that did not ruin its domestic producers, and thereby actually take advantage of the opportunity to acquire goods at prices that were below full costs. The country that sells at less than full-cost prices only hurts itself as long as other countries restrict their trade with that country to a volume that does not ruin their own producers. That, of course, would not be free trade. There is clearly a conflict between free trade and a national policy of internalization of external costs. External costs are now so important that the latter goal should take precedence. In this case there is a clear argument for tariffs to protect not an inefficient industry, but an efficient national policy of internalizing external costs into prices.

Of course, if all trading nations agreed to common rules for defining, evaluating, and internalizing external costs, then this objection would disappear and the standard arguments for free trade could again be made in the new context. But how likely is such agreement? Even the small expert technical fraternity of national income accountants cannot agree on how to measure environmental costs in the system of national accounts, let alone on rules for internalizing these costs into prices at the firm level. Politicians are not likely to do better. Some economists will argue against uniform cost internalization on the grounds that different countries have different tastes for environmental services and amenities, and that these differences should be reflected in prices as legitimate reasons for profitable trade. Certainly agreement on uniform principles, and proper extent of departure from uniformity in their application, will not be easy. Nevertheless, suppose that this difficulty is overcome so that all countries internalize external costs, using the same rules applied in each case to the appropriate degree in the light of differing tastes and levels of income.

Just Distribution: Wage levels vary enormously between countries and are largely determined by the supply of labor, which in turn depends on population size and growth rates. Overpopulated countries are naturally low-wage countries, and if population growth is rapid they will remain low-wage countries. This is especially so because the demographic rate of increase of the lower class (labor) is frequently twice or more that of the upper class (capital). For most traded goods, labor is still the largest item of cost and consequently the major determinant of price. Cheap labor means low prices and a competitive advantage in trade. (The theoretical possibility that low wages reflect a taste for poverty and therefore a legitimate reason for cost differences is not taken seriously here.) But adjustment economists do not worry about that because economists have proved that free trade between high-wage and low-wage countries can be mutually advantageous thanks to comparative advantage.

The doctrine of comparative advantage is quite correct given the assumptions on which it rests, but unfortunately one of those assumptions is that capital is immobile internationally. The theory is supposed to work as follows: when in international competition the relatively inefficient activities lose out and jobs are eliminated, at the same time the relatively efficient activities (those with the comparative advantage) expand, absorbing both the labor and capital that were disemployed in activities with a comparative disadvantage. Capital and labor are reallocated within the country, specializing according to that country's comparative advantage. However, when both capital and goods are mobile internationally, then capital will follow absolute advantage to the low-wage country rather than reallocate itself according to comparative advantage within its home country. It will follow the highest absolute profit, which is usually determined by the lowest absolute wage.

Of course, further inducements to absolute profits such as low social insurance charges or a low degree of internalization of environmental, social, health and safety costs also attract capital, usually toward the very same low-wage countries. But we have assumed that all countries have internalized costs to the same degree in order to focus on the wage issue. Once capital is mobile then the entire doctrine of comparative advantage and all its comforting demonstrations become irrelevant. The consequence of capital mobility would be similar to that of international labor mobility—a strong tendency to equalize wages throughout the world.

Given the existing overpopulation and high demographic growth of the Third World, it is clear that the equalization will be downward, as it has indeed been during the last decade in the U.S. Of course, returns to capital will also be equalized by free trade and capital mobility, but the level at which equalization will occur will be higher than at present. U.S. capital will benefit from cheap labor abroad followed by cheap labor at home, at least until checked by a crisis of insufficient demand due to a lack of worker purchasing power resulting from low wages. But that can be forestalled by efficient reallocation to serve the new pattern of effective demand resulting from the greater concentration of income. More luxury goods will be produced and fewer basic wage goods. Efficiency is attained, but distributive equity is sacrificed.

The standard neoclassical adjustment view argues that wages will eventually be equalized worldwide at high levels, thanks to the enormous increase in production made possible by free trade. This increase in production presumably will trigger the automatic demographic transition to lower birth rates—a doctrine that might be considered a part of the adjustment package in so far as any attention at all is paid to population. Such a thought can only be entertained by those who ignore the issue of scale, as neoclassicists traditionally do. For all 5.7 billion people presently alive to consume resources and absorptive capacities at the same per capita rate as Americans or Europeans is ecologically impossible. Much less is it possible to extend that level of consumption to future generations. Development as it currently is understood on the U.S. model is only possible for a minority of the world's population over a few generations—that is, it is neither just nor sustainable. The goal of sustainable development is, by changes in allocation, distribution, and scale, to move the world toward a state in which "development," whatever it concretely comes to mean, will be for all people in all generations. This is certainly not achievable by more finely tuned "adjustment" to the standard growth model, which is largely responsible for having created the present impasse in the first place.

Of course, if somehow all countries decided to control their populations and to adopt distributive and scale limiting measures such that wages could be equalized worldwide at an acceptably high level, then this problem would disappear and the standard arguments for free trade could again be evoked in the new context. Although the likelihood of that context seems infinitesimal, we might for purposes of a fortiori argument consider a major problem with free trade that would still remain.

Fostering Community: Even with uniformly high wages, made possible by universal population control and redistribution, and with uniform internalization of external costs, free trade and free capital mobility still increase the separation of ownership and control and the forced mobility of labor, which are so inimical to community. Community economic life can be disrupted not only by fellow citizens who, though living in another part of your country, might at least share some tenuous bonds of community with you, but by someone on the other side of the world with whom you have no community of language, history, culture, law, and so on. These foreigners may be wonderful people; that are not the point. The point is that they are very far removed from the life of the community that is affected significantly by their decisions. Your life and your community can be disrupted by decisions and events over which you have no control, no vote and no voice.

Specialization and integration of a local community into the world economy does offer a quick fix to problems of local unemployment, and one must admit that carrying community self-sufficiency to extremes can certainly be impoverishing. But short supply lines and relatively local control over the livelihood of the community remain obvious prudential measures which require some restraint on free trade if they are to be effective. Libertarian economists look at *Homo economicus* as a self-contained individual who is infinitely mobile and equally at home anywhere. But real people live in communities, and in communities of communities. Their very individual identity is constituted by their relations in community. To regard community as a disposable aggregate of individuals in temporary proximity only for as long as it serves the interests of mobile capital is bad enough when capital stays within the nation. But when capital moves internationally it becomes much worse.

The fact that we are fellow citizens of the same country creates no obligations on my part, then admittedly not much community remains, and it is not hard to understand why Indian worker would be indifferent to the nationality of his or her employer. Indeed, if local community is more respected by the foreign company than by the displaced American counterpart, then the interests of community could conceivably be furthered by foreign ownership in some specific cases. But this could not be counted as the rule, and serves only to show that the extent of pathological disregard for community in India has not yet been equaled by others. In any event the further undercutting of local and national communities (which are real) in the name of a cosmopolitan world "community" which does not exist, is a poor trade, even if we call it free trade. The true road to international community is that of a federation of communities and communities of communities – not the destruction of local and national communities in the service of a single cosmopolitan world of footloose money managers who constitute, not a community, but merely an interdependent, mutually vulnerable, unstable coalition of short-term interests.

Controlling the Macro Economy: Free trade and free capital mobility have interfered with macroeconomic stability by permitting huge international payments imbalances and capital transfers resulting in debts that are not repayable in many cases and excessive in others. Efforts to service these debts can lead to unsustainable rates of exploitation of exportable resources, and to an eagerness to make new loans to get the foreign exchange with which to pay old loans, with a consequent disincentive to take a hard look at the real productivity of the project for which the new loan is being made. Efforts to pay back loans and still meet domestic obligations have lead to government budget deficits and monetary creation with resulting inflation. Inflation, plus the need to export to pay off loans, leads to currency devaluations, giving rise to foreign exchange speculation, capital flight, and hot money movements, disrupting the macroeconomic stability that adjustment was supposed to foster.

To summarize so far: free trade sins against allocative efficiency by making it hard for nations to internalize external costs; it sins against distributive justice by widening the disparity between labor and capital in high-wage countries; it sins against community by demanding more mobility and by further separating ownership and control; and it sins against macroeconomic stability. Finally, it also sins against the criterion of sustainable scale in a more subtle manner that will now be considered.

Keeping Scale Manageable: It has already been mentioned in passing that part of the free trade dogma of adjustment thinking is based on the assumption that the whole world and all future generations can consume resources at the levels current in today's high-wage countries without inducing ecological collapse. So in this way, free trade sin is against the criterion of sustainable scale. But, in its physical dimensions, the economy really is an open subsystem of a materially closed, non-growing, and finite ecosystem with a limited throughput of solar energy. The proper scale of the economic subsystem relative to the finite total system really is a very important question. Free trade has obscured the scale limit in the following way.

Sustainable development means living within environmental constraints of absorptive and regenerative capacities. These constraints are both global (e.g., climate change, ozone shield damage) and local (e.g., soil erosion, deforestation). Trade between nations or regions offers a way of loosening local constraints by importing environmental services (including waste absorption) from elsewhere. Within limits this can be quite reasonable and justifiable, but carried to extremes in the name of free trade it becomes destructive. It leads to a situation in which each country is trying to live beyond its own absorptive and regenerative capacities by importing these capacities from elsewhere. Of course environmental capacity-importing countries pay for the capacities they import, and all is well as long as other countries have made the complementary decision—namely, to keep their own scale well below their own national carrying capacity in order to be able to export some of their environmental services. In other words, the apparent escape from scale constraints enjoyed by some countries via trade depends on other countries' willingness and ability to adopt the very discipline of limiting scale that the importing country is seeking to avoid. What nations have actually made this complementary choice? All countries now aim to grow in scale, and it is merely the fact that some have not yet reached their limits that allows other nations to import carrying capacity. Free trade does not remove carrying capacity constraints; it just guarantees that nations will hit that constraint more or less simultaneously rather than sequentially. It converts differing local constraints into an aggregated global constraint. It converts a set of problems, some of which are manageable, into one big unmanageable problem. Evidence that this is not understood is provided by the countless occasions when someone who really should know better points to The Netherlands or Hong Kong as both examples to be emulated, and as evidence that all countries could become as densely populated as these two. How it would be possible for all countries to be net exporters of goods and net importers of carrying capacity is not explained.

Of course the drive to grow beyond carrying capacity has roots other and deeper than the free trade dogma. The point is that free trade makes it very hard to deal with these root causes at a national level, which is the only level at which effective social controls over the economy exist. Standard economists will argue that free trade is just a natural extension of price adjustment across international boundaries, and that "right prices" must reflect *global* scarcities and preferences. But if the unit of community is the nation, the unit in which there are institutions and traditions of collective action, responsibility, and mutual help, the unit in which government tries to carry out policy for the good of its citizens, then "right prices" should not reflect the preferences and scarcities of other nations. Right prices should differ between national communities. Such differences traditionally have provided the whole reason for international trade in goods—trade that can continue if balanced, that is, if not accompanied by the free mobility of capital (and labor) that homogenizes preferences and scarcities globally, while reducing national economic policy to ineffectiveness unless agreed upon by all freely trading nations.

It is admitted by neoclassical economists that externalities resulting from overpopulation can spill over to other nations, and thus provide a legitimate reason against free immigration, however uncongenial to liberal sentiments[143][144]. But externalities of overpopulation in the form of cheap labor can spill over into other countries through free migration of capital toward abundant labor, just as much as through free migration of labor toward abundant capital. The legitimate case for restrictions on labor immigration are therefore easily extended to restrictions on capital emigration for any country not wanting to suffer the consequences of another country's overpopulation[145].

The nation state certainly has many historical sins to atone for, but it is where community exists in the sense that it is the main unit in which policies are taken for the common good. To say that national boundaries are just lines on the map, and that we should all be environmental earth citizens is nice rhetoric, but not very realistic. Given the urgency of action, and the reality of transnational corporate power eager to take over, we have no alternative but to work within the existing institution of the nation state. Certainly population and per capita consumption will not be controlled at a global level. It will be done by nations. But the nations will have to cooperate and make binding international agreements.

For example, while all countries must worry about both population and per capita consumption, it is evident that the South needs to focus more on population, and the North more on per capita consumption. This fact will likely play a major role in all North/South treaties and discussions. Why should the South control its population if the resources saved thereby are merely gobbled up by Northern overconsumption? Why should the North control its overconsumption if the saved resources will merely allow a larger number of poor people to subsist at the same level of misery? Global problems are indeed global, but their solutions require national policies supported by international treaties. Nations have to be able to enact and enforce national policies agreed to in international treaties. If a nation's borders are porous to the flow of goods and services, capital, and labor then that country is in a poor position to carry out any national policy, including those it agreed to in international treaties.

References

1. Costanza, R. and B.C. Patten (1995), Defining and Predicting Sustainability. *Ecological Economics* 15:193–196.
2. Max-Neef, M. (1995), Economic Growth and the Quality of Life: A Threshold Hypothesis. *Ecological Economics* 15:115–118.
3. Max-Neef, M. (1995), Economic Growth and the Quality of Life: A Threshold Hypothesis. *Ecological Economics* 15:115–118.
4. Max-Neef, M. (1995), Economic Growth and the Quality of Life: A Threshold Hypothesis. *Ecological Economics* 15:115–118.
5. Ekins, P. (1992), A Four-capital Model of Wealth Creation. In P. Ekins and M. Max-Neef (eds.), *Real-life Economics: Understanding Wealth Creation*, pp. 147–155. London: Routledge.
6. Funtowicz, S.O. and J.R. Ravetz (1991), A New Scientific Methodology for Global Environmental Problems. In R. Costanza

(ed.), *Ecological Economics: The Science and Management of Sustainability*, pp. 137–152. New York: Columbia University Press.

7. Costanza, R. (1980), Embodied Energy and Economic Valuation. *Science* 210:1219–1224.

   —Cleveland, C.J., R. Costanza, C.A.S. Hall, and R. Kaufmann (1984), Energy and the United States Economy: A Biophysical Perspective. *Science* 225:890–897.

8. Daly, H.E. (1992), Allocation, Distribution, and Scale: Toward an Economics that is Efficient, Just, and Sustainable. *Ecological Economics* 6:185–194.

9. Bishop, R.C. (1993), Economic Efficiency, Sustainability, and Biodiversity. *Ambio* 22:69–73.

10. Daly, H.E. and J. Cobb (1989), *For the Common Good: Redirecting the Economy Towards Community, the Environment, and a Sustainable Future*. Boston: Beacon Press.

11. Young, M.D. (1992), *Sustainable Investment and Resource Use: Equity, Environmental Integrity and Economic Efficiency*. Park Ridge, NJ: Parthenon.

12. Boulding, K.E. (1966), The Economics of the Coming Spaceship Earth. In H. Jarrett (ed.), *Environmental Quality in a Growing Economy*, pp. 3–14. Baltimore, MD: Resources for the Future/ Johns Hopkins University Press.

13. Georgescu-Roegen, N. (1971), *The Entropy Law and the Economic Process*. Cambridge, MA: Harvard University Press.

14. Vitousek, P.M., et al. (1986), Human Appropriation of the Products of Photosynthesis. *BioScience* 34(6):368–373.

15. Ahmad, Y.J., S. El Serafy, and E. Lutz (1989), *Environmental Accounting for Sustainable Development*. A UNEP-World Bank Symposium. Washington, DC: The World Bank.

16. Cleveland, C.J. (1994), Reallocating Work between Human and Natural Capital in Agriculture. In A.-M. Jansson, M. Hammer, C. Folke, and R. Costanza (eds.), *Investing in Natural Capital: The Ecological Economics Approach to Sustainability*, pp. 179–199. Washington, DC: Island Press.

17. Odum, E.P. (1989), *Ecology and Our Endangered Life-support Systems*. Sunderland, MA: Sinauer Associates.

18. Holling, C.S. (1987), Simplifying the Complex: The Paradigms of Ecological Function and Structure. *European Journal of Operational Research* 30:139–146.

19. Holling, C.S., D.W. Schindler, B.H. Walker, and J. Roughgarden (1995), Biodiversity in the Functioning of Ecosystems: An Ecological Synthesis. In C.A. Perrings, K.-G. Mäler, C. Folke, C. S. Holling, and B.-O. Jansson (eds.), *Biodiversity loss: Ecological and economic issues*, pp. 44–83. Cambridge, U.K.: Cambridge University Press.

20. Holling, C.S., D.W. Schindler, B.H. Walker, and J. Roughgarden (1995), Biodiversity in the Functioning of Ecosystems: An Ecological Synthesis. In C.A. Perrings, K.-G. Mäler, C. Folke, C. S. Holling, and B.-O. Jansson (eds.), *Biodiversity loss: Ecological and economic issues*, pp. 44–83. Cambridge, U.K.: Cambridge University Press.

21. Perrings, C. and B.H. Walker (1995), Biodiversity Loss and the Economics of Discontinuous Change in Semi-arid Rangelands. In C. A. Perrings, K.-G. Mäler, C. Folke, C. S. Holling, and B.-O. Jansson (eds.), *Biodiversity loss: Ecological and economic issues*, pp. 190–210. Cambridge, U.K.: Cambridge University Press.

22. Knowlton, N. (1992), Thresholds and Multiple Stable States in Coral Reef Community Dynamics. *American Zoologist* 32:674–682.

23. Scheffer, M., S.H. Hosper, M.-L. Meyjer, B. Moss, and E. Jeppsen (1993), Alternative Equilibria in Shallow Lakes. *Trends in Ecology and Evolution* 8:275–285.

24. Costanza, R., L. Wainger, C. Folke, and K.-G. Mäler (1993), Modeling Complex Ecological Economic Systems: Toward an Evolutionary, Dynamic Understanding of Humans and Nature. *BioScience* 43(8):545–555.

25. Naeem, S., L. J. Thompson, S.P. Lawler, J.H. Lawton, and R.M. Woodfin (1994), Declining Biodiversity can Alter the Performance of Ecosystems. *Nature* 368:734–737.

26. Folke, C. (1991), Socioeconomic Dependence on the Life-supporting Environment. In C. Folke and T. Kåberger (eds.), *Linking the natural environment and the economy: Essays from the Eco-Eco group*, pp. 77–94. Dordrecht, the Netherlands: Kluwer Academic Publishers.

—Holling, C.S., D.W. Schindler, B.H. Walker, and J. Roughgarden (1995), Biodiversity in the functioning of ecosystems: An ecological synthesis. In C.A. Perrings, K.-G. Mäler, C. Folke, C. S. Holling, and B.-O. Jansson (eds.), *Biodiversity loss: Ecological and economic issues*, pp. 44–83. Cambridge, U.K.: Cambridge University Press.

—Tilman, D. and J.A. Downing (1994), Biodiversity and Stability in Grasslands. *Nature* 367:363-365.

27. Barbier, E.B., J.C. Burgess, and C. Folke (1994), *Paradise Lost? The Ecological Economics of Biodiversity*. London: Earthscan.

28. Schneider, E. and J.J. Kay (1994), Complexity and thermodynamics: Towards a new ecology. *Futures* 24:626-647.

29. Günther, F. and C. Folke (1993), Characteristics of Nested Living Systems. *Journal of Biological Systems* 1(3):257-254.

30. Holling, C.S., D.W. Schindler, B.H. Walker, and J. Roughgarden (1995), Biodiversity in the Functioning of Ecosystems: An Ecological Synthesis. In C.A. Perrings, K.-G. Mäler, C. Folke, C. S. Holling, and B.-O. Jansson (eds.), *Biodiversity loss: Ecological and economic issues*, pp. 44-83. Cambridge, U.K.: Cambridge University Press.

31. See further along in this chapter and Ulanowicz, R.E. (1980), An Hypothesis on the Development of Natural Communities. *Journal of Theoretical Biology* 85:223-245.

    Ulanowicz, R.E. (1986), *Growth and Development: Ecosystems phenomenology*. New York: Springer-Verlag.

32. Mageau, M., R. Costanza, and R.E. Ulanowicz (1995), The Development, Testing, and Application of a Quantitative Assessment of Ecosystem Health. *Ecosystem Health* 1:201-213.

33. Barbier, E.B., J.C. Burgess, and C. Folke (1994), *Paradise Lost? The Ecological Economics of Biodiversity*. London: Earthscan.

34. de Groot, R.S. (1992), *Functions of Nature*. Groningen, the Netherlands: Wolters Noordhoff BV.—Ehrlich, P. R. and A. E. Ehrlich. 1992. The value of biodiversity. *Ambio* 21:219-226.—Ehrlich, P. R. and H. A. Mooney. 1983. Extinction, substitution and ecosystem services. *BioScience* 33:248-254. —Folke, C. 1991. Socioeconomic dependence on the life-supporting environment. In C. Folke and T. Kåberger (eds.), *Linking the natural environment and the economy: Essays from the Eco-Eco group*, pp. 77-94. Dordrecht, the Netherlands: Kluwer Academic Publishers.

35. Cairns, J. and J.R. Pratt (1995), The Relationship between Ecosystem Health and Delivery of Ecosystem Services. In D.J. Rapport, C.L. Gaudet, and P. Calow (eds.), *Evaluating and monitoring the health of large-scale ecosystems*, pp. 63-93. New York: Springer-Verlag.

36. Costanza, R., L. Wainger, C. Folke, and K.-G. Mäler (1993), Modeling Complex Ecological Economic Systems: Toward an Evolutionary, Dynamic Understanding of Humans and Nature. *BioScience* 43(8):545–555. – Perrings, C. A., K.-G. Mäler, C. Folke, C. S. Holling, and B.-O. Jansson (eds.). 1995. *Biodiversity loss: Ecological and Economic Issues*. Cambridge, U.K.: Cambridge University Press.

37. Costanza, R. and B.C. Patten (1995), Defining and Predicting Sustainability. *Ecological Economics* 15:193–196, p. 194.

38. Roedel, P.M. (ed.). (1975), *Optimum Sustainable Yield as a Concept in Fisheries Management*. Special Publication No. 9. Washington, DC: American Fisheries Society.

39. Ludwig, D., R. Hilborn, and C. Walters (1993), Uncertainty, Resource Exploitation, and Conservation: Lessons from history. *Science* 260:17, 36.

40. Holling, C.S. (1987), Simplifying the Complex: The Paradigms of Ecological Function and Structure. *European Journal of Operational Research* 30:139–146.

41. This distinction is explicit in the dictionary's first definition of each term. To grow means literally "to increase naturally in size by the addition of material through assimilation or accretion." To develop means "to expand or realize the potentialities of; bring gradually to a fuller, greater, or better state" (*The American Heritage Dictionary of the English Language*).

42. Lovins, A.B. (1977), *Soft Energy Paths*. Friends of the Earth International. Cambridge, MA: Ballinger. – Lovins, A. B. and L. H. Lovins. 1987. Energy: The avoidable oil crisis. *The Atlantic* December:22–30.

43. Cleveland, C.J., R. Costanza, C.A.S. Hall, and R. Kaufmann (1984), Energy and the United States Economy: A Biophysical Perspective. *Science* 225:890–897. – Costanza, R. 1980. Embodied energy and economic valuation. *Science* 210:1219–1224.

– Gever, J., R. Kaufmann, D. Skole, and C. Vorosmarty (1986), *Beyond oil*. Cambridge, MA: Ballinger. – Hall, Charles A. S., Cutler J. Cleveland, and Robert Kaufman. 1986. *Energy and Resource Quality: The Ecology of the Economic Process*. New York: John Wiley and Sons.

44. WCED (1987), *Our Common Future*. World Commission on Environment and Development (The Brundtland Report). Oxford: Oxford University Press.

45. MacNeil, J. (1990), *Sustainable Development, Economics, and the Growth Imperative.* Workshop on the Economics of Sustainable Development, Background Paper No. 3, Washington, DC, p. 13.

46. Rawls, J. (1987), The Idea of an Overlapping Consensus. *Oxford Journal of Legal Studies* 7:1-25.

47. AGENDA 21. (1992), United Nations Environment Program. New York: United Nations.

—WCED (1987), *Our Common Future.* World Commission on Environment and Development (The Brundtland Report). Oxford: Oxford University Press.

48. Costanza, R. (ed.). (1991), *Ecological Economics: The Science and Management of Sustainability.* New York: Columbia Press.—Goodland, R. and H.E. Daly. 1996. Environmental ability: Universal and non-negotiable. *Ecological Applications* 6:1002–1017. —WCED. 1987. *Our common future.* World Commission on Environment and Development (The Brundtland Report). Oxford: Oxford University Press.

49. Bodansky, D. (1991), Scientific Uncertainty and the Precautionary Principle. *Environment* 33:4–44.

50. Costanza, R.,and H.E. Daly (1992), Natural Capital and Sustainable Development. *Conservation Biology* 6:37–46. —El Serafy, S. 1991. The environment as capital. In R. Costanza (ed.), *Ecological economics: The Science and Management of Sustainability,* pp. 168–175. New York: Columbia Press.—Pearce, D. W. and R. K. Turner. 1989. Economics of natural resources and the environment. Brighton: Wheatsheaf.

51. Daly, H.E. (1990a), Boundless Bull. *Gannett Center Journal* 4(3):113–118.—Daly, H. E. 1990b. Toward some operational principles of sustainable development. *Ecological Economics* 2:1–6.

52. Bernard Gilliand, as cited in Demeny, P. (1988), Demography and the Limits to Growth. In M. S. Teitelbaum and J. M. Winter (eds.), *Population and resources in Western intellectual traditions,* pp. 213–244. Supplement to vol. 14 of *Population and Development Review* (winter), pp. 224–225.

53. Clark, C. (1958), World Population. *Nature* May 3:1235–1236. Reprinted in W. Y. Davis (ed.). 1971. *Readings in human population ecology,* pp. 101–106. Englewood Cliffs, NJ: Prentice-Hall.

54. Revelle (1976).

55. Brown, H. (1954), *The Challenge of Man's Future: An Inquiry Concerning the Condition of Man during the Years that Lie Ahead.* New York: Viking.

56. Demeny, P. (1988), Demography and the Limits to Growth. In M.S. Teitelbaum and J.M. Winter (eds.), *Population and Resources in Western Intellectual Traditions,* pp. 213–244. Supplement to vol. 14 of *Population and Development Review* (winter).

57. Cohen, J. (1995), *How Many People can the Earth Support?* New York: Norton.

58. Blaikie, P. and H. Brookfield (1987), *Land Degradation and Society.* London: Metheun.

59. Daly, H.E. (1977), *Steady State Economics.* San Francisco: W. H. Freeman.

60. Caldwell, L.K. (1984), *International Environmental Policy: Emergence and Dimensions.* Durham, NC: Duke University Press.

61. Blaikie, P. and H. Brookfield (1987), *Land Degradation and Society.* London: Metheun.

62. Ehrlich, P. (1989), The Limits to Substitution: Metaresource Depletion and a New Economic–ecologic Paradigm. *Ecological Economics* 1(1):9–16, p. 20.

63. Boserup, E. 1965 [1974], *The Conditions of Agricultural Growth.* Chicago: Aldine.

64. Simon (1990).

65. Lappe, F.M. and R. Schurman (1988), *The Missing Piece in the Population Puzzle.* San Francisco: Institute for Food and Development Policy.

66. Durning, A.T. (1992), *How Much is Enough?: The Consumer Society and the Future of the Earth.* New York: Norton.

67. OECD (Organisation for Economic Co-operation and Development) (1991), *Environmental Indicators.* Paris: OECD.

68. Daly, H.E. and J. Cobb (1989), *For the Common Good: Redirecting the Economy Towards Community, the Environment, and a Sustainable Future.* Boston: Beacon Press.

69. Costanza, R. and L. Cornwell (1992), The 4P Approach to Dealing with Scientific Uncertainty. *Environment* 34:12–20, 42.

70. Brown, L.R. (1997a), *State of the World.* Washington, DC: Worldwatch Institute (annual).

71. Brown, L.R. (1997b), *Vital Signs*. Washington, DC: Worldwatch Institute (annual).

72. Wachtel, P.L. (1983), *The Poverty of Affluence: A Psychological Portrait of the American Way of Life*. New York: Free Press.

73. Sherman, H.J. (1966), *Elementary Aggregate Economics*. Meredith, NY: Appleton-Century-Crofts.

74. Sherman, H.J. (1966), *Elementary Aggregate Economics*. Meredith, NY: Appleton-Century-Crofts, pp. 30–31.

75. Sherman, H.J. (1966), *Elementary Aggregate Economics*. Meredith, NY: Appleton-Century-Crofts, emphasis added, pp. 52–53.

76. Eckstein, O. (1983), The NIPA Accounts: A User's View. In Murray F. Foss (ed.), *The U.S. National Income and Public Accounts*. Chicago: University of Chicago Press.

77. Ruggles, R. (1983).

78. Eckstein, O. (1983), The NIPA Accounts: A User's View. In Murray F. Foss (ed.), *The U.S. National Income and Public Accounts*. Chicago: University of Chicago Press, p. 316.

79. Fisher, I. (1906), *The Nature of Capital and Income*. London: Macmillan.

80. Ruggles, R. (1983), p. 17.

81. Ruggles, R. (1983), p. 332.

82. Ruggles, R. (1983), p. 332.

83. Ruggles, R. (1983).

84. Ruggles, (1983), pp. 41–43.

85. Hicks, J.R. (1948), *Value and Capital* (2nd ed.). Oxford: Clarendon, p. 172.

86. WCED (1987), *Our Common Future*. World Commission on Environment and Development (The Brundtland Report). Oxford: Oxford University Press.

87. El Serafy, S. (1988), The Proper Calculation of Income from Deployable Natural Resources. In E. Lutz and S. El Serafy (eds.), *Environmental and resource accounting and their relevance to the measurement of sustainable income*. Washington, DC: World Bank.

88. Nordhaus, W. and J. Tobin (1972), Is Growth Obsolete? In *Economic Growth*. National Bureau of Economic Research General Series #96E. New York: Columbia University Press.

89. Nordhaus, W. and J. Tobin (1972), Is Growth Obsolete? In *Economic growth.* National Bureau of Economic Research General Series #96E. New York: Columbia University Press, p. 4.
90. Nordhaus, W. and J. Tobin (1972), Is Growth Obsolete? In *Economic Growth.* National Bureau of Economic Research General Series #96E. New York: Columbia University Press, p. 6.
91. Nordhaus, W., and J. Tobin (1972), Is Growth Obsolete? In *Economic Growth.* National Bureau of Economic Research General Series #96E. New York: Columbia University Press, p. 5.
92. Nordhaus, W. and J. Tobin (1972), Is Growth Obsolete? In *Economic Growth.* National Bureau of Economic Research General Series #96E. New York: Columbia University Press.
93. Nordhaus, W. and J. Tobin (1972), Is Growth Obsolete? In *Economic Growth.* National Bureau of Economic Research General Series #96E. New York: Columbia University Press, p. 13.
94. Nordhaus, W., and J. Tobin (1972), Is Growth Obsolete? In *Economic Growth.* National Bureau of Economic Research General Series #96E. New York: Columbia University Press, p. 8–9.
95. Jaszi, G. (1973), Comment. In M. Moss (ed.), *The Measurement of Economic and Social Performance.* New York: National Bureau of Economic Research, Columbia University Press.
96. Nordhaus, W. and J. Tobin (1972), Is Growth Obsolete? In *Economic Growth.* National Bureau of Economic Research General Series #96E. New York: Columbia University Press, pp. 8–9.
97. Nordhaus, W. and J. Tobin (1972), Is Growth Obsolete? In *Economic Growth.* National Bureau of Economic Research General Series #96E. New York: Columbia University Press, p. 17.
98. In fact, the growth rate of per capita MEW from 1929 to 1965 was only 1.0% per year, as opposed to 1.1%. The correct evaluation can be found in table 18 on p. 56 of Nordhaus and Tobin's study. (Nordhaus, W. and J. Tobin. 1972. Is growth obsolete? In *Economic growth.* National Bureau of Economic Research General Series #96E. New York: Columbia University Press, p. 17.)
99. We have chosen to compare per capita MEW with per capita GNP rather than with per capita NNP as Nordhaus and Tobin (Nordhaus, W. and J. Tobin. 1972. Is growth obsolete? In *Economic growth.* National Bureau of Economic Research General Series #96E. New York: Columbia University Press, p. 17) have done. We do this for the sake of consistency with other studies (especially the one by Zoltas [Zoltas, X. 1981. *Economic growth*

and declining social welfare] discussed below). The differences in annual growth rates are not large, though the growth of per capital NNP is slightly slower than for per capita GNP.

100. Interestingly, though Nordhaus and Tobin (Nordhaus, W. and J. Tobin (1972), Is Growth Obsolete? In *Economic growth*. National Bureau of Economic Research General Series #96E. New York: Columbia University Press, p. 17.) Calculate the growth rate of per capita NNP and per capita sustainable MEW for the period 1929–1947 and 1947–1965 (see Table 18 on p. 56 of their text), they never refer to the remarkable difference between those two periods in their discussion. To do so would have required them to explain why the growth rate for per capita sustainable MEW had flattened out, even as per capita NNP kept rising.
101. Nordhaus, W. and J. Tobin (1972), Is Growth Obsolete? In *Economic growth*. National Bureau of Economic Research General Series #96E. New York: Columbia University Press.
102. Nordhaus, W. and J. Tobin (1972), Is Growth Obsolete? In *Economic growth*. National Bureau of Economic Research General Series #96E. New York: Columbia University Press, p. 39.
103. Nordhaus, W. and J. Tobin (1972), Is Growth Obsolete? In *Economic Growth*. National Bureau of Economic Research General Series #96E. New York: Columbia University Press, p. 13.
104. Nordhaus (1977), p. 197.
105. Daly, H.E. and J. Cobb (1989), *For the Common Good: Redirecting the Economy Towards Community, the Environment, and a Sustainable Future*. Boston: Beacon Press.
106. Zoltas, X. (1981), *Economic Growth and Declining Social Welfare.*
107. Nordhaus, W. and J. Tobin (1972), Is Growth Obsolete? In *Economic Growth*. National Bureau of Economic Research General Series #96E. New York: Columbia University Press.
108. Zoltas, X. (1981), *Economic Growth and declining Social Welfare.*
109. Daly, H.E. and J. Cobb (1989), *For the Common Good: Redirecting the Economy Towards Community, the Environment, and a Sustainable Future*. Boston: Beacon Press.
110. Max-Neef, M. (1995), Economic Growth and the Quality of Life: A Threshold Hypothesis. *Ecological Economics* 15:115–118.
111. Max-Neef, M. (1992), Development and Human Needs. In P. Ekins and M. Max-Neef (eds.), *Real-life Economics: Understanding Wealth Creation*, pp. 197–213. London: Routledge.

112. Max-Neef, M. (1992), Development and Human Needs. In P. Ekins and M. Max-Neef (eds.), *Real-life economics: Understanding wealth creation*, pp. 197–213. London: Routledge, pp. 199–200.

113. Ekins, P. (1992), A Four-capital Model of Wealth Creation. In P. Ekins and M. Max-Neef (eds.), *Real-life Economics: Understanding wealth creation*, pp. 147–155. London: Routledge.

114. Ekins, P. (1992), A Four-capital Model of Wealth Creation. In P. Ekins and M. Max-Neef (eds.), *Real-life Economics: Understanding Wealth Creation*, pp. 147–155. London: Routledge, p. 151.

115. Paul Hawken in the forward to Prugh, T., R. Costanza, J.H. Cumberland, H. Daly, R. Goodland, and R.B. Norgaard (1995), *Natural Capital and Human Economic Survival.* Solomons, MD: ISEE Press.

116. Daly, H.E. and J. Cobb (1989), *For the Common Good: Redirecting the Economy Towards Community, the Environment, and a Sustainable Future.* Boston: Beacon Press.

– Page, T. (1977), *Conservation and Economic Efficiency.* Baltimore, MD: Johns Hopkins University Press.

– Norton, B.G. (ed.). (1986), *The Preservation of Species: The Value of Biological Diversity.* Princeton, NJ: Princeton University Press.

117. Science Advisory Board (1990), *Reducing Risk: Setting Priorities and Strategies for Environmental Protection.* SAB-EC-90-021. Washington, DC: U.S. EPA.

118. Thompson, P.B. (1986), Uncertainty Arguments in Environmental Issues. *Environmental Ethics* 8:59–76.

119. Weinberg, A.M. (1985), Science and Its Limits: The Regulator's Dilemma. *Issues in Science and Technology* 2:59–73.

120. Cameron, J. and J. Abouchar (1991), The Precautionary Principle: A Fundamental Principle of Law and Policy for the Protection of the Global Environment. *Boston College International and Comparative Law Review* 14:1–27.

121. Perrings, C. (1991), Reserved Rationality and the Precautionary Principle: Technological Change, Time and Uncertainty in Environmental Decision Making. In R. Costanza (ed.), *Ecological Economics: The Science and Management of Sustainability*, pp. 153–166. New York: Columbia University Press. p. 154.

122. Funtowicz, S.O. and J.R. Ravetz (1991), A New Scientific Methodology for Global Environmental Problems. In R. Costanza

(ed.), *Ecological economics: the science and management of sustainability*, pp. 137-152. New York: Columbia University Press.

123. Peskin, H.M. (1991), Alternative Environmental and Resource Accounting Approaches. In R. Costanza (ed.), *Ecological Economics: The Science and Management of Sustainability*, pp. 176-193. New York: Columbia University Press.

124. Barnett, H.J. and C. Morse (1963), *Scarcity and Growth: The Economics of Natural Resource Availability*. Baltimore: Johns Hopkins.

125. Meadows, D.H., D.L. Meadows, J. Randers, and W.W. Behrens (1972), *The Limits to Growth*. New York: Universe.

126. Clark, C.W. (1973), The Economics of Overexploitation. *Science* 181:630-634.

127. Hardin, G. (1968), The Tragedy of the Commons. *Science* 162:1243-1248.

128. Costanza, R. (1987), Social Traps and Environmental Policy. *BioScience* 37:407-412. —Costanza, R. and C. Perrings. 1990. A flexible assurance bonding system for improved environmental management. *Ecological Economics* 2:57-76.

—Costanza, R. and W. Shrum (1988), The Effects of Taxation on Moderating the Conflict Escalation Process: An Experiment using the Dollar Auction Game. *Social Science Quarterly* 69:416-432. —Cross, J.G. and M.J. Guyer. 1980. *Social Traps*. Ann Arbor: University of Michigan Press. —Platt, J. 1973. Social traps. *American Psychologist* 28:642-651. —Teger, A. I. 1980. *Too much invested to quit*. New York: Pergamon.

129. Brockner, J. and J.Z. Rubin (1985), *Entrapment in Escalating Conflicts: A Social Psychological Analysis*. New York: Springer-Verlag. —Costanza, R. and W. Shrum. 1988. The Effects of Taxation on Moderating the Conflict Escalation Process: An Experiment using the Dollar Auction Game. *Social Science Quarterly* 69:416-432.

—Edney, J.J. and C. Harper (1978), The Effects of Information in a Eesource Management Problem: A Social Trap Analog. *Human Ecology* 6:387-395. —Teger, A. I. 1980. *Too much invested to quit*. New York: Pergamon.

130. Heiner, R. (1983), The Origin of Predictable behavior. *American Economic Review* 73:560-595.

131. Cross, J.G. and M.J. Guyer (1980), *Social Traps*. Ann Arbor: University of Michigan Press.

132. Shubik, M. (1971), The Dollar Auction Game: A Paradox in Noncooperative Behavior and Escalation. *Journal of Conflict Resolution* 15:109–111.

133. Teger, A.I. (1980), *Too Much Invested to Quit*. New York: Pergamon.

134. Costanza, R. and W. Shrum (1988), The Effects of Taxation on Moderating the Conflict Escalation Process: An Experiment Using the Dollar Auction Game. *Social Science Quarterly* 69:416–432.

135. Costanza, R. and W. Shrum (1988), The Effects of Taxation on Moderating the Conflict Escalation Process: An Experiment Using the Dollar Auction Game. *Social Science Quarterly* 69:416–432.

136. Daly, H.E. (1993), The Perils of Free Trade. *Scientific American* November:50–57.

—Daly, H.E. and R. Goodland (1994), An Ecological-economic Assessment of Deregulation of International Commerce Under GATT. *Environment* 15:399–427, 477–503.

137. Whitehead, A.N. (1925), *Science and the Modern World*. New York: Macmillan.

138. Daly, H.E. and J. Cobb (1989), *For the Common Good: Redirecting the Economy Towards Community, the Environment, and a Sustainable Future*. Boston: Beacon Press.

—Marglin, S.A. (1963), The Social Rate of Discount and the Optimal Rate of Investment. *Quarterly Journal of Economics* 77:95–112. —Weiss, E.B. 1989. *In Fairness to Future Generations: International Law, Common Patrimony, and Intergenerational Equity*. Ardsley-on-Hudson, NY: Transnational Publishers.

139. Howarth, R.B. and R.B. Norgaard (1992), Environmental Valuation Under Sustainable Development. *American Economic Review* 82:473–477.

140. Giddens, A. (1990), *The Consequences of Modernity*. Stanford, CA: Stanford University Press.

141. Norgaard, R.B. (1992), Environmental Science as a Social Process. *Environmental Monitoring and Assessment* 20:95–110.

142. Costanza, R. and B.C. Patten (1995), Defining and Predicting Sustainability. *Ecological Economics* 15:193–196.

143. Economists tend to dismiss such wage effects as merely "pecuniary externalities" that deserve less attention than

"technological externalities." The latter refers to costs or benefits shifted to third parties in a manner external to the price system; the former refers to third-party effects that operate through the price system. Since lowering the price of labor by free migration is a cost to the pre-existing labor force and a benefit to employers and foreign laborers that is mediated by the wage rate, it is classed as a pecuniary externality and not given much consideration in economic theory—i.e., it is "merely a matter of distribution."

144. Baumol, W.J. (1971), *Environmental Protection, International Spillovers, and Trade*. Stockholm: Almqvist and Wicksell.

145. Culbertson, J.M. (1971), *Economic Development: An Ecological Approach*. New York: Alfred A. Knopf.

4

General and Specific of Environmental Policies: A Fresh Look

"...while purity is an uncomplicated virtue for olive oil, sea air, and heroines of folk tales, it is not so for systems of collective choice."

– Amartya Sen[1]

In this section we discuss some general and specific policy ideas that follow from the previously discussed principles, and introduce instruments that may be useful in implementing these policies[2]. We advocate a broad, democratic process to discuss and achieve consensus on these important issues. This is distinct from the polemic and divisive political process that seems to hold sway in many countries today. What is needed is deep discussion and consensus about long-term goals, not constant quibbling over short-term details[3].

Democracy is not merely the process of voting. The two are far from the same thing. Voting, without broad-based discussion, information exchange, and, most importantly, agreement on shared goals and visions for the future, is merely the façade of democracy. We have a long way to go to actually achieve the kind of participatory, "living democracy" which Frances Moore Lappé and Paul DuBois, and many others advocate[4]. It is within this context of living, participatory democracy that the policies and instruments we describe below need to be evaluated. They are not answers; they are inputs to the process of living democracy, which must involve all of society in a meaningful way. The starting point is the development of a shared vision of the goals of society.

The Need to Develop a Shared Vision of a Sustainable Society

A broad, overlapping consensus is forming around the goal of sustainability, including its ecological, social, and economic aspects as described above. But movement toward this goal is being impeded not so much by lack of knowledge, or even lack of "political will," but rather by a lack of a *coherent, relatively detailed, shared vision of what a sustainable society would actually look like.* Developing this shared vision is an essential prerequisite to generating any movement toward it. The default vision of continued, unlimited growth in material consumption is inherently unsustainable, but we cannot break away from this vision until a credible and desirable alternative is available. The process of collaboratively developing this shared vision can also help to mediate many short-term conflicts that will otherwise remain irresolvable. There has actually been quite a lot of success in using envisioning and "future searches" in organizations and communities around the world[5]. This experience has shown that it is actually quite possible to get disparate (even adversarial) groups to collaborate on envisioning a desirable future, given the right forum. The process has been successful in hundreds of cases at the level of individual firms and communities up to the size of large cities. The challenge is to scale it up to whole states, nations, and the world.

Meadows[6] discusses why the processes of envisioning and goal-setting are so important (at all levels of problem solving); why envisioning and goal-setting are so underdeveloped in our society; and how we can begin to train people in the skill of envisioning and begin to construct shared visions of a sustainable society. She tells the personal story of her own discovery of that skill and her attempts to use the process of shared envisioning in problem solving. From this experience, several general principles emerged, including:

- In order to envision effectively, it is necessary to focus on what one really wants, not what one will settle for. For example, the lists below show the kinds of things people really want, compared to the kinds of things they often settle for.
- A vision should be judged by the clarity of its values, not the clarity of its implementation path. Holding to the vision and being flexible about the path is often the only way to find the path.
- Responsible vision must acknowledge, but not get crushed by, the physical constraints of the real world.
- It is critical for visions to be shared because only shared visions can be responsible.
- Vision has to be flexible and evolving.

Really Want	*Settle For*
Self-esteem	Fancy car
Serenity	Drugs
Health	Medicine
Human happiness	GNP
Permanent prosperity	Sustainable growth

Probably the most challenging task facing humanity today is the creation of a shared vision of a sustainable and desirable society, one that can provide permanent prosperity within the biophysical constraints of the real world in a way that is fair and equitable to all of humanity, to other species, and to future generations. This vision does not now exist, although the seeds are there. We all have our own private visions of the world we really want and we need to overcome our fears and skepticism and begin to share these visions and build on them, until we have built a vision of the world we want.

In the previous sections we have sketched out the general characteristics of this world—it is ecologically sustainable, fair, efficient, and secure—but we need to fill in the details in order to make it tangible enough to motivate people across the spectrum to work toward achieving it. The time to start is now.

Nagpal and Foltz[7] have begun this task by commissioning a range of individual visions of a sustainable world from around the world. They laid out the following challenge for each of their "envisionaries":

> Individuals were asked not to try to predict what lies ahead, but rather to imagine a *positive* future for their respective region, defined in any way they chose—village, group of villages, nation, group of nations, or continent. We asked only that people remain within the bounds of plausibility, and set no other restrictive guidelines.

The results were revealing. While these independent visions were difficult to generalize, they shared at least one important point. The "default" Western vision of continued material growth was not what people envisioned as part of their "positive future." They envisioned a future with "enough" material consumption, but where the focus has shifted to maintaining high-quality communities and environments, education, culturally rewarding full employment, and peace.

Much more work is necessary to implement living democracy and within that to create a truly shared vision of a desirable and sustainable future. This ongoing work needs to engage all members of society in a substantive dialogue about the future they desire and the policies and instruments necessary to bring it about. In the following sections we discuss the history of some current Western institutions and policy instruments that have been used to address environmental issues, and offer some new ideas to expand this range. They are not "solutions" to the problems of environmental management or sustainability, but rather inputs to the broad democratic discussion of options and futures. They need to be used in various combinations and modified to fit different cultural contexts. They also can serve as the starting point for development of new policies and instruments which are better adapted to unique circumstances.

History of Environmental Institutions and Instruments

As noted above, severe anthropogenic damage to some regions of the earth began as soon as humans learned to apply entropy-increasing technology processes to agriculture, and was sharply escalated by factory production in Europe during the industrial revolution. Massive loss of life from the spread of water-borne disease continued to be accepted as part of the human condition until advances in scientific knowledge concerning the role of microorganisms prompted public health research to develop sewage treatment systems. Vast urban expenditures on such systems eventually reduced the enormous loss of human capital from the uncontrolled discharge of sanitary waste into waterways. The application of appropriate science, appropriate technology, and community will was necessary to reduce the costly loss of human capital which had resulted from unprecedented population expansion, concentration of humans into unplanned urban areas, and uncontrolled appropriation of open-access resources.

In the U.S., pollution of harbor waters, fear of human disease, and financial loss from contamination of oyster fisheries in the Chesapeake Bay finally forced the city of Baltimore to become the first major city in the nation to construct, during the period from 1909 to 1912, a municipal sewage treatment plant, with Washington, D.C., not following suit until the late 1930s[8]. The Bethlehem Steel Company persuaded the State of Maryland to permit the company to run Baltimore City's sewage effluent through the company's plant as coolant. This was arranged on terms very favorable for the company, but to the considerable discomfort of the labor force in the plant[9].

Unfortunately no such zeal was applied to the removal or treatment of toxic wastes from this steel plant or other factories polluting the Chesapeake Bay and the estuaries, rivers, lakes, and oceans of the earth until late in the last half of the 20th century. Appropriate policies and management instruments had been discussed by physical and social scientists, but the political will necessary to confront the economic power of the dominant industrial establishment was unequal to the task. Under the federal system in the U.S., the central government left environmental management to the states. This was a system which virtually guaranteed environmental degradation, since competition among states for economic growth was a convenient excuse for avoiding effective regulation. Nor, in the face of abdication of environmental responsibility by all levels of government, could victims of environmental damage count on redress in the court system. Although award of damages for injury was a time-honored principle of common law, the burden of proof was on the plaintiff and it was formidable. Victims had to prove not only that they had suffered injury, but that a specific party had caused the injury, to the exclusion of other sources of the injury.

This combination of institutionalized pollution permissiveness and lack of recourse from government or courts, combined with the global expansion of energy and material throughput into a finite environment following World War II, set the stage for a series of ecological catastrophes. These events not only energized the then small community of those concerned about the ecological health of the earth, but they also increased the awareness of some leaders that ecological damage could reduce the profitability of economic systems, which had been their primary concern. Although academic scientists and even a small minority of economists were on record with their serious concerns about what they perceived as a collision course with ecological catastrophe, it took a best-seller authored by a scientist, Rachel Carson's *Silent Spring*[10], to capture the public imagination. Silent Spring presented a dramatic message in a lyrical form which alerted the public to the long-run ecological consequences of the toxics-laden waters, urban smog, and accumulating litter, which were becoming all too evident to increasing numbers of citizens. Local but increasingly severe and frequent environmental catastrophes such as the Cuyahoga River catching fire in Cleveland, the near death of Lake Erie, ubiquitous toxic spills, toxic dumps, fatal smog incidents in Pennsylvania, and smog in the Grand Canyon gradually convinced the majority of

Americans that action was needed. Similar reactions followed in Western Europe. Finally a new and intensive inquiry into the state of the earth and the policies and instruments needed for its protection could begin. The public awareness of the need for innovation in policy, however, moved far in advance of recognition of the need for innovation in instruments for carrying out these policies.

The U.S. legislative response to accelerating environmental damage was President Richard Nixon's National Environmental Protection Act of 1969. The goal was to halt the accelerating environmental degradation, and the policy instrument for implementing this objective was the traditional recourse to direct regulation. Reflecting the conventional wisdom of the time, the federal government legislated broad policy guidelines in general terms, leaving implementation primarily to the states. State compliance was sought through the pragmatic U.S. practice of offering generous federal grants for participation combined with potential federal intervention in cases where states failed to formulate effective plans. This federal approach had served the nation well since the early federal period when it was introduced by President Thomas Jefferson in the era of "internal improvements"[11].

Given the legislative history of the U.S., as polluters were forced to recognize that some form of control was inevitable, they reluctantly accepted the familiar regulatory approach as that with which they were most familiar, and which they could most easily manipulate to their own advantage. Legislators and bureaucrats recognized new opportunities for funding, power, and careers at both the federal and state levels, which was the time-honored formula and quid pro quo for gaining acceptance of innovative programs.

Unfortunately, the new environmental regulations, though designed for acceptance by the major interest groups, lacked two dimensions that were essential for adequately confronting the accelerating pollution problems: sound scientific grounding and economic efficiency. Predictably, environmental protection lagged behind the expanding throughput of pollutants into air and water, and onto the land.

The major objection to the inefficiency of the regulatory approach came initially from the economics profession, in which a small minority had broken with the traditional preoccupation with promoting economic growth to focus on evaluating and ameliorating the unanticipated detrimental side effects of growth, especially pollution. The existence of these spillover phenomena, now termed *externalities*, had been recognized in the economics literature since their identification by A. C. Pigou[12], but were regarded as more of an academic anomaly than a real-world problem. Ayers and Kneese[13] confronted the economics profession with the proposition that pollution externalities, far from being an anomaly, were actually pervasive in industrial economies with their massive throughputs. Furthermore, regulatory approaches were not proving equal to the task of coping with the vast throughput of mass and energy with which industrial economies were converting low-entropy inputs into high-entropy pollutants. More-efficient instruments of pollution control were needed.

The scientific basis for this phenomenon had actually been worked out in impressive detail by another economist, Nicholas Georgescu-Roegen[14], who, as noted above, argued eloquently for the need to reformulate economic thinking and models for consistency with the fundamental physical laws of thermodynamics and entropy, hitherto almost totally neglected by the profession. Casting the environmental problem in terms of externalities, a concept familiar to economists, focused attention directly on policy instruments since Pigou had demonstrated that an offsetting tax on detrimental externalities, such as pollution, could restore economic efficiency and increase welfare in otherwise competitive economies. Thus, a large literature emerged in support of replacing inefficient regulations with economically efficient taxes on pollution. This notion failed initially to gain wide support outside of the economics profession, but, because of its compelling potential efficiency gains, has begun more recently to become imbedded in U.S. and other management programs, as will be explored below. As society was forced in Western nations to expand the amount of real resources allocated to protecting their populations and resources, the need for greater economic efficiency in the use of these scarce resources became more urgent. However, strict application of the efficiency principle appeared to neglect distributional issues and to threaten the now vested interests of polluters and regulators alike, delaying and limiting its acceptance in the political arena. And, as we have previously noted, the issue of sustainable scale had not yet been recognized and incorporated.

As the U.S. and other nations began curbing some of the grosser environmental insults from point source emissions of pollutants, ecologists and resource managers could begin to address more subtle but more ominous phenomena, such as sharp declines in species diversity, natural habitats, and ecosystem health. Ecologists and others began to point out that the human economy was a subsystem of the earth's total ecology, and could not long function sustainably or even efficiently without a healthy life-support system[15]. This brings us to ecological economics' efforts to reintegrate social and natural science around the three goals of sustainable scale, fair distribution, and efficient allocation.

Despite this growing awareness of threats to the global ecology, the intensity of the Cold War simultaneously accelerated the generation of nuclear wastes, along with other long-lived toxic wastes, and diminished the will to contain or to control them. The greater openness in both the East and the West since the end of this 40-year arms race is beginning to reveal the appalling extent of the chemical, nuclear, and biological wastes produced, stored, and discarded both deliberately and accidentally. Without drastic and costly remedial action, vast areas of the earth will remain contaminated and unfit for habitation for long periods. The seriousness of this problem and its complexity demonstrate the need for a new generation of policies and instruments which will be based upon science, which is sufficiently sophisticated to deal with the complexity of the problem, economically efficient enough to accomplish the goals with the funds available, and socially equitable enough to win the consensual, democratic support required nationally and internationally. Ecological economics offers just such a trans-disciplinary approach for approaching these formidable challenges.

Various conclusions can be drawn from this brief overview of the evolution of thinking about environmental policy instruments. The management structure developed by a society for protection of its environment tends to reflect the distribution of economic and political power of interest groups within that society. However, without the inclusion of broader scientific perspectives such as ecology, thermodynamics, uncertainty, and sustainability, and without broader social concepts such as fairness, equity, and ethical values, the most well-intentioned efforts at environmental protection will be overwhelmed by the continued exponential growth of production, consumption, technology, and population. The magnitude of remedial work to be accomplished means that the instruments used must be economically efficient. But they must at the same time be fair and lead to an ecologically sustainable scale of activity. The following sections investigate these issues in more detail.

Successes, Failures, and Remedies

For purposes of achieving the environmental and other social values identified here, society has created an array of interlocking institutions. For satisfying material needs and wants, competitive markets have evolved as efficient though not perfect institutions. For addressing market failures, pursuing equity goals, and other community purposes, governmental institutions have evolved, though few would defend them as totally satisfactory. Therefore, in order to address the intervention failures of government, citizens have banded together to form voluntary non-governmental organizations. However, it should come as no surprise that even these NGOs have their failures and shortcomings, as will be examined below. These formal institutions, markets, governments, and voluntary organizations, though potent forces, should not cause us to overlook the most fundamental source of power in an open society, namely, the actions and values of individuals.

Individual actions and values are the ultimate determinants of environmental quality and of the possibility for sustainability. Individual decisions about what to purchase, consume, wear, and drive, about where and how to live, what jobs to seek, how many children to have, will decide the future. Each of these consumption decisions determines what resources, renewable or irreplaceable, must be used in its production, and what pollutants will be emitted when they become waste, as all produced goods inevitably must become sooner or later. It is individual and family choices about family size, lifestyle, residential style, career paths, and voting choice that will determine the viability of the environment, the life span of our natural resources, the diversity of the biosphere, and the possibility of global sustainability. Obviously, the amount of freedom and latitude we have in making these choices varies widely and is a function of affluence and education. Therefore it follows that the responsibility for wise choice (and example) falls most heavily on the rich, the privileged, the educated, the famous, and the powerful. Choosing sustainability is thus ultimately a matter of moral, ethical choice and thus a result of individuals' fundamental values. Although these human values are basically independent of the biophysical constraints that limit their realization, we nevertheless believe that they are affected in part by knowledge. Knowledge about ecology, about economics, and about their interrelationships will help modify some of the values that lead to excessive consumerism, to the search for satisfaction in materialism, and to the search for social salvation through quantitative growth of economic throughput.

The Policy Role of Non-Government Organizations

Although governments are now (since the 1970s) staffed at many levels with agencies nominally charged with environmental protection, it is difficult, upon close examination of the performance of these agencies, for those working for effective environmental management to avoid disillusionment. Indeed, it would be naive to have any other expectation than that these agencies will faithfully reflect the distribution of political and economic power of the society in which they are embedded. Therefore, environmental agencies have not only been limited in their ability to achieve environmental improvement, they have at times obstructed it and even dismantled environmental programs. James Watt as Secretary of the U.S. Department of Interior and Ann Gorsuch Burford as Administrator of the U.S. EPA are examples of officials who were appointed to turn back the clock on environmental protection, and who succeeded in creating damage that will be difficult to repair. The 1996 "contract with America," despite good intentions, envisions even greater environmental retrogression.

It is one of the strengths of a pluralistic society that alternative institutions emerge in order to protect vital interests. One response to governmental intervention failures in managing the environment is the emergence of NGOs (non-governmental organizations). Work by Buchanan[16] and others in the public choice field helps explain this phenomenon of intervention failures. While there are many able, idealistic public servants who are dedicated to the public interest, with Watt and Burford being extreme examples of those serving special interests, few would argue that government alone; relying upon current practices can be depended upon for environmental protection. However, some steps should be taken in order to make existing institutions more effective in carrying out their legal responsibilities for protecting and managing environmental resources. One, for example, would be to establish awards that would provide additional financial and professional incentives with which to reward resource managers who perform outstandingly efficient, innovative work in environmental protection.

Another step would be for citizens to provide more support for conservation groups such as the Sierra Club, the Nature Conservancy, the Chesapeake Bay Foundation, and the Natural

Resources Defense Council which have responsible records in providing environmental protection where public agencies have failed, and for these groups to coordinate their programs.

Adaptive Ecological Economic Assessment and Management

It is undeniable that technological innovation has generated significant advances in human welfare. However, in retrospect, not all technologies have resulted in positive net improvements in human welfare. Nor have advanced technologies been managed responsibly. The most obvious cases of technologies without which humanity would be better off are the military technologies of mass destruction, such as nuclear and biochemical weapons, which society is struggling to ban. Additionally, it is possible to cite some nonmilitary technologies, such as nuclear energy, agricultural chemicals, and even the internal combustion engine, which have had large unintended negative environmental consequences. Certainly the final judgment of history has yet to be rendered on these technologies, but at the minimum, all but the most doctrinaire libertarians would concede that there is room for better management of these technologies. However, once these technologies are introduced, it is difficult to squeeze the genie back into the bottle. A reasonable inference to be drawn from experience is that lessons might be gained from history that can guide and manage the introduction of massive technological systems which potentially have far-reaching consequences for humanity.

Granted that the law of unintended consequences makes it impossible to anticipate all of the impacts for better or for worse of technology, this does not mean that it is totally impossible or undesirable to devise minimal guidelines in advance of introduction for assessing and managing technologies, especially those having global implications. While technological laissez faire may have been appropriate in a relatively empty world, now that humans have the capability of rendering the earth uninhabitable, we no longer can afford to let survival depend upon the benevolence and wisdom of naive technological enthusiasts.

The shaping of policies and instruments for technology assessment is a difficult task requiring transdisciplinary research of a high order, but some minimal guidelines can be offered[17].

- Exceptional caution should be exercised before the introduction of high-entropy systems, such as fossil fuels and nuclear energy.
- Low-entropy systems, such as solar energy, are less irreversible and less damaging than high-entropy systems.
- Technologies that depend upon a high ratio of human intelligence and information to material and energy throughput have a higher probability of advancing human welfare than do high-entropy technologies.

Examples of low-entropy technologies depending upon high input ratios of intelligence and information to mass and energy include notably the telescope, the microscope, reading glasses, the compass, the sextant, the chronometer, and other navigational instruments that literally opened up new worlds to humanity. It remains to be seen whether the much higher entropy exploration of space will bring comparable benefits to humanity. Other examples of benevolent technologies are transistors and silicon chips, which have made possible the computer, yet save energy.

Obviously, any technology, even that characterized by lowest entropy can be applied to antisocial purposes of crime and warfare, so no guarantees of benevolence can be realistically expected, and the distinction must be made between the potential environmental impact of the technology and the purposes to which it is applied. What technology essentially does is to extend the power of humans to accomplish constructive or destructive ends. Thus the mastery of technology requires both its assessment before adoption and the responsible social control of its application as well as a realistic understanding of human motivation.

Several guidelines for the management of technology can be drawn from regrettable lessons of history. We should have now learned that before adopting new systems, it would be desirable to examine the full life cycle of the technology. This elementary precaution could save us from such disasters as making major commitments to nuclear energy before understanding the problems of storing radioactive wastes, safeguarding them from terrorists, and decommissioning contaminated plants.

Another guideline for the management of technologies is to require, before the acceptance and adoption of new systems, the implementation of mass balance and energy balance accounting systems so that a comprehensive tracking of wastes is assured.

Habitat Protection, Intergenerational Transfers, and Equity

Many options exist for habitat protection, including purchase, easements, and gifts, each having a role[18]. Protection should begin as soon as possible, before adverse uses and property rights are established. This section explores priorities for acquisition and relates habitat protection to equity across regions, groups, and generations.

The central point of this section is that in selecting the stock of environmental resources to be passed along to future generations, emphasis should be given to such resources as large-scale living ecosystems containing species diversity, complex interrelationships between species, and, above all, the capability of supporting evolutionary processes over sufficiently long enough time frames that species can evolve and adapt to both man-made and natural changes in climate and other environmental conditions. Obvious candidates include rain forests, estuaries, wetlands, lakes, river basins, grasslands, Polar Regions, and coral reefs. However, the ultimate selection of the highest priorities for protection of sustainable ecosystems should be made by trans-disciplinary teams including not only ecologists, but other representatives of life sciences, earth sciences, physical sciences, and social sciences preferably with insights also from the arts and humanities.

After the identification of the scientific principles and priorities for selecting sustainable ecosystems for intergenerational transfer, the challenge of designing the most effective policy measures for acquiring and protecting these ecosystems will remain.

A major challenge will be gaining acceptance for large-scale current sacrifices that will produce uncertain benefits in an uncertain future. Another complicating factor is the need for consensus on goals for global cooperation in implementation. The fact that serious intra-generational inequalities exist in the distribution of current income and wealth will make it difficult to achieve consensus on the need for intergenerational transfers and will complicate the problem of apportioning sacrifices. A related problem is that, in an uncertain future, the continuity of a commitment to pass on ecological resources cannot be guaranteed for future generations that are not parties to the agreement. Therefore, intermediate generations may be tempted to consume all or part of an inheritance that was intended for the more distant future. There is the danger of a prisoners' dilemma in which uncertainty about the action of intermediate generations could reduce the welfare of more distant future generations. However, as successful experience is gained in protecting intergenerational transfers, uncertainties could be reduced and welfare gains increased.

Well known public goods problems could pose additional difficulties in making intergenerational transfers, to the extent that future benefits will be shared by all regardless of which group made the sacrifice to provide them. In the case of global public goods like the atmosphere and oceans, those groups making current sacrifices to protect the resources could not reap the entire benefits. This free-rider problem could reduce incentives to sacrifice unless measures could be designed to spread the burden widely.

Therefore, in choosing policy instruments for acquiring and protecting sustainable ecosystems, new courses must be charted utilizing what limited insights are available from the fields of public choice and policy science. It is unlikely that acceptable policies can be derived from any one discipline such as economics, with its primary focus on efficiency, or ecology with its limited institutional content, or from any other single discipline. Therefore, it seems self-evident that policy instruments for intergenerational transfers must be drawn from a trans-disciplinary approach.

Given the fact that making bequests requires sacrifices and therefore involves scarcity problems, economic efficiency concepts can be helpful in achieving the maximum amount of resource protection for a given amount of resources available, or they can assist in achieving specified resource endowments at minimum total cost. The field of economics can also offer some limited insights into problems of distribution and equity. An especially important concept is that of Pareto improvement, which suggests that policies are most likely to gain acceptance if they can be designed so that there are no losers, or alternatively so that the gains from the policy are great enough to compensate the losers and that compensation actually occurs.

The criteria for ecological bequests must be based upon good science which should emphasize protecting species diversity and minimizing entropy increase. Finally, in order to gain acceptance, policies for making intergenerational transfers must be realistically based upon acceptance by the major interest groups involved. Society has already begun the process of making intergenerational environmental transfers in the form of wilderness areas, wildlife sanctuaries, protected parts of the Polar Regions, and similar set-asides. These programs have been initiated not only by local, state, national, and international governmental organizations, but also by non-governmental organizations (NGOs) such as the Nature Conservancy. Significantly, many families and individuals have demonstrated the value they place upon intergenerational environmental transfers through their willingness to bear the opportunity cost of holding land and resources in their natural state. These public and private initiatives in protecting living ecosystems offer guideposts for the much greater future efforts that will be necessary for achieving sustainable global environments.

In cases where governments already own very large tracts, such as in the western United States, the task of acquisition and set-aside can be relatively easily accomplished. Setting aside tracts currently held by governments has the advantage of not requiring additional expenditure, but it must be recognized that there is an opportunity cost equal to the value of the highest alternative use to which the asset could be put. The least-cost way of protecting valuable ecosystems is through simple appropriation, but this approach may fail the equity test. In cases where high-priority ecosystems are in private hands, a wide array of policy instruments for acquisition is available. The most straightforward method is through purchase, which has the equity advantage of fully compensating current owners, but has the budgetary disadvantage of being very costly. The funds available for acquiring ecosystems can be stretched through the purchase of easements strong enough to protect the desired ecological feature but sufficiently permissive to grant current owners lifetime estates or limited use in return for long-run protection.

In the cases where funds are raised by the government for acquisition, the cost to current generations is made explicit through the taxing and budgeting process, and in democratic societies can be achieved only through consensus. Transfers of funds from the general public to the current owners of the ecologies are made explicit under this procedure. An important economic consideration is what the taxpayers must give up in order to make the transfer possible, and what the recipients of the funds do with the proceeds. Thus, when government purchases of ecological assets occur, redistribution occurs not only between generations, but within current generations.

Policy Instruments

An important element in the evolution of ecological economics has been a serious concern not only with the goals, policies, and programs needed for environmental sustainability but also with the design of improved and innovative policy instruments needed for the successful accomplishment of these goals. Thus far, we have emphasized the basic principles of ecological economics and derived from them an agenda of programs that seem to us to be essential in changing our course from the current policy of looting the planet to that of protecting species diversity and of building a sustainable human society on earth with concern for equity among groups, regions, and generations.

However, one critical factor which is often given short shrift in discussions of environmental protection is analysis of the policy instruments which are fundamental to the achievement of program objectives. For example, Gore's *Earth in the Balance*[19] provides a visionary set of programs which, if implemented, could advance us significantly toward the goal of a sustainable society. However, he gives much less attention to the policy instruments needed for achieving the admirable goals he enumerates. This is not intended as criticism, but as an observation that even some of the most serious and dedicated environmentalists, among whom Gore has certainly been in the forefront, are more comfortable in dealing with the large issues of goals and purposes than with the technical aspects of instruments for achieving them. We, on the other hand, believe that a serious approach to environmental management must include analysis of the management instruments to be used as an integral part of the program to be implemented.

One reason for the typical neglect of policy instruments is the widespread dependence, especially in the U.S., on a regulatory approach to environmental management. Beginning with the National Environmental Protection Act of 1969 which established the EPA, the primary approach to environmental protection has continued to be the promulgation of regulations intended to achieve the desired objectives. This approach has achieved a great deal and unquestionably has left the U.S. in a much better position than we would have been in without it. However, few would agree that the results have been entirely satisfactory, and questions must be raised:

- Might some other approaches have given better results?

- Are present approaches inadequate for dealing with the growing problems of the future?
- Can improved policy instruments be designed to provide better results, or lower costs, or both?

Many who have studied these problems have concluded that all of these questions can be answered in the affirmative. Although pollution is only one of the many causes of environmental damage, it is the one that best illustrates the evolution of policy instruments, and from which insights can be drawn for addressing related environmental issues. For controlling pollution, policy makers have devised a wide menu of instruments, ranging all the way from moral exhortation to imprisonment. Some of the most important include regulating emissions, taxing emissions, taxing products whose use pollutes, requiring permits to pollute, paying polluters to abate, labeling products as to contents, educating consumers, and imposing deposit-refund systems on polluting products. One useful way of classifying this wide range of options is to divide them into two general categories: conventionally defined as either regulatory or the incentive-based (IB) use of economic measures.

The regulatory approach is sometimes referred to, especially by those who disapprove of it, as the command-and-control or CAC approach. However, the CAC terminology is more appropriately applied to central planning for an entire economy, such as that of the former Soviet Union, rather than as a description of a subset of environmental policy instruments, which are entirely consistent as a correction to market failures in a predominantly market economy.

Rather than casting the evaluation of policy instruments in terms of regulatory versus incentive systems, a more constructive approach is to investigate the conditions under which incentives yield better results as compared with conditions under which regulations make more sense. Cropper and Oates[20], among others, have provided much needed insight into this issue.

Incentive systems are potentially more appropriate for the control of some pollutants rather than others. For example, regulation will continue to be the preferred instrument in the case of severe threats to human health, such as radionuclide and severely toxic carcinogens, where the optimal level of emission approaches zero. The prevalence of scientific uncertainty about all but the most simple damage functions is a powerful argument for explicitly recognizing the limitations on knowledge and for acknowledging them in formulating pollution control policies. Therefore environmental policies such as the precautionary principle and instruments such as assurance bonding, which are discussed further on, have been developed in order to preserve the advantages of economic incentives in the face of incomplete scientific knowledge about the effects of pollutants and about the interactions among them.

In the face of uncertainty, appropriate public policy is to prevent emissions (which is usually much cheaper than cleaning them up), and thus to limit exposure initially. This can be achieved by ending the assumption of safety for emissions unless damage has been proven and by shifting the burden of proof to emitters by requiring the demonstration of safety by the emitter before use, rather than the more costly procedure of requiring regulators to prove damage. Economic incentives can be effective instruments for this purpose, particularly when used in conjunction with regulations.

Policy instruments based upon economic incentives can be powerfully efficient methods for achieving allocation objectives, but it is important to avoid the error in logic into which the economics literature often lapses of assuming that markets, just because they can be such powerful guides in achieving allocative goals, are equally valid for determining the other two critical goals: sustainable scale and equitable distribution. We need to put in place separate instruments for achieving the prior goals of sustainable scale and equitable distribution before applying efficient methods of reaching them.

Regulatory Systems

Environmental management in the U.S., as noted above, is based upon a federal regulatory system under which the

Congress has enacted national guidelines for regulations, with implementation left largely to the states. This approach evolved from growing recognition in the second half of this century that serious environmental damage could not be prevented by relying exclusively upon state and local governments, whose competition for economic development was an impediment to effective local environmental management. Federal efforts to implement environmental management have been characterized as the regulatory system to distinguish them from alternative approaches such as the use of economic incentives, or incentive-based (IB) systems. In the United States, the regulatory approach predominates. For stationary sources of air pollution each state is required to develop a State Implementation Plan (SIP) to ensure that emissions of particulate matter, sulfur oxides, and nitrogen oxides are in compliance with national air quality standards. In all these cases, enforcement is left primarily to the states. In theory, failure to meet local air quality standards is penalized by termination of federal subsidies for major highway and other programs. However, continued failure to achieve local air quality goals in many major metropolitan areas with strong political and economic power has resulted in repeated postponement of deadlines for meeting air quality goals. The Clean Air Act of 1990 was intended to provide an improved approach to these problems.

U.S. water pollution control also relies upon a state-federal division of responsibilities with emphasis upon both emissions and ambient quality. Ambient quality is defined not in terms of quantitative standards but in terms of more qualitative objectives, such as fitness for supporting swimming and fishing.

The regulatory approach has had only limited success in achieving the desired levels of environmental protection in the U.S. market economy and the system has failed disastrously in the centrally directed economies of the former USSR[21] and Eastern Europe. In general, the regulatory system can work well where there are clear environmental goals with overwhelming political consensus, similar costs of abatement across all actors, relative certainty about what is being emitted, and easy and effective enforcement. These conditions hold in all too few cases and we have already identified and controlled many of them (i.e., large industrial point sources and sewage treatment plants). Making further progress with only the regulatory system will be much more difficult.

The limits of the regulatory approach in achieving acceptable levels of environmental protection and the high cost of these traditional policies have led economists and others to propose less costly, more effective incentive-based management instruments, such as pollution charges, marketable emission permits, and performance and assurance bonds. The lack of widespread acceptance to date of alternatives to regulation suggests that current practices are viewed as possessing superior political and historical acceptability, or at least of not being as unacceptable as the proposed innovations. Among the nominal advantages of regulation are:

- Simplicity, familiarity, and acceptance.
- Historical U.S. reliance upon legislative regulation in order to deal with perceived problems.
- Acceptance by major emitters and interest groups.
- Long-term incorporation into the legal system.

However, despite these advantages, the regulatory approach has failed to meet rising expectations for environmental quality and contains numerous inherent disadvantages, especially in the case of diffuse, chronic, non-point-source pollution. These disadvantages include:

- Effective regulation requires a level of technical and proprietary information which is seldom available to regulators.
- Successful enforcement of regulation requires high monitoring and enforcement costs.
- The costly bureaucracies associated with regulation result in high expenditure per unit of pollution reduction.

- Environmental regulations are easily evaded or avoided.
- The lack of strong incentives to reduce pollution below the mandated level reduces motivation for technological advance and for preventing pollution before it is generated.
- Polluters are permitted to ignore the costs their actions impose upon society at the time decisions are made.

In addition, the regulatory system, having its roots in the legal system, is based on a presumption of no damage on the part of polluters until they can be proven to have violated the regulations or to have caused demonstrable damages. Given the high degree of uncertainty about the fate and effects of pollutants, this presumption can lead to significant difficulties, especially in those cases where this uncertainty is high.

Despite these limitations associated with regulatory systems, especially with respect to problems like pollution where incentives are significant, regulatory systems still have a major role to play in addressing the basic environmental problems of concern here: population, technology, habitat, and species diversity. Our point is that the efficiency of regulatory systems can be substantially enhanced by incorporating economic incentives within them.

Incentive-Based Systems: Alternatives to Regulatory Control

The urgent need for alternative approaches to environmental management that are less costly and more efficient than traditional approaches has long been recognized[22]. The major, but not only, alternatives suggested to the regulatory approach have been based on some form of economic incentives[23].

The accumulating evidence suggests that the present regulatory approach to environmental management in the U.S. and throughout much of the earth, though leaving us better off than we would have been without any management system, does not inspire confidence in its adequacy for addressing the twin challenges of explosive global population growth coupled with growing expectations of exponential increases in per capita consumption by the growing billions of passengers on spaceship earth. We therefore emphasize that problems of achieving sustainable scale and distributional equity are basic to the human condition. Once these goals have been addressed, it becomes important to devise efficient instruments for accomplishing them. Unfortunately, it is inefficiency that characterizes most of the regulatory environmental control instruments now in place, though they have gained grudging acceptance. These shortcomings of the current regulatory approach are evident in the limited results from the excessive levels of bureaucracy and expenditures involved, compounded by the inadequate scientific basis for current programs. Reform efforts must therefore aim at improving both the efficiency of environmental protection programs and the scientific bases upon which they rest. We turn first to the role of economic efficiency, and to its limitations.

The Role of Economic Efficiency

From the perspective of economic efficiency, the regulatory approach appears to be both cumbersome and costly. Indeed, now that most of the nations on earth have rejected command and control methods in favor of competitive markets for guiding economic policy, it seems anachronistic to rely so heavily upon regulatory techniques for organizing environmental policy rather than attempting to reap in the policy arena some of the efficiency advantages that economic incentives have demonstrated in the organization of markets.

Proposals for economic incentive-based (IB) instruments for environmental management encompass a wide range of alternatives, including:

- taxes on pollution emissions (Pigouvian taxes or charges)
- product charges (levied on products whose use causes environmental damage, such as CFCs, carbon fuels, agricultural chemicals, and fertilizers)
- subsidies for pollution abatement (similar to taxes in concept but not in distributional consequences), especially for agriculture and sewage treatment
- marketable permits for pollution emissions

- creation of property rights for open access and other environmental resources
- creation of economic incentives for acting in the common interest

Several themes run through the literature that advocate more extensive use of these IB instruments as alternatives or supplements to current regulatory policies. The most important is the achievement of economic efficiency through correction of market failures such as:

- Externalities, especially pollution
- open-access resources
- inadequate provision of public goods (because of non-excludability and non-depletability)
- poorly defined property rights
- uncertainty and incomplete information
- myopic time discounting

IB instruments are designed to correct or offset these market failures as shown below.

Pollution Fees and Subsidies

The classic incentive-based alternative to regulation of pollution is a tax, fee, or charge per unit of pollution emitted,

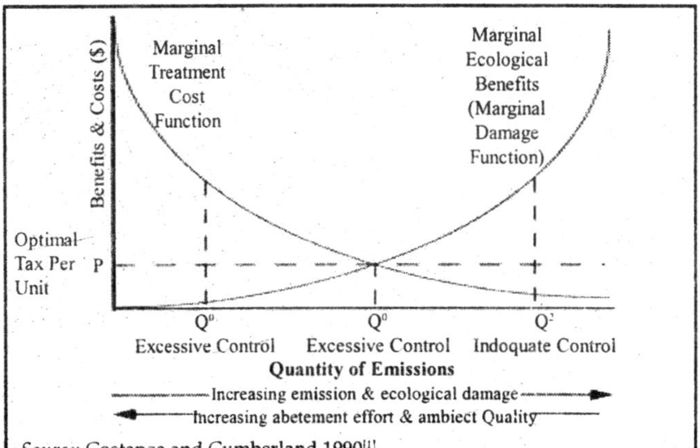

Source: Costanza and Cumberland 1990[1]

Figure 1: Optimal Pollution Control and Environmental Quality

known as a Pigouvian tax after A.C. Pigou[24]. However, the intellectual foundation for the incentive approach is Adam Smith's concept of the invisible hand operating in free, competitive markets. In this model, which emphasizes economic efficiency, rational utilitarian consumers attempting to maximize utility, and competitive producers attempting to maximize profits, will automatically generate optimal allocation of scarce resources. Thus free competitive markets are assumed to permit the pursuit of self-interest by producers and consumers to result in socially desirable outcomes, except where the (rigorous) conditions for competitive markets are not achieved and any of a number of well-defined market failures (listed above) are present.

The significance of this approach for environmental management is that if markets existed, or could be created, for environmental goods and services, consumers could purchase the types and quantities of environmental quality and sustainability they desired relative to their means and their competing wants, just as they do now for marketed goods and services. Obviously, for the true believer the market approach is a compelling one since, if it could be made to work, it would effectively dispose of the environmental problem, which would then be reduced to a level of seriousness no greater than, say, of selecting one's household detergent. For readers interested in economic theory and graphics, a simple diagram typically found in texts on environmental economics (a version of which is presented and discussed in Figure 1) is provided.

Popular Critiques of the Incentives for Efficiency Approach

Given the strong theoretical case in favor of IB pollution controls[25], it is appropriate to inquire into the reasons for their low level of acceptance in the U.S. Some objections to IB pollution controls are based upon popular misconceptions, myths, and imagery, and interest group pressures. Other objections to IB policies are more firmly based upon legitimate concerns, and merit thorough analysis. They include concerns about data requirements, spatial differentiation, gaps in scientific knowledge, and inadequate trans-disciplinary research. These are valid objections, but they may also be raised with respect to regulatory instruments or any other environmental control instruments.

As we have discussed, a criticism to which economic efficiency policy instruments are vulnerable is that of inadequate sensitivity to issues of sustainability, equity, welfare, and fairness. Indeed, much of the economics literature explicitly accepts the dichotomy and trade-off between equity and efficiency, recognizing that while efficiency is the proper concern of economics, it generally speaks with less credibility about equity, and has until recently ignored sustainability. We have noted, however, one principle dealing with equity that appears throughout the economics literature and which is relevant to policy analysis. This is the concept of Pareto fairness. This concept is drawn from the more general notion of Pareto optimality worked out by the Italian sociologist Vilfredo Pareto[26], dealing with the necessary conditions for efficient general equilibrium solutions[27]. However, inherent in the more general case of Pareto optimality is the concept of Pareto fairness, which in its simplest form requires that changes in policies or other arrangements should not be undertaken unless they make some people (or even one person) better off without making any party worse off. Although this theorem has extensive and significant implications for the analysis of human welfare[28], we only note here that policy changes are more likely to be acceptable and successful if they can be designed to make no one worse off.

This Pareto fairness principle is one reason for proposing that marketable pollution permits be given without charge to existing polluters, even though there may be objections to this course on both efficiency and ethical grounds. The same principle can be used to justify compensating property owners at public expense for potential losses resulting from zoning changes, and for other "takings." Compensation, though costly to the public, may be a valid price to pay in other cases where the general welfare is improved by a policy change. These are all examples of the equity vs. efficiency conflict emphasized above.

In terms of popular misconceptions, real and imaginary, opponents of incentive-based systems have persuaded large elements of the public that emission charges constitute a "license to pollute" and that this is somehow reprehensible. Actually both pollution charges and the current system of regulations represent "licenses to pollute," or property rights to pollute, but these rights now are free to the polluter in the case of the regulatory system and there are no dynamic incentives for polluters to reduce pollution below the currently permitted levels. The IB system would require payment for each unit of emission and thus would generate the appropriate continuous dynamic economic incentives to reduce pollution further, develop new pollution control technologies, and generate public revenue which could be used for mitigation of the remaining pollution or for other public purposes.

In terms of interest group pressures, emitters object to emission charges because they would then have to pay for the privilege of expropriating common property resources (the assimilative capacity of air and water) which they now enjoy without charge. Estimates of the costs of emission permits and revenue raised from emission charges on only particulate and sulfur oxides from stationary sources range from \$1.8 to 8.7 billion in 1984 in 1982 dollars[29]. Initially, the switch from free emissions to charges would amount to a transfer of income and wealth from emitters to the general public. The political and economic obstacles to such an innovation are obvious. In the long run, however, since the IB system leads to a improvement of economic efficiency, both the emitters and public would benefit. It is this initial short-run hurdle that must be overcome if IB systems are ever to be implemented.

One way of addressing this interest group problem, as noted above, would be to give, rather than sell, emission permits to present emitters. This has the ethical disadvantage of "grandfathering in" present polluters who would stand to benefit in direct proportion to the damage they are currently imposing upon the environment but it also has the advantage of creating property rights which could generate incentives to reduce pollution in that unused permits could be sold, adding efficiency to the system thereafter[30].

In addition to the political and interest group objections to incentive-based pollution control methods, there are also substantive scientific problems of knowledge and uncertainty, especially in terms of optimizing approaches. Derivation of optimal pollution charges (Figure 1) requires knowledge of the marginal treatment cost function and the marginal damage functions. Conceptually, marginal treatment cost functions should be computable from engineering and other data[31]. Computing marginal environmental damage functions is more difficult and involves at least three steps even in the simplest case of damage to a single species from a single pollutant at one point:

- Estimating the reduction in ambient concentrations associated with reductions in emission levels.
- Estimating biological damage functions associated with levels of ambient concentrations.
- Assigning economic values to the relevant levels of biological damage.

Early assumptions by economists about the existence of damage functions for individual pollutants derivable by scientists from dose--response relationships and relevant for efficiency-based policy, appear to have been overly optimistic, now that ecological economists are learning actually to develop trans-disciplinary working relationships with physical scientists. Clearly, the more realistic case of multiple emission sites, multiple species, plus positive and negative synergism between multiple pollutants involves formidable problems of research, analysis, and uncertainty[32]. The formal information requirements for deriving optimal water quality standards and optimal emission charge for ecologies as complex as estuaries are so demanding that they may never be fully met.

Epidemiological research on human exposure to toxic chemicals has revealed some of the limits of science in determining safe standards, given problems of gender, age, concentration, genetic heritage, synergism, and other variables.

However, this situation need not preclude efforts to establish standards based upon best current scientific judgment. This is particularly essential in the case of multiple pollutants, as in an estuary, where interrelationships among toxic substances are most likely to be synergistic and nonlinear. In such cases, damage functions could be estimated on the basis of best current judgment for the total mix of pollutants, and average emission charges applied to the discharge of every pollutant. The use of economic incentives could provide a least-cost (i.e., cost-effective) route to achieving environmental goals; however they are set, and thus is not dependent upon achieving an improbable level of scientific certainty (i.e., optimization).

Advantages and Disadvantages of Incentive-Based Systems of Regulation

In a realistic, dynamic situation, the use of IB pollution charges has several potential efficiency advantages over regulation. The most important advantage is that there are differences in the costs of pollution control between firms and the regulatory approach gives inadequate incentives to abate for lower-cost firms. With an IB system, more modern firms with lower-cost pollution control technologies will undertake more abatement rather than pay the charges, while firms with higher pollution control costs will prefer to pay the charges rather than abate. Society will then obtain more pollution control at lower total costs than if all firms, including those with higher abatement costs, are required to impose the same level of control, as is typical under a regulatory approach.

Comparable cost savings and efficiency increases might be achievable in water pollution control as well. Under the effluent charges system, more of the total clean-up is performed by low-cost firms than is the case under regulation. The potential cost savings are greatest when there are significant differences in treatment costs among polluters. Incentives are greater for continual improvements in pollution abatement technology under a pollution charge system than under a regulatory system under which all firms abate equally or under which abatement technology is specified.

Under an alternative IB system based upon transferable pollution permits (TP), firms have economic incentives to find cost-saving abatement technology because of the property rights they then have in their unused abatement permits which can be sold to firms having higher cost abatement technologies. These cost-reduction incentives have the merit of shifting the marginal treatment cost curve downward and to the left (Figure 1), further increasing the optimal level of environmental quality. If competitive markets could be created for transferable pollution permits, their price per unit of emission would approximate the same shadow price as that for pollution charges (P in Figure1).

Incentive-based pollution control policies have many other potential advantages over regulatory approaches:

- They have the ethical advantage of consistency with the OECD "polluter pays" principle.
- They raise public revenues.
- They pass the cost of pollution control along to the consumer of pollution-intensive products, providing the public with the proper signals for modifying consumer behavior and imposing the costs of environmental damage upon those who cause it and those who benefit from it.
- They provide polluters with economic incentives to prevent pollution, thus saving society the much greater cost of attempting to clean up the pollution after it occurs.
- Marketable permits do not require that regulators have the level of technical proprietary information required for efficient regulation.
- They can provide incentives for shifting the burden of monitoring from the government to the polluter.
- They offer profitable opportunities for industry to undertake development projects for improvements in pollution abatement technology.

- They can shift the incidence of tax burdens away from socially desirable objectives (incomes and jobs) toward reducing socially undesirable phenomena (pollution).

On the other side of the balance sheet, a number of substantive problems limit the applicability of the market approach to environmental management. Among the most serious are that market theory does not directly address the issues of:

- sustainable scale;
- income distribution, or equity, and therefore of unequal access to environmental protection among individuals, nations, regions, and generations;
- limitations of scientific information and of knowledge by individuals may impair their ability to make wise choices; and
- Additionally, the market failures that would need correction in order to make markets work for environmental quality are numerous and pervasive. They include externalities, excessive time discounting, common property resources, open-access resources, public goods, and noncompetitive markets.

Recognition in recent decades of the pervasiveness of market failures has resulted in much effort by economists to develop a wide range of compensatory methods for offsetting market failures. The conventional economic wisdom has been that, although market failures are serious impediments to economic efficiency, most markets are sufficiently robust that with the judicious application of corrective measures such as taxes on pollution, the overwhelming efficiency advantages of market economies can be retained and are well worth saving.

The major problem with the strictly efficiency-based economic approach to environmental management is that even if all market failures could be corrected or offset by compensating countermeasures such as pollution taxes, the resulting outcomes, though economically efficient, would not necessarily be universally perceived as an improved state of affairs. Society does not exist for or by economic efficiency alone. Though economic efficiency is important, and should be an element in any successful management approach, society will also insist upon the protection of other crucial, deep-seated values such as fairness, equity, scientific validity, democratic pluralism, and political acceptability. Therefore one lesson that can be drawn from environmental management practices to date and from efforts to reform them, is that unidimensional approaches, whether regulatory, efficiency-based, or science-dominated, have a low probability of success as compared to more broadly based, multi-objective, eclectic, trans-disciplinary approaches. It is for this reason that ecological economists have developed a range of policy instruments that meet all of the above criteria of equity, efficiency, scientific validity, and political acceptability. Examples of policy instruments designed to meet these multiple public policy criteria are given in the following sections.

Three Policies to Achieve Sustainability

In this section three fairly broad, interdependent proposals are described and discussed. Taken together they would go a long way toward achieving sustainability. The market incentive-based instruments suggested to implement the policies are intended to do the job with relatively high efficiency and effectiveness. They are not the only possible mechanisms to achieve these goals, but there is considerable evidence that they could work rather well in certain cultural and legal circumstances. By focusing on specific policies and instruments, we can also address the essential changes that need to be made in the system and begin to build a broad enough consensus to implement these changes. Various aspects of the proposals have appeared in various other forms elsewhere[33]. This section represents an attempt to synthesize and generalize them as the basis for developing an "overlapping consensus"[34] . A consensus that is affirmed by opposing theoretical, religious, philosophical and moral doctrines is most likely to be fair and just, and is also most likely to be resilient and to survive over time.

In summary, the policies are:

- a broad natural capital depletion tax to assure that resource inputs from the environment to the economy are sustainable, while giving strong incentives to develop. new technologies and processes to minimize impacts[35];
- application of the precautionary polluter pays principle (4P) to assure that the full costs of outputs from the economy to the environment are charged to the polluter in a way that adequately deals with the huge uncertainty about the impacts of pollution and encourages technological innovation[36]; and
- a system of ecological tariffs as one way (short of global agreements that are difficult to negotiate and enforce) to allow countries to implement the first two proposals without putting themselves at an undue disadvantage (at least on the import side) relative to countries that have not yet implemented them.

Natural Capital Depletion (NCD) Tax

One way to implement the sustainability constraint of no net depletion of natural capital is to hold throughput (consumption of total natural capital) constant at present levels (or lower truly sustainable levels) by taxing natural capital consumption, especially energy, very heavily. Nobel Laureate Robert Solow has emphasized the importance of replacing depleted natural capital by an amount of human-made capital sufficient to maintain the aggregate social capital intact in order to ensure sustainability and intergenerational equity[37]. Not everyone would share Solow's optimism about the extent to which other forms of capital can be substituted for natural capital, but to the extent that this is feasible, a NCD tax would be an efficient instrument for achieving it. Society could raise most public revenue from such a natural capital depletion tax, and compensate by reducing the income tax, especially on the lower end of the income distribution, perhaps even financing a negative income tax at the very low end. Technological optimists who believe that efficiency can increase by a factor of ten should welcome this policy which raises natural resource prices considerably and would powerfully encourage just those technological advances in which they have so much faith. Skeptics who lack that technological faith will nevertheless be happy to see the throughput limited since that is their main imperative in order to conserve resources for the future. The skeptics are protected against their worst fears; the optimists are encouraged to pursue their fondest dreams. If the skeptics are proved wrong and the enormous increase in efficiency actually happens, then they will be even happier (unless they are total misanthropists). They got what they wanted, but it just cost less than they expected and were willing to pay. The optimists, for their part, can hardly object to a policy that not only allows but offers strong incentives for the very technical progress on which their optimism is based. If they are proved wrong at least they should be glad that the rate of environmental destruction has been slowed.

Implementation of this policy does not hinge upon the precise measurement of natural capital, but the valuation issue remains relevant in the sense that the policy recommendation is based on the perception that we are at or beyond the optimal scale. The evidence for this perception consists of the greenhouse effect, ozone layer depletion, acid rain, and the general decline in many dimensions of the quality of life. It would be helpful to have better quantitative measures of these perceived costs, just as it would be helpful to carry along an altimeter when we jump out of an airplane. But we would all prefer a parachute to an altimeter if we could take only one thing. The consequences of an un-arrested free fall are clear enough without a precise measure of our speed and acceleration. But we would need at least a ballpark estimate of the value of natural capital depletion in order to determine the magnitude of the suggested NCD tax. This, we think, is possible, especially if uncertainty about the value of natural capital is incorporated in the tax itself, using, for example, the refundable assurance bonding system discussed below.

The political feasibility of this policy is an important and difficult question. It certainly represents a major shift in the way we view our relationship to natural capital and would have major social, economic, and political implications. But these implications are just the ones we need to expose and face squarely if we hope to achieve sustainability. Because of its logic, its conceptual simplicity, and its built-in market incentive structure leading to sustainability, the proposed NCD tax may be the most politically feasible of the possible alternatives to achieving sustainability.

We have not tried to work out all the details of how the NCD tax would be administered. In general, it could be administered like any other tax, but it would most likely require international agreements or at least national ecological tariffs (as discussed below) to prevent some countries from flooding markets with untaxed natural capital or products made with untaxed natural capital (see further on). By shifting most of the tax burden to the NCD tax and away from income taxes, the NCD tax could actually simplify the administration of the taxation system while providing the appropriate economic incentives to achieve sustainability.

The Precautionary Polluter Pays Principle (4P)

One of the primary reasons for the problems with current methods of environmental management is the issue of scientific uncertainty. At issue are not just its existence, but the radically different expectations and modes of operation that science and policy have developed to deal with it. If we are to solve this problem, we must understand and expose these differences about the nature of uncertainty and design better methods to incorporate it into the policy-making and management process.

Problems arise when regulators ask scientists for answers to unanswerable questions. For example, the law may mandate that the regulatory agency come up with safety standards for all known toxins when little or no information is available on the impacts of these chemicals. When trying to enforce the regulations after they are drafted, the problem of true uncertainty about the impacts remains. It is not possible to determine with any certainty whether the local chemical company contributed to the death of some of the people in the vicinity of their toxic waste dump. One cannot *prove* the smoking/lung cancer connection in any direct, causal way (i.e., in the courtroom sense), only as a statistical relationship.

As they are currently set up most environmental regulations, particularly in the United States, demand certainty, and when scientists are pressured to supply this nonexistent commodity there is not only frustration and poor communication but mixed messages in the media as well. Because of uncertainty, environmental issues can often be manipulated by political and economic interest groups. Uncertainty about global warming is perhaps the most visible current example of this effect.

The "precautionary principle" is one way the environmental regulatory community has begun to deal with the problem of true uncertainty. The principle states that rather than await certainty, regulators should act in anticipation of any potential environmental harm in order to prevent it. The precautionary principle is so frequently invoked in international environmental resolutions that it has come to be seen by some as a basic normative principle of international environmental law[38].

Implementing this view of science requires a new approach to environmental protection that acknowledges the existence of true uncertainty rather than denying it, and includes mechanisms to safeguard against its potentially harmful effects, while at the same time encouraging development of lower impact technologies and the reduction of uncertainty about impacts. The precautionary principle sets the stage for this approach, but the real challenge is to develop scientific methods to determine the potential costs of uncertainty, and to adjust incentives so that the appropriate parties pay this cost of uncertainty and have appropriate incentives to reduce its detrimental effects. Without this adjustment, the full costs of environmental damage will continue to be left out of the accounting[39], and the hidden subsidies from society to those who profit from environmental degradation will continue to provide strong incentives to degrade the environment beyond sustainable levels[40].

Over the past two decades there has been extensive discussion about the efficiency that can theoretically be achieved in environmental management through the use of market mechanisms[41]. These mechanisms are designed to alter the pricing structure of the present market system to incorporate the total, long-term social and ecological costs of an economic agent's activities. Suggested incentive-based mechanisms, in addition to pollution taxes, and tradable pollution discharge permits discussed above, include financial responsibility requirements and deposit–refund systems. Dealing with the pervasive uncertainty inherent in environmental problems in a precautionary way is possible using some new versions of these incentive-based alternatives.

An innovative incentive-based instrument currently being researched to manage the environment for precaution under uncertainty is a flexible environmental assurance bonding system[42]. This variation of the deposit–refund system is designed to incorporate both known and uncertain environmental costs into the incentive system and to induce positive environmental technological innovation. It works in this way: in addition to charging an economic agent directly for known environmental damages, an assurance bond equal to the current best estimate of the largest potential future environmental damages would be levied and kept in an interest-bearing escrow account for a predetermined length of time. In keeping with the precautionary principle, this system requires the commitment of resources now to offset the potentially catastrophic future effects of current activity. Portions of the bond (plus interest) would be returned if and when the agent could demonstrate that the suspected worst-case damages had not occurred or would be less than originally assessed. Funds tied up in bonds could continue to be used for other economic activities. The only cost would be the difference (plus or minus) between the interest on the bond and the return that could be earned by the firm had they invested in other activities. On average one would expect this difference to be minimal. In addition, the "forced savings" which the bond would require could actually improve overall economic performance in economies like the U.S. that chronically under-save.

By requiring the users of environmental resources to post a bond adequate to cover uncertain future environmental damages (with the possibility for refunds), the burden of proof (and the cost of the uncertainty) is shifted from the public to the resource user. At the same time, agents are not charged in any final way for uncertain future damages and can recover portions of their bond (with interest) in proportion to how much better their performance is than the worst case.

Deposit–refund systems, in general, are not a new concept. They have been successfully applied to a range of consumer, conservation, and environmental policy objectives[43]. The most well-known examples are the systems for beverage containers and used lubricating oils that have both proven to be quite effective and efficient. Another precedent for environmental assurance bonds is the producer-paid performance bonds often required for federal, state, or local government construction work. For example, The Miller Act (40 U.S.C. 270), a 1935 federal statute, requires contractors performing construction contracts for the federal government to secure performance bonds. Performance bonds provide a contractual guarantee that the principal (the entity that is doing the work or providing the service) will perform in a designated way. Bonds are frequently required for construction work done in the private sector as well.

Performance bonds are frequently posted in the form of corporate surety bonds, which are licensed under various insurance laws and, under their charter, have legal authority to act as financial guarantee for others. The unrecoverable cost of this service is usually 1–5% of the bond amount. However, under the Miller Act (FAR 28.203-1 and 28.203-2), any contract above a designated amount ($25,000 in the case of construction) can be backed by other types of securities, such as U.S. bonds or notes, in lieu of a bond guaranteed by a surety company. In this case, the contractor provides duly executed power of attorney and an agreement authorizing collection on the bond or notes if they default on the contract[44]. If the contractor performs all the obligations specified in the contract, the securities are returned to the contractor and the usual cost of the surety is avoided.

Environmental assurance bonds would work in a similar manner (by providing a contractual guarantee that the principal would perform in an environmentally benign manner) but would be levied for the current best estimate of the *largest* probable potential future environmental damages. Funds in the bond would be invested and would produce interest that could be returned to the principal. An "environmentally benign" investment strategy would probably be most appropriate for a bond such as this.

These bonds could be administered by the regulatory authority that currently manages the operation or procedure (for example, in the U.S. the Environmental Protection Agency could be the primary authority). But a case can be made that it is better to set up a completely independent agency to administer the bonds. The detailed design of the institutions to administer the bond is worthy of considerable additional thought and analysis, and will depend on the details of the particular situation (see further on).

The bond would be held until the uncertainty or some part of it was removed. This would provide a strong incentive for the principals to reduce the uncertainty about their environmental impacts as quickly as possible, either by funding independent research or by changing their processes to ones which are less damaging. A quasi-judicial body would be necessary to resolve disputes about when and how much refund on the bonds should be awarded. This body would utilize the latest independent scientific information on the worst-case ecological damages that could result from a firm's activities, but with the burden of proof falling on the economic agent that stands to gain from the activity, not the public. Protocol for worst-case analysis already exists within the U.S. EPA. In 1977 the U.S. Council on Environmental Quality required worst-case analysis for implementing NEPA

(National Environmental Protection Act of 1969). This required the regulatory agency to consider the worst environmental consequences of an action when scientific uncertainty was involved[45].

One potential argument against the bond is that it would select for relatively large firms that could afford to handle the financial responsibility of activities that are potentially hazardous to the environment. This is true, but it is exactly the desired effect, since firms that cannot handle the financial responsibility should *not* be passing the cost of potential environmental damage on to the public. In the construction industry, small "fly-by-night" firms are prevented (through the use of performance bonds) from cutting corners and endangering the public in order to underbid responsible firms.

This is not to say that small businesses would be eliminated. Far from it, they could either band together to form associations to handle the financial responsibility for environmentally risky activities, or, preferably, they could change to more environmentally benign activities that did not require large assurance bonds. This encouragement of the development of new environmentally benign technologies is one of the main attractions of the bonding system, and small, start-up firms would certainly lead the way.

The individual elements of the 4P system have broad theoretical support, and have been implemented before in various forms. The precautionary principle is gaining wide acceptance in many areas where true uncertainty is important. Incentive-based environmental regulation schemes are also gaining acceptance as more efficient ways to achieve environmental goals. For example, the U.S. Clean Air Act reauthorization contains a tradable permit system for controlling air pollution. Both the precautionary and the polluter pays principles are also incorporated in Agenda 21, the final resolutions of the 1992 United Nations Conference on Environment and Development[46]. By linking these two important principles we can begin to effectively deal with uncertainty in an economically efficient and ecologically sustainable way.

In a sense, we are already moving in the direction of the 4P system. As strict liability for environmental damages becomes more the norm, farsighted firms have already started to protect themselves against possible future lawsuits and damage claims by putting aside funds for this purpose. The 4P system is, in effect, a requirement that all firms be farsighted. It is an improvement on strict liability because it:

- explicitly moves the costs to the present, where they will have the maximum impact on decision making[47];
- provides "edge-focused, second-order scientific" assessments of the potential impacts from a comprehensive ecological economic perspective in order to ensure that the size of the bond is large enough to cover the worst-case damages;
- ensures that appropriate use of the funds is made in case of a partial or complete default.

Because of its logic, fairness, efficiency, ability to implement the precautionary and polluter pays principles in a practical way, and use of legal and financial mechanisms with long and successful precedents, the 4P system promises to be both practical and politically feasible. We think it can do much to help head off the current environmental crisis before it is too late.

Ecological Tariffs: Making Trade Sustainable

If all countries in the world were to adopt and enforce the 4P system and NCD taxes there would be no problem (at least from an ecological point of view) in allowing "free" trade. Given recent commitments of the global community to the idea of sustainable development[48] it does not seem totally out of the question that a global agreement along these lines could someday be worked out. But in the meantime, there are alternative instruments that could allow individual countries or trading blocks to apply the 4P system and NCD taxes in their local economies without forcing producers overseas to do so. It is within at least the spirit of the GATT guidelines to allow countervailing duties to be assessed to impose the same ecological costs on internally produced and imported products. The key is fairness. A country cannot impose duties on imports that it does not also impose on domestically produced products. But if a country chose to adopt the 4P and NCD tax systems domestically, it could also adopt a system of ecologically based tariffs that would impose equivalent costs on imports. This is a different use for tariffs than the usual one. In the past, tariffs have been used to protect domestic industries from foreign competition. The proposed (and more defensible) use of tariffs (in conjunction with the 4P and NCD taxes) is to protect the domestic (and global) environment from private polluters and non-sustainable resource users, regardless of their country of origin or operation. The mechanisms for imposing tariffs are well established. All that we are changing is the motive and the result. The proposed ecological tariffs would result in patterns of trade that do not endanger sustainability.

Toward Ecological Tax Reform

Taken together, the three policy instruments suggested above [Natural Capital Depletion (NCD) taxes, the Precautionary Polluter Pays Principle (4P), and Ecological Tariffs (ETs)] would go a long way toward assuring ecological sustainability, while at the same time taking advantage of market incentives to achieve this result at high efficiency. They represent components of what is coming to be called "ecological tax reform."

There is a growing consensus among a broad range of stakeholder groups in the U.S., and even more so in Europe, concerning the need to reform tax systems to tax "bads" rather than "goods." Taxes have significant incentive effects which need to be considered and utilized more effectively. The most comprehensive proposed implementation of this idea is coming to be known under the general heading of "ecological tax reform"[49]. Earlier discussions of similar schemes were given by Page[50] who considered a national severance tax, and Daly[51] who discussed a depletion quota auction.

The basic idea is to limit the throughput flow of resources to an ecologically sustainable level and composition, thus serving the goal of a sustainable scale of the economy relative to the ecosystem, a goal that was neglected until recently. The more traditional goal of efficient allocation of resources is also served by this instrument because it raises the tax on bads and lowers the tax on goods—it internalizes externalities in a blunt general way, without getting stuck in the informational tar baby of calculating Pigouvian taxes and fretting over "second best" problems. The third goal of distributive equity is both helped and hindered. Since the throughput tax is basically a capturing for public purposes of the scarcity rent to natural capital as economic and demographic growth increases its value, it has some of the equity appeal of Henry George's rent tax. However, like all consumption taxes it is regressive. This could be counteracted by retaining a zero tax bracket for very low incomes, and a progressive income tax structure for the rest of the population. Of the three major goals of economic policy (sustainable scale, efficient allocation, and just distribution) ecological tax reform serves the first two quite well, and the third partially, requiring some supplement from a progressive income tax structure.

The idea is to gradually shift much of the tax burden away from "goods" like income and labor, and toward "bads" like ecological damages and consumption of nonrenewable resources. Such a shift would have far-reaching implications, and should simultaneously encourage both employment and ecologically sustainability.

There are three basic problems that need to be addressed: (1) *the research problem*: what would be the quantitative effects of various forms of ecological tax reform on the three policy goals discussed above? Would it significantly induce efficient resource-saving technologies? Would that raise or lower employment? What taxes would most effectively limit scale? How close can we come to the efficient and equitable ideal of taxing mainly rent? What are the implications for international trade of raising revenue by ecological taxes rather than income taxes? (2) *the communication problem*: how do we adequately develop and communicate with the relevant stakeholder groups the options for ecological tax reform and their implications? and (3) *the political problem*: how could such an idea be implemented in the current political climate? We believe that these three problems are best addressed in an integrated and coordinated manner, as described above.

The time for action is running short, but the political will to implement significant changes seems to be finally at hand. The tax reforms suggested embody the mix of environmental protection and economic development potential necessary to make them politically feasible. The next steps are to further elaborate and test the instruments, and to build a broad, overlapping consensus to allow their ultimate implementation. It is not too late to protect our natural capital and achieve sustainability.

A Trans-disciplinary Pollution Control Policy Instrument

As pointed out earlier, when economists deal with common environmental issues but analyze these issues with the use of models that are both differing and partial, they may arrive at conflicting policy prescriptions. Above we emphasized the complexity of these issues and the need to find common ground. In moving on from policy prescriptions to policy instruments for implementing policies, it is therefore not surprising to find economists in disagreement (e.g., pollution taxes vs. tradable permits) not only among themselves, but, more to the point, to find economists in disagreement with ecologists (nature sanctuaries vs. ecotourism), who in turn are opposed by regulators who prefer a bureaucratic command-and-control structure. If sustainable development is to be achieved, the need to find common ground is compelling. This section suggests how the search for common ground might contribute to the design of a policy instrument for pollution control.

The proposed trans-disciplinary framework, which supplements economic insights through a team approach by explicitly including concepts from ecology and the physical sciences as well as concerns for equity, distribution, and political feasibility, is illustrated in Figure 2[52].

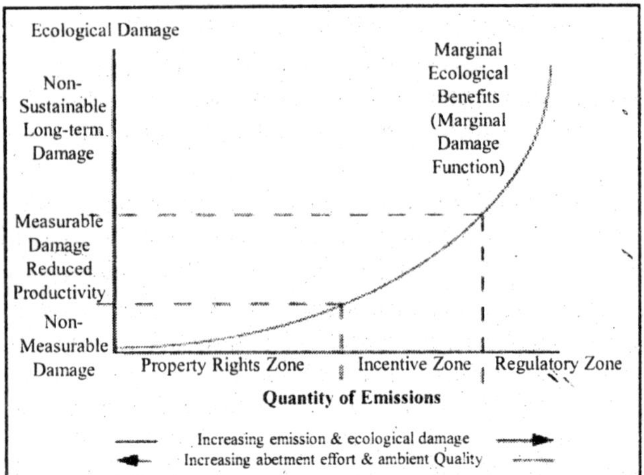

Source: Cumberland 1994[2]

Figure 2: An Ecological Economic Approach to Pollution Control

This model is proposed as an alternative to the purely economic model, which is predicated upon marginal damage and treatment cost functions whose intersection yields a single uniquely efficient level of pollution tax, treatment, and environmental quality. In contrast, the proposed approach recognizes three separate ranges of environmental quality or levels of ecological health, each with its appropriate policy measure. The model allows for a range, band, or zone of low levels of emissions within which damage is too low to measure, or too low to reduce the productivity of the system. Until emissions and concentrations of pollutants reached a level at which damage could be detected, emitters would be permitted to release waste within legal limits without charge as under the present practice in the U.S. This is termed the property right zone. For equity reasons, emitters are not taxed for emission levels below which (1) no damage occurs, (2) no accumulation results, and (3) ecological productivity is not impaired. Here emissions fall well within the assimilative capacity of the environment. Within this range or band of emissions, the marginal cost of monitoring and administration would probably exceed marginal ecological damage, and thus not justify the expense of administration costs.

The next level of policy concern is that at which ecological criteria indicate that pollution emissions and concentrations have measurably damaged the environment and threatened the productivity of the system. Within this emission range, a pollution charge, calibrated like the optimal tax in Figure 4.1, and set at a level sufficient to prevent transgressing into the cumulative damage zone is imposed upon each additional unit of pollution emitted. This is termed the incentive range because the pollution tax is used as an economically efficient measure for confronting emitters with financial incentives to reduce pollution to efficient levels, as in Figure 4.1. Despite an understandable reluctance by regulators to place exclusive reliance on financial incentives, establishing an incentive range or band could serve the important goal of achieving the highest level of environmental safety per unit of social cost. The establishment of an incentive zone also creates a discrete threshold within which emitters are given the incentives to limit their emissions to non-damaging, assailable levels. The central importance of the incentive zone here and of IB policies in general is that they apply the powerful forces of competition to the reduction of pollution through economic rewards to those who act in the public interest. Thus, they shift entrepreneurial talents away from regulatory evasion toward efficient, less entropic technical improvement. Within these first two management bands, the proposed instrument is similar to a Pigouvian tax.

However, even the ability and willingness to pay pollution taxes should not permit the privilege of purchasing rights to unconstrained emissions beyond ecologically acceptable limits. A third level of policy concern is therefore reached when pollution emissions and concentrations threaten to rise to the point that ecological criteria indicate irreversible, non-sustainable damage to the system. This is the regulatory zone, because at this threshold, the option of pollute-and-pay would be superseded by regulatory prohibition of any further increases in emissions. While an efficient pollution tax would have been designed to preclude taxed emissions from reaching an unsustainable level, back-up regulatory authority would serve as a safeguard against miscalculation and uncertainty.

There is an efficiency disadvantage in the proposed approach. Strict efficiency requires that each unit of emission be taxed at the same rate. However, in this proposal, those emitting within a no-damage range could continue to emit at initial levels even after new emissions pushed the total into the taxable incentive range. This equity–efficiency trade-off in the incentive zone is introduced in order to provide a measure of protection to existing firms against the possible impact of future entrants having greater market power. Also, the absolute cutoff of further emissions once the regulatory range has been reached would preclude the entry of new, more efficient firms.

Both the equity and efficiency goals, however, could be served by a variant of this tripartite approach, using tradable permits instead of charges. Provided that markets could be established for them, permits would be issued without charge in the property right range of no measurable damage. After the threshold of measurable damage was crossed, additional permits would be offered for sale on the open market, but their number would be limited to a level set by ecological criteria to prevent irreversible damage and transgression into the regulatory range. Therefore, additional emission permits would not be available at any price once the regulatory range had been reached. Economic efficiency would automatically result from the equilibrium price of permits set by bidders in the market.

Thus, limitations on sales of marketable permits to ecologically safe levels combine the best features of both regulation and economic incentives. The option of selling emission permits in competitive markets would automatically allow new and technologically efficient producers to emerge and to phase out those more pollution intensive producers, but only if the latter found this to be an attractive option. Resale of permits would also automatically adjust markets for inflation, unlike Pigouvian emission charges which would require administrative action for efficient response to price level changes. In fact, transferable permits for emissions in all ranges would have efficiency advantages over limiting charges to the incentive range by permitting new, efficient emitters to purchase permits and by requiring all emitters to pay the same price per unit of emission rather than merely cutting off all new emissions beyond the efficiency limit.

Implementation and Operational Considerations

Clearly, practical problems would have to be faced in implementing these proposals, depending upon local and other conditions. In deriving the damage and treatment cost functions, difficult decisions would have to be made concerning multiple pollutants, multiple species affected, and multiple spatial jurisdictions, depending upon the availability of data and knowledge. For example, Tietenberg has discussed techniques for dealing with multiple sources and multiple receptors of pollution damage[53]. Fine tuning would require different tax levels appropriate spatially and temporally for different pollutants, again depending upon the state of data and knowledge. Given the limitations of scientific knowledge and the extent of uncertainty, a pragmatic approach could require simply proceeding on the basis of scientific consensus concerning the best current information. Given problems of assessing the differential impacts and synergisms among different pollutants, simple estimates of relative toxicity could serve as the basis for setting pollution charges or permit fees subject to the accumulation of additional data. Monitoring and enforcement would be essential. Nevertheless, it must be emphasized that these imperatives are just as compelling for all environmental management systems, including those now in place.

Some of the features of this proposal would be precluded in places where pollutants were already causing measurable damage, which is unfortunately already the case in much of the world. In such instances, the property right zone would be forfeited and pollution taxes would become relevant on all emissions. Rates on these taxes could then be increased to keep damages within the incentive range and prevent spillover into the non-sustainable damage range. Where non-sustainable damage has already occurred, drastic regulatory and punitive (negative incentive) action is justified. Examples include the fines and damage judgments incurred from oil spills and the damage assessments against hazardous waste disposal under the U.S. Superfund program[54].

It should be noted that a variant of this approach has already been applied in the Netherlands[55]. Farmers are permitted to discharge the manure equivalent of 125 kg of phosphate per hectare per year without charge. However, beyond that level, they are then charged the equivalent of 0.1 ECU ($0.11) per kg from 125 to 200 kg per hectare. Above 200 kg, the charge increases progressively to 0.2 ECU ($0.22) per kg per hectare per year, with a typical charge per farm of about 730 ECU ($810) annually. This innovative policy instrument, though similar in many respects to the tripartite approach suggested in this paper, utilizes in place of a regulatory level of capped maximum discharges a level of increased emission charges at twice that in what is termed here the incentive zone. The two approaches can be made to converge formally by raising the emission charge in the zone of unacceptable damages to a prohibitively high level. Like the proposals here, the practice in the Netherlands diverges from the strict efficiency rule of taxing each unit of emission at the same price in order to provide some equity consideration to emitters.

Appropriate Policies, Instruments, and Institutions for Governance at Different Levels of Spatial Aggregation

The Local Level

Although the legal and institutional framework for environmental management is typically determined at the national level, and for some issues is shifting slowly to the international level, the individual events which in total determine environmental quality actually occur at the local level. Examples are the conversion of natural habitats to agriculture, subdivision of land for residential, commercial, or industrial development, and construction of a factory and the disposal of its waste. More generally, the most important decisions made at the local level are those dealing with land use. Land use decisions affect the full spectrum of environmental problems, from those of human habitat to those of habitat for protection of species diversity. The basic problem is that market processes do not necessarily result in land use densities that are consistent with local carrying capacity or with growth on a scale that is sustainable.

Just as most political issues are said ultimately to be local (Tip O' Neill), so are the sources of most environmental impacts. Therefore, although broad environmental policy issues should be coordinated at higher levels of governance, the struggle for ecological sustainability must ultimately be won or lost at the local level. While the NIMBY (Not In My Back Yard) response to local economic development[56] threats is deprecated by growth advocates, this type of local feedback provides valuable information that merits serious consideration in the planning and decision processes. "Not in my backyard" can be a perfectly rational and responsible local reaction which sophisticated developers as well as ultimate decision makers are learning to factor into the management process, since this is where the detrimental externalities are felt most acutely. A recent example is the decision of Disney to cancel plans to build a multimillion dollar theme park near Washington, DC, close to Civil War battlefields and open countryside, in the face of strong opposition by historians and local citizens. The lesson to be learned from this experience is that the professional developers usually prevail (because of their well-financed mastery of legal and political intricacies of the development process, which indeed they have designed precisely for this purpose) except in those rare cases where conservationists mobilize the resources and will required to organize the legal, public relations, planning, and other professional skills needed to defend their rights and environment[57]. Unfortunately, few communities have the means and resolution available in Middleburg, Virginia, and environmental activists too often confine their efforts to their own backyards. Therefore there is opportunity and urgent need for NGOs to make their experience and expertise more widely available to local communities facing serious environmental damage from ill-advised, poorly designed development projects.

Although this section emphasizes policy instruments, discussion of these instruments should involve some reference to the interest groups that affect them, the management agencies that apply them, and the processes through which they are applied.

A major obstacle to environmental protection that is readily verifiable through observation at the level of local government is the heavy bias of economic and political power toward growth and against ecological preservation. There are many reasons for this:

- Local economic growth decisions are typically based upon private cost and benefit, rather than upon total social cost and benefit.
- The economic benefits of particular development projects are immediately observable in quantifiable terms and measurable in monetary terms, while the benefits of ecological protection are often qualitative, future oriented, and therefore heavily discounted.
- The beneficiaries of development are sharply focused and can command the financial resources required to retain the top, politically connected legal talent which controls the development process and can persevere until they achieve their objectives. The economic and political power of the development establishment becomes institutionalized in the laws and procedures governing land use and environmental regulation.
- Local development establishments sub optimize by competing for growth with other jurisdictions and by subsidizing growth to inefficient, unsustainable levels.
- Though the total benefits of a decision to preserve ecology may significantly outweigh the benefits of development, the beneficiaries of environmental protection are less sharply focused, are scattered throughout the general public and, unless they can

rally thinly spread organized environmental associations to their cause, must rely upon part-time volunteers to protect their interests.

- The diffused nature of environmental benefits inclines many of the potential beneficiaries of ecological protection to become "free riders" on the activism of the minority, reducing their apparent total representation to below a socially warranted level.
- Subsidies from all levels of governance to transportation via cheap energy and infrastructure aggravate the bias toward excessive levels of local economic growth.

Together, these factors all contribute to the current dilemma of biases toward excessive, ecologically unsustainable rates of local economic growth. The problem is made particularly acute by the fact that the efforts of the local growth establishment to privatize the beneficial externalities of common property resources such as estuaries, public waterways, wetlands, forests, scenic areas, parklands, and other stocks of natural capital, too often target economic growth in the most sensitive ecological areas.

As the results of these biases toward development, the resulting privatization of natural capital assets began in the 1970s to cause unacceptably polluted air, water, and land, and the need to correct some of the developmental excesses became more obvious. This is why the NGOs have been able to assume a major role in providing the public with environmental protection against major polluters, protection that is particularly crucial in cases where government agencies at all levels have been sufficiently co-opted by those they were established to control that they have in effect abdicated their obligations to the public interest. Such incidents have been cited in the case of the Chesapeake Bay[58].

Institutional biases toward local economic growth have been resulted both in excessive aggregate levels of economic growth and economic growth concentrated in ecologically sensitive areas. Belated recognition of this problem has led to the emergence of policy instruments for its control, but these instruments are demonstrably not adequate to the task.

In the U.S., the primary policy instrument for management of land use and economic growth is the planning and zoning process. This is a regulatory process that typically reflects accurately the distribution of local political and economic power. Consequently, local land use decisions tend to be made on the basis of private rather than community benefits and costs.

Improving the quality of local land use will depend most importantly upon giving appropriate weight to:

- assigning priority to net social welfare gains over net private gains;
- scientific evaluation, protection, and management of local ecological resources for sustainability;
- equitable participation in the decision process by all affected parties;
- oversight and review at higher levels of governance to prevent interregional competition for growth from degenerating into competitive sacrifice of natural capital and of critical areas.

Specific policy instruments are necessary for achieving these objectives. Rather than the present policy of subsidizing excessive levels of local economic growth, policy instruments are needed that confront developers with the full economic and social costs of growth. One such instrument is full-cost pricing of local government services.

Land Purchasing and Conservation Easements

Another alternative policy instrument for managing local land use and protecting sensitive ecosystems is outright acquisition of sensitive ecosystems through purchase by governments, by other agencies, by citizens, by the Nature Conservancy, or by other NGOs as discussed elsewhere. Before approving land for development it should be evaluated in terms of soil type, hydrology, habitat, archaeological significance, and other scientific criteria. Strengthening local land use authorities through strong trans-disciplinary science input is essential to sustainable land use. Evaluation of land for development suitability prior to development could have saved residents of Los Angeles, to cite a single example, billions of dollars in losses from fire, flood, landslides, and earthquakes. Many of these losses are shifted to the general public, who pay the bills for publicly subsidized insurance relief efforts and often for rebuilding in the same disaster areas. The lethal combination of federally subsidized insurance and incompetent, development-biased local planning and zoning has caused billions of dollars worth of social and personal loss not only in California, but also along the floodplains of the Mississippi and the hurricane alleys of the American Southeast.

In terms of equity and Pareto fairness, when specific parcels of land are taken from owners or are subjected to prohibition from all uses because of ecological and other scientific or public purposes, compensation is a reasonable policy instrument to be considered. However, no such equity consideration is appropriate in the case of speculative pursuit of gain at public expense, since real estate activities should be recognized as subject to both profit and loss possibilities. The case for compensation is weak when some land uses are affected by broad federal, state, or local planning, zoning, or legislation, as has been widely recognized by the courts. The misnamed "wise use" movement to block environmental legislation by threatening compensation demands in retaliation for the exercise of legitimate governmental functions is an effort to carry the compensation principle far beyond reasonable limits.

Full-Cost Pricing

Local taxes, utility fees, and other services should reflect the full cost to society of additional residential, commercial, and industrial growth, both during the period of construction and throughout the life of the project. Among the un-priced social costs of residential, commercial, and industrial real estate development are environmental impacts from sewage disposal, storm water non-point-source runoff of silt and sediment, runoff of lawn and garden chemicals, and loss of open space. Unless local land prices and taxes fully reflect all of these costs, the resulting subsidization of the real estate and economic growth establishment causes excessive densities and misallocation of land resources.

The typical practice of avoiding full-cost pricing subsidizes new growth at the expense of current residents. The use of impact fees on new developments is a variant of this full-cost approach. In addition to these initial fees, continuing monthly fees should be set at levels sufficiently high to cover the full cost of sustainable environmental protection. The adoption of full-cost pricing may not be a sufficient policy instrument for achieving sustainability, but it is a necessary condition for confronting developers with the social cost of their actions and for sending proper signals to purchasers concerning the full social cost of moving to environmentally sensitive areas. Economically efficient instruments of this type can assist in limiting population densities to the carrying capacity of the local environment.

Getting the prices right may seem to be a rather simplistic instrument for achieving the many important goals of good land use and it obviously must be supplemented with other regulatory instruments such as regional planning for watersheds, air sheds, and life-support ecologies. However, incorporating full social and ecological costs into land prices is a potentially powerful instrument for achieving ecologically responsible development decisions. To the extent that consumer sovereignty can be preserved in free societies, getting the prices right is a necessary precondition for assisting markets to make decisions that serve the public interest. Most advanced societies found early on that rather than relying exclusively on markets to make land-use decisions, the introduction of planning and zoning was essential for capturing the benefits of positive externalities and avoiding the costs of negative externalities.

The Regional Level: Reducing Counterproductive Interregional Competition for Growth

Although this section addresses policies that regional governments can utilize in pursuing sustainable development, it should also be recognized that national governments play a major role in setting the rules of the game for interregional competition and they bear the responsibility for providing for sustainability. The goal of national policy should be to assure that the means used by states and localities in interregional competition lead constructively toward improving the quality of development, and not merely toward the competitive subsidization of quantitative growth. Incentives to standards-lowering competition among states should be avoided, just as among nations. This problem is particularly egregious when states engage in competitive bidding wars to attract such facilities as factories, sports arenas, theme parks, industrial parks, housing developments, shopping centers, and industrial complexes. The now familiar give-away instruments used for such competition include tax relief, relaxation of zoning and environmental standards, subsidization of access roads and public facilities, and the disguised transfer of funds through the issuance of tax-free municipal bonds[59].

Although these types of subsidies to regional growth have become so widespread as to seem commonplace, it is important to recognize that they run against the public interest by violating the principles of efficiency, equity, and sustainability in numerous ways. They are inefficient because those projects that are economically viable would have been undertaken in any event without public subsidies. Therefore, from the national perspective, the subsidy is unnecessary and merely represents an unjustifiable transfer of publicly raised tax revenues from taxpayers to private developers in a zero-sum game. The bidding contest among states may influence where the project will actually be located, but it may not since fiscal subsidies are only one factor and usually a minor factor entering into the benefit–cost calculus of developers. In such cases the subsidy is an unnecessary public-to-private transfer from the viewpoint of both the region and the nation. In cases where the project actually would not proceed without subsidization, this indicates that its proponents are unable or unwilling to pay for its fair share of public services, and that it should probably not be built at all.

In the best-case scenario, a state may succeed in out-competing other states for the location of a new activity. An example is the case of a theme park, for which a typical benefit-cost study indicates total state economic benefits exceeding total state economic costs, including the cost of the subsidy. If resources can be raised to finance it, an objective, professional benefit–cost study should be undertaken in advance of any major local development. However, benefit–cost studies typically deal only with totals, and rarely with the environmental, distributional, and equity issues of which groups receive the benefits and which groups bear the costs. Typically, the promised new jobs go to immigrants from outside the region, and the promised tax relief gets transformed into tax increases needed to pay for the new social services caused by the development. Obviously, the beneficiaries of growth are the economic development establishment, the tourism industry, and related activities. Not coincidentally, these are the groups which have the economic and political incentives to dominate planning, zoning, and development processes. Despite possible net economic benefits to these groups, heavy economic and other costs fall upon local taxpayers, residents, and commuters, all of whom are affected by the widespread environmental and ecological externalities imposed by large-scale economic growth. All economic growth increases throughput, accelerates entropy, and threatens sustainability.

Although subsidizing the location of growth (which would occur in any event) is, from the national viewpoint, a zero sum game, there are other constructive forms of interregional competition that can benefit both the competing regions and the larger society. States and regions can compete in terms of improving the quality of public services, such as education and environmental management, thus making their areas more attractive to innovative firms whose major location requirements are the need to attract and retain highly trained, highly paid, but highly mobile human resources[60]. This might be termed "standards-raising competition," in contrast to standards-lowering competition to reduce taxes, regulations, and so on.

Rather than perpetuating the spread of economic inefficiency, distributional inequity, and environmental damage through allowing competitive interregional subsidization of economic growth, national governments could encourage interregional competition in the quality of development by disallowing fiscal transfers from state and local governments to private firms. This could easily and appropriately be accomplished through minor changes in the internal revenue code.

The National Level: Toxic Release Inventory and the Public's Right to Know

The hard-won democratic right to freedom of information can be especially valuable as an instrument for improving environmental management[61]. In particular, the collection and public release of environmental data on emissions could, if more widely used, serve as a powerful management instrument. For example, a promising first step toward a system of materials balance and waste tracking has already been put into place in the U.S. EPA Toxic Release Inventory (TRI). Following the 1984 disaster at the Union Carbide plant in Bhopal, India, which killed more than 2,000 persons and injured some 500,000, the EPA began requiring chemical manufacturers in the U.S. to file annual reports on releases of toxic substances into the air, water, and land. In 1986, the Emergency Planning and Right to Know legislation was passed over the objections of the Reagan administration and industry groups, requiring disclosure of toxic chemical releases by some 24,000 U.S. chemical plants[62].

The potential policy leverage of this approach is illustrated by a recent publication in the popular press that listed by name the 10 cleanest major U.S. corporations, the 10 "most improved," and the 10 "laggards," along with analyses of their environmental policies[63]. Although it would not be realistic to attribute the entire decline in toxic releases achieved since this system was initiated in 1986 to this one factor, the 30% reduction that has occurred does illustrate its public relations impact.

An excellent example of the effective use state and regional authorities can make of TRI data is the study done under the EPA's Chesapeake Bay Program by Maryland, Pennsylvania, Virginia, and the District of Columbia[64]. The potency of this study lays not only in the detail presented in terms of types of releases and water basin and sub-basin affected, but in that the names of emitters, both public and private, are cited along with the estimated pounds per year of each type of pollutant released by each establishment. The policy significance of this information lies in the fact that while the fact of "regulatory capture" through economic and political power can limit the ability of regulators to curb pollution, citizens' associations and NGOs can and has used this type of information in the courts to obtain judgments against polluters when regulators have not acted. The data show the worst polluter of the Chesapeake to be the Bethlehem Steel Corporation plant at Sparrows Point near Baltimore. As would be expected, in addition to steel producers, chemical plants, meat processors, and electric power plants are major offenders. Somewhat less expected are the huge pollution loadings released from public wastewater treatment plants. This enormous and ironic pollution impact by the very facilities intended to reduce pollution reflects in part the failure of public environmental policy and the huge amount of pollutants illegally discharged by polluters into public sewers.

This TRI system, if extended to all existing toxics producers and made a requirement before new operations could begin, could provide comprehensive information on total waste flows and be integrated with the improved social accounting systems discussed elsewhere in this study.

The EIS as a National Policy Instrument

We noted above that as the results of biases toward local development began in the 1970s to become painfully obvious in terms of unacceptably polluted air, water, and land, the need to correct some of the developmental excesses became more acute. An effort was made principally in the U.S. through the National Environmental Policy Act of 1969 to constrain uncontrolled environmental damage and to initiate environmental protection, especially at the national level. One key provision of this Act, as noted above, almost inadvertently gave a new weapon to local residents provided that they develop the skills to use it. This was the section of the Act requiring development promoters to file environmental impact statements. The EIS deserves recognition as an important policy innovation, since for the first time, it also gave the general public national opportunities heretofore systematically withheld from them to learn about and participate in decision making about environmentally impacting programs affecting their lives. These decision-making processes had previously been closely controlled by polluters and their often captive regulators. The EIS process provided new opportunities for citizens to confront the organized political and economic power of polluters.

We emphasized above the potential empowerment local communities could gain from using the environmental impact statement as a weapon against the imposition upon them of detrimental externalities from local economic growth excesses. This same policy instrument can be used effectively by citizens' groups and NGOs at the national level. One of its earliest and most successful applications in India was to cite estimates of the probable extent of sonic boom damage to prevent the costly federally subsidized development of a commercial supersonic transport aircraft.

Ecological Labeling

After prolonged resistance by the food industries, India has recently begun to label foods as to their nutritional and other contents providing an urgently needed source of information to consumers. The urgency of this need was aggravated by the billions of dollars spent annually by the food industries on the bombardment of consumers by advertising which spreads false and misleading information in unconscionable pursuit of consumers' expenditures.

In the interest of truth in advertising, exciting opportunities exist for introducing ecological labeling, comparable to nutritional labeling, on a wide range of products, goods, and services. Some obvious candidates for information to be included in ecological labeling per unit of product are inputs per unit of energy, recycled vs. virgin materials, amounts and types of toxic and other wastes generated in both the product's production and consumption, amounts of nonrenewable vs. renewable resources used, and related information. Such eco-labeling could become a powerful instrument for informing consumers, persuading producers to improve products, and rewarding good practices.

Other National Policies

In order to highlight the potential contributions of incentives, we have drawn a sharp contrast above between IB and regulatory national policy instruments. In reality, there are many instruments that combine features of both, as well as other altogether different types of options. Since government procurement is a major portion of many markets and products, government purchase directly and by example can influence environmental policy. Examples include:

- purchase of recycled paper and other products;
- purchase of vehicle fleets that operate on natural gas and other alternative fuels;
- construction and operation of energy-efficient public structures;
- management, cleanup, and prevention of wastes on military and civilian government installations.

In addition to using their procurement powers for green purposes, governments can take direct steps such as subsidizing the shift from use of nonrenewable to renewable energy sources and subsidizing research and development of sustainable technologies. Besides forging cost-effective new policies and instruments for environmental protection, national governments already have at their disposal efficient and virtually cost-free opportunities for making major environmental improvements by eliminating expensive subsidies and other obsolete programs which currently add to environmental damage. These perverse national policies have been referred to as "intervention failures" since they result from deliberately undertaken government actions which, whether purposely or inadvertently, cause environmental damage.

Examples include:

- underpricing the sale of publicly owned timber;
- underpricing the sale of public lands for mining;
- subsidizing the construction of roads for private harvesting of timber in national forests;
- subsidizing grazing and permitting overgrazing on public lands;
- subsidizing the sale of irrigation water to special-interest users;
- subsidizing the production of crops in excess supply (e.g., sugar cane in the Everglades), or which damage human health (e.g., tobacco);
- subsidizing highly entropic technologies for which no generally acceptable method of waste management has yet been found and which are regarded by the private insurance industry as too hazardous to qualify for commercial insurance (e.g., nuclear power);
- subsidizing the use of virgin materials and penalizing recycling by imposing uneconomically high transportation rates on the former;
- subsidizing the construction of costly environmentally damaging dams, levees, and irrigation projects.

Obviously, special interest groups, the subsidized polluters, benefit handsomely from the public largesse expended upon such programs, but continuation of such subsidies cannot be justified on public policy principles. Taxing citizens and using their money to pay the subsidized polluters to then damage these taxpayers is a double insult. A politically unlikely but perfectly rational alliance of conservatives concerned about downsizing government and liberal environmentalists concerned about governmentally sponsored environmental damage is emerging under the banner of "green scissors." They regard these and similar intervention failures as expensive self-inflicted ecological wounds whose early termination would permit immediate damage control and generate significant net public benefits. Intervention failures become particularly egregious at the regional level when they damage entire ecosystems such as estuaries, like the Chesapeake Bay.

The International Level and the Third World

The end of the Cold War and reductions in expenditures on weapons of mass destruction offer opportunities for addressing neglected international environmental issues that have been held hostage to the armament race for almost a half century. One of the most comprehensive proposals for meeting this challenge is embodied in Vice President Gore's plan for a global Marshall Plan. It is based upon the U.S. program which succeeded brilliantly in achieving the economic reconstruction for both our allies and adversaries after World War II. Although the analogy is not exact, the same spirit of common purpose and the growing recognition of the urgency for shifting from the present policy of devastating our habitat to one of lengthening the human tenure on earth could reactivate the idealism and generosity, which after that cataclysm proved to be major sources of enlightened self-interest for the U.S. We have suggested that funding for international environmental protection could be made self-financing through a system of Pigouvian pollution charges[65]. A modest international tax on carbon emissions, which would be an obvious candidate with which to begin, could have many advantages of the type discussed above in the sections on economic efficiency. Positive financial incentives would accrue to nations and enterprises which reduced emissions, innovated cleaner technologies, and conserved resources. The charges would raise revenue that could be used for research, administration, and compensation in hardship cases. The global threat of climate change would be reduced, and equity adjustments could be made in hardship cases and for developing nations.

Further recognition of the special needs of developing nations is embodied in the "debt-for-nature swaps." Unfortunately, many nations have borrowed so heavily that crushing pressures of servicing their debts are forcing them to deplete their environmental capital at rates that are causing problems not only internally, but which are of global concern, as in the Amazon Basin. The discount at which this debt is traded in international capital markets, and which unfortunately provides de facto evidence of its excess, also fortunately provides low-cost opportunities for purchasing this debt economically and liquidating it in return for the debtor nations' agreements to undertake specific environmental projects. Although excessive borrowing should not be encouraged, debt-for-nature swaps are a constructive policy instruments for salvaging ecological benefits from previous mistakes.

Economic incentives can contribute positively to environmental protection in developing nations especially through the strengthening of property rights by making these rights explicit, enforceable, and marketable. A problem of developing nations that threatens all of the fundamental goals of sustainability, equity, and efficiency is the loss of rain forests and other habitats, which not only damages indigenous cultures, but destroys forever endangered species. In some cases, rain forests can yield higher economic returns if left in their natural state than if destroyed for timber cutting and grazing. Rain forests are now recognized as vast reservoirs of potential life-saving drugs and sustainable non timber products. However, in the absence of property rights to these products, incentives are inadequate for their discovery and cultivation as contrasted to the clear-cutting of the forests.

Various policy instruments are available to mitigate this tragedy of the commons. One of the best ways to protect rain forests and other vital habitats is to create and protect property rights to the sustainable yields these resource systems can produce on a continuing basis in their natural state, rather than clear-cutting them for unsustainable short-run profits.

The creation of property rights can be established in the form of patents, royalties, and discovery rights. These would be paid by developed nations to create incentives in the LDCs to protect and harvest these resources sustainably, rather than destroying them forever for short-term gain. Another promising approach is that pioneered in Costa Rica, which has negotiated a "prospecting fee" with Merck Pharmaceuticals, giving the company rights for two years to screen forest products for valuable drugs. In return, the nation has agreed to set aside and protect the extraordinary amount of one quarter of its total land. Potential benefits to both parties could be great, and Costa Rica has undertaken an action that makes it a world leader in the struggle for sustainable development. Other similarly situated nations could benefit from this and similar initiatives.

Innovative as this Costa Rica–Merck agreement is, turning points out a major opportunity for improving such policies[66]. Emphasizing the importance of secure property rights and tenure in the management of resources, he notes that vesting these rights in central government agencies is one step toward correcting the tragedy of the commons. However, if it ignores the rights of indigenous tribes, in addition to being unfair to them, it results in a loss of their traditional knowledge of how to manage these resources for sustainable harvest of medicinal and other products. Thus, from the perspective of our approach, providing secure property rights to indigenous people in the management of forests, fisheries, and other environmental resources could provide significant improvements with respect to all of our criteria of scale, equity, efficiency, acceptability, and sustainability.

The Global Level

Increasingly, environmental and ecological problems are spilling over national borders and becoming not only transboundary phenomena, but, more seriously, threats to the global commons. Recognition of these increasingly serious global dimensions of the problem will require international solutions. One proposal, as noted above, has been to empower international agencies, such as OECD or the UN, to impose emission charges on transboundary pollutants with the proceeds used for monitoring, enforcement, and research[67].

One of the potentially most serious global environmental problems is that of greenhouse gases. Although much uncertainty remains concerning atmospheric science, there is considerable consensus that the growing concentration of carbon dioxide and other greenhouse gases in the atmosphere since the industrial revolution will, at current rates of accumulation, eventually raise global temperatures. The release of other gases, such as chlorofluorocarbons (CFCs) depletes the earth's protective atmospheric ozone, even causing periodic holes in this shield. Probable consequences include higher incidence of skin cancer, damage to human immune systems, to marine larvae, and to germinating crops. The accelerated melting of glaciers and polar ice caps could raise sea levels around the globe, inundating low-lying cities and coastal regions.

Reducing damage to the atmosphere is even more difficult than dealing with transboundary problems because atmospheric emissions eventually encircle the globe, affecting all nations, not just two or several. Furthermore, the atmosphere is a truly global public good, because only a small fraction of the benefits from any efforts to protect or improve it can accrue to those nations taking individual action. This is a classical situation almost guaranteed to result in suboptimal control efforts unless international efforts are undertaken[68].

As demonstrated by the 1992 UN Rio Conference, international efforts to protect the atmosphere are fraught with multiple problems. Among the most serious, in addition to scientific uncertainty, are those of national sovereignty, North-South value conflicts, and population issues. The Montreal Accords to control the emissions of CFCs was a step in the proper direction, establishing a program of phased future reductions for all parties. However, much greater efforts will be necessary in the future for a comprehensive approach to protect the ozone shield, atmosphere, and climate. As has been noted throughout this book, successful policy measures must meet the multiple criteria of scientific validity, interregional and intergenerational fairness, political acceptability, and economic efficiency. Richard E. Schuler[69] has discussed a promising effort to address these issues and meet these criteria by the United Nations Environmental Program (UNEP).

The UNEP proposal addresses equity by protecting the interests of all stakeholders in developing as well as industrial nations. It addresses the national sovereignty issue by making the program voluntary with a distribution of emission rights (ERs) to all signatories, recognizing the two fundamental realities of high current emissions by industrial nations and growing Third World populations. This would be accomplished by basing the ERs on the average per capita emissions of greenhouse gases of the five most advanced industrial nations and by allocating them to nations according to their current (but not future) populations. Economic efficiency would be achieved by making the ERs marketable. Developing nations would benefit by receiving large population-based allocations of currently unused permits, which they could choose either to hold for use in prospect of future industrialization or sell, using the proceeds in lieu of growth. These nations could also be awarded additional ERs in return for protecting forests and grasslands which offset greenhouse gases, benefiting themselves and other nations through incentives for managing population and growth. Each nation would thus have options for choosing its preferred development strategy. The marketable value of these permits would also reduce the temptation for the LDCs to attempt to reduce the initial distributions to levels that would create problems for industrialized nations.

Industrialized nations would benefit from having the alternative opportunities of reducing emissions and thus freeing permits for sale or purchasing permits from others if this appeared less costly in their particular situation. Choice and market incentives would encourage economic efficiency and technological advance. The incentives for industrial nations to press for high numbers of initial distributions would be tempered by awareness of the global danger from having excessive unused permits in existence, jeopardizing the planet in the event of their simultaneous future use.

Ecological goals would be served under this scheme by phased proportional reductions in each nation's ERs. Scientific validity would be served by using the best current transdisciplinary scientific consensus as the basis for the periodic changes in the number of total allowable permits.

Numerous refinements of this approach are possible, including a central banking feature under which the UN or other international organizations such as OECD could make a market for buying and selling the permits. Carrying this concept to the point of permitting nations to borrow permits from the future for current use, however, would create the potential for intergenerational inequity by letting current populations increase damage to the planet at the expense of as yet unborn future generations who would thus have no voice in the decision, despite its effects upon them.

Schuler's paper[70] concludes with the observation that a critical requirement for implementing this type of regime is estimates of the value of current and future reductions in the risk of global climate change. We consider that creating a transdisciplinary ecological economic research program would be an appropriate and challenging means for addressing the complex issues involved in this problem. This could serve as a model for dealing with other global environmental problems that confront the planet.

Warfare, especially that using technologies of mass destruction, is the ultimate environmental threat, as the environmental aggression against the Kuwaiti oil fields demonstrated during the 1992 Desert Storm conflict. Following this war, the Iraqi draining of marshes in order to drive out the tribes who have inhabited them since Biblical times is an unprecedented example of turning ecological fragility into a form of environmental genocide.

The accumulation of nuclear waste from weapons production and testing during the Cold War leaves a deadly heritage that will require costly monitoring for thousands of years, longer than the total life span of any human civilization to date. Even the peacefully intended use of nuclear energy has left a similar problem for which acceptable solutions have yet to be found. We suggest that the quest for policy instruments capable of addressing these global issues be guided and facilitated by observing the above criteria of equity, efficiency, and scientific validity.

Conclusions

In retrospect, some obvious conclusions can be drawn about the human efforts to date to manage our global habitat. The adoption of industrial technology has both satisfied and, with positive feedback, accelerated human appetites for material consumption, thereby generating throughputs of materials and energy far in excess of the capacity of the earth's ecosystems to assimilate sustainably. Exponential expansion of human populations has crowded out other species. The 40-year armament race during the Cold War both absorbed resources which might have been devoted to environmental protection and weakened the resolution needed for reversing centuries of damage to the global habitat. The end of the Cold War has unveiled a heritage of nuclear and toxic wastes that leaves vast areas at risk or even uninhabitable in both the East and the West.

But the end of the Cold War also creates a historic worldwide opportunity to reallocate resources away from looting the planet and toward restoring a sustainable human habitat. The former global competition for dominance precluded serious efforts to replace economic growth with sustainable development (qualitative improvement without increasing throughput). The barriers to acceptance of sustainable development will be well-entrenched consumer materialism in developed societies and the understandable aspirations of the Third World to emulate Western material affluence. Success in meeting and overcoming these barriers will require learning from the historical record, avoiding the mistakes of the past, and creating innovative solutions for the future. One mistake of the past to be avoided is that of letting appetites for material consumption blur our sensitivity to the conditions essential for sustainable development. Another lesson we must learn with respect to population growth is that a positive exponential growth rate, no matter how limited, of any variable (such as population) in a closed system (such as the earth) will eventually overpower the system, and cannot be sustained. Kenneth Boulding warned during the height of the Cold War that citizens of all nations are passengers on a single, finite Spaceship Earth, whose continued existence is totally dependent upon a more fundamental understanding of its owner's manual and operating instructions. Among the most important of the earth's operating instructions are the policy instruments we use as tools for maintenance, safe operation, and repair. In the past, we have attempted to make do with a tool kit of insufficient and faulty tools.

Our tools and instruments for operating our spaceship have been designed too much for administrative regulation of what comes out of smokestacks and not enough for providing economic incentives for limiting throughputs of energy and materials to sustainable levels. Our management of habitats has been based excessively upon highly entropic conversion of land, forest, and water resources with unsustainable levels of harvesting and cultivation and too little upon scientific understanding of the complexity of ecological interrelationships. Our management of species diversity has been dominated more by market exploitation of open-access resources than by responsible stewardship of our common heritage and infrastructure. Our debate over human population growth has been dominated more by doctrinaire ideological confrontation and defense of male power structures than by a good-faith search for common ground. Our management of energy resources has been based too much upon short-run market considerations, excessive discounting of the interests of future generations, and too little sensitivity to either intergenerational equity or intra-generational justice.

In short the historical record indicates that our efforts to protect our earthly environment have been defective with respect to scientific understanding, economic efficiency, and equity as between individuals, regions, and generations. The early warning indicators and their combined patterns as perceived by Rachel Carson, Kenneth Boulding, and others suggest that if we continue on the current trajectory of naive growth-man-ship, the probable ultimate consequence will be overshoot and collapse of painful proportions. Our choices lie between using our educational and democratic institutions for gaining acceptance of consensual solutions, or of continuing on into disaster and social chaos, from which democratic processes are unlikely to survive. Forging a new set of policies and tools capable of meeting these new challenges is urgent. We are in a race between educating ourselves about how the planet functions, and destroying it through acts of greed and hubris, against which the better part of human wisdom has warned since the time of the Greeks. Forging a new set of policies and tools capable of meeting these new challenges will require the emerging science of complex systems, the search for true economic sufficiency that acknowledges nature as an equal partner, and the concern for fair and participatory democratic processes that have been emphasized throughout this work.

Clearly, the momentous adjustments required for moving onto a path of sustainable development will require a global commitment by all nations. Daly has emphasized the opportunity offered by a global social contract between North and South. The North, which accounts for most of the global throughput, should undertake to abandon mindless quantitative growth in favor of sustainable qualitative development. The North should also emphasize intra-generationally equitable distribution by aiding the South to achieve levels of welfare which will permit a demographic transition to stable populations and intergenerational equity through restoring the stock of natural capital. The South, in response, could undertake to stabilize human populations and provide permanently protected habitats needed for assuring species diversity.

Making this transition from the present unsustainable course of plundering the earth to a sustainable course is the major challenge to humankind today, but it can be accomplished by learning from past mistakes and overcoming the failures we have discussed throughout this work. Although many of our institutions have served us well, we must continue to reduce the economic failures in markets, the intervention failures in governments, and even the failures in the non-governmental organizations that we have created to offset failures in markets and in governments. Above all, and in many ways most difficult of all, we must confront personal failure in our individual choices about consumption, lifestyles, habitation, and work styles, and recognize that these are the decisions that ultimately determine environmental quality. Furthermore, the more affluence and education we are privileged to enjoy, the greater our opportunities and moral responsibilities are for making personal choices consistent with a sustainable civilization for the planet.

The new transdiscipline of ecological economics attempts to draw wisdom from our past in order to provide new generations with both the capability to envision a desirable and sustainable future and the navigational instruments with which to find the way.

References

1. From Costanza and Cumberland, 1990.
2. Cumberland, John H. (1994), Ecology, Economic Incentives, and Public Policy in the Design of a Transdisciplinary Pollution Control Instrument. In J.C. J.M. van den Bergh and J. van der Straaten (eds.), *Toward sustainable development: Concepts, methods and policy*. Washington, DC: Island Press.
3. Sen, Amartya K. (1979), *Collective Choice and Social Welfare*. Amsterdam: North-Holland, p. 200.
4. Button, D. (1996), Interview with Frances Moore Lappé and Paul Martin DuBois. *Ecological Economics Bulletin* 1(1):10–11,14, 28–29.
5. Weisbord, M. (ed.). (1992), *Discovering Common Ground*. San Francisco: Berrett-Koehler.

   —Weisbord, M., and S. Janoff (1995), *Future Search: An Action Guide to Finding Common Ground in Organizations and Communities*. San Francisco: Berrett-Koehler.

6. Meadows, D.H. (1996), Envisioning a Sustainable World. In Robert Costanza, Olman Segura, and Juan Martinez-Alier (eds.), *Getting down to earth: Practical applica2tions of ecological economics*, pp. 117–126. Washington, DC: Island Press.
7. Nagpal, T., and C. Foltz (1995), *Choosing our Future: Visions of a Sustainable World*, Washington, DC: World Resources Institute.
8. Capper, John, Garrett Power, and Frank R. Shivers (1983), *Chesapeake Waters, Pollution, Public Health, and Public Opinion*. Centreville, MD: Tidewater Publishers.
9. Reutter, Mark (1988), *Sparrows Point, Making Steel – The Rise and Ruin of American Industrial Might*. New York: Summit Books.
10. Carson, Rachel (1962), *Silent Spring*. Boston: Houghton Mifflin.
11. Cumberland, John H. (1971), *Regional Development: Experiences and Prospects in the United States of America*. Paris: Mouton, United Nations Research Institute for Social Development.
12. Pigou, A.C. (1920), *The Economics of Welfare*. London: Macmillan.
13. Ayres, R.U., and A.V. Kneese (1969), Production, Consumption, and Externalities. *American Economic Review* 54(3).
14. Georgescu-Roegen, Nicholas (1971), *The Entropy Law and the Economic Process*. Cambridge, MA: Harvard University Press.
15. Costanza, R. (ed.). (1991), *Ecological Economics: The Science and Management of Sustainability*. New York: Columbia Press.
16. Buchanan, James M. (1987), The Constitution of Economic Policy. *American Economic Review* 177:243–290.
17. Cumberland, John H. (1990a), Public Choice and the Improvement of Policy Instruments for Environmental Management. *Ecological Economics* 2:149–162.
18. Cumberland, John H. (1991), Intergenerational Transfers and Ecological Sustainability. In R. Costanza (ed.), *Ecological Economics: The Science and Management of Sustainability*, pp. 355–366. New York: Columbia University Press.
19. Gore, A. (1992), *Earth in the Balance: Ecology and the Human Spirit*. New York: Houghton Mifflin Co.
20. Cropper, M.L., and W.E. Oates (1992), Environmental Economics: A Survey. *Journal of Economic Literature* 30:675–740.
21. Feshbach, Murray, and Alfred Friendly, Jr. (1992), *Ecocide in the USSR: Health and Nature Under Siege*. New York: Basic Books.

22. Baumol, William J., and Oates, Wallace E. (1975), *The Theory of Environmental Policy*. Cambridge: Cambridge University Press.

23. Anderşon, Robert C., Lisa A. Hofmann, and Michael Rusin (1991), *The Use of Economic Incentive Mechanisms in Environmental Management*. Research Paper #051. Washington, DC: American Petroleum Institute Research. —Baumol, William J., and Oates, Wallace E. 1975. The theory of environmental policy. Cambridge: Cambridge University Press.

24. Pigou, A.C. (1920), *The Economics of Welfare*. London: Macmillan.

25. Cropper, M.L., and W.E. Oates (1992), Environmental Economics: A Survey. *Journal of Economic Literature* 30:675–740.

26. Pareto, Vilfredo (1927), *Manuel d'economie politique* (2nd ed.). Paris: Girard.

27. Randall, Alan (1987), *Resource Economics* (2nd ed.). New York: John Wiley and Sons.

28. Randall, Alan (1987), *Resource Economics* (2nd ed.). New York: John Wiley and Sons.

29. David Terkla, quoted in Cropper, M.L., and W.E. Oates (1992), Environmental Economics: A Survey. *Journal of Economic Literature* 30:675–740.

30. Cumberland, John H. (1990a), Public Choice and the Improvement of Policy Instruments for Environmental Management. *Ecological Economics* 2:149–162.

31. Cumberland and Kahn (1984).

32. Cumberland, John H. (1990a), Public Choice and the Improvement of Policy Instruments for Environmental Management. *Ecological Economics* 2:149–162.

33. cf. Bishop, Richard C. (1993), Economic Efficiency, Sustainability, and Biodiversity. *Ambio* 22:69–73. —Costanza, R. (ed.). 1991. *Ecological economics: The science and management of sustainability*. New York: Columbia Press. —Costanza, R., and L. Cornwell. 1992. The 4P approach to dealing with scientific uncertainty. *Environment* 34:12–20, 42.—Cropper, M. L., and W. E. Oates. 1992. Environmental economics: A survey. *Journal of Economic Literature* 30:675–740. —Daly, H. E. 1990a. Boundless bull. *Gannett Center Journal* 4(3):113–118. —Pearce, D. W., and R. K. Turner. 1989. *Economics of natural resources and the environment*. Brighton: Wheatsheaf.

– Perrings, C. (1991), Reserved Rationality and the Precautionary Principle: Technological Change, Time and Uncertainty in Environmental Decision Making. In R. Costanza (ed.), *Ecological economics: the science and management of sustainability*, pp. 153–166. New York: Columbia University Press. – Young, M. D. 1992. *Sustainable investment and resource use: Equity, environmental integrity and economic efficiency*. Park Ridge, NJ: Parthenon.

34. Rawls, J. (1987), The Idea of an Overlapping Consensus. *Oxford Journal of Legal Studies* 7:1–25.

35. Costanza, R., and L. Cornwell (1992), The 4P Approach to Dealing with Scientific Uncertainty. *Environment* 34:12–20, 42.

36. Costanza, R., and L. Cornwell (1992), The 4P Approach to Dealing with Scientific Uncertainty. *Environment* 34:12–20, 42.

37. Solow, Robert M. (1993), Sustainability: An Economist's Perspective. In R. Dorfman and N. Dorfman (eds.), *Economics of the environment: Selected readings*, pp. 179–187. New York: W.W. Norton and Company.

38. Cameron, J., and J. Abouchar (1991), The Precautionary Principle: A Fundamental Principle of Law and Policy for the Protection of the Global Environment. *Boston College International and Comparative Law Review* 14:1–27.

39. Peskin, H.M. (1991), Alternative Environmental and Resource Accounting Approaches. In R. Costanza (ed.), *Ecological economics: The science and management of sustainability*, pp. 176–193. New York: Columbia University Press.

40. Cameron, J., and J. Abouchar (1991), The Precautionary Principle: A Fundamental Principle of Law and Policy for the Protection of the Global Environment. *Boston College International and Comparative Law Review* 14:1–27.

41. Brady, G.L., and R.D. Cunningham (1981), The Economics of Pollution Control in the U.S. *Ambio* 10:171–175. – Cropper, M. L., and W. E. Oates. 1992. Environmental Economics: A Survey. *Journal of Economic Literature* 30:675–740.

42. Costanza, R., and C. Perrings (1990), A Flexible Assurance Bonding System for Improved Environmental Management. *Ecological Economics* 2:57–76.

43. Bohm (1981).

44. PRC Environmental Management (1986), *Performance Bonding*. A Final Report prepared for the U.S. Environmental Protection Agency, Office of Waste Programs and Enforcement, Washington, DC.

45. Fogleman, V.M. (19870, Worst Case Analysis: A Continued Requirement Under the National Environmental Policy Act? *Columbia Journal of Environmental Law* 13:53.

46. AGENDA 21 (1992), United Nations Environment Program. New York: United Nations.

47. Several studies of "social traps" have shown that the timing of information about costs is more important than the actual expected magnitude (cf. Brockner, J., and J. Z. Rubin. 1985. *Entrapment in escalating conflicts: A social psychological analysis*. New York: Springer-Verlag; Costanza, R. 1987. Social traps and environmental policy. *BioScience* 37:407–412; Costanza, R., and W. Shrum. 1988. The effects of taxation on moderating the conflict escalation process: An experiment using the dollar auction game. *Social Science Quarterly* 69:416–432; Cross, J. G., and M. J. Guyer. 1980. *Social traps*. Ann Arbor: University of Michigan Press; Platt, J. 1973. Social traps. *American Psychologist* 28:642–651; Teger, A. I. 1980. *Too much invested to quit*. New York: Pergamon).

48. AGENDA 21. (1992), United Nations Environment Program. New York: United Nations.

49. Costanza, R., and H.E. Daly (1992), Natural Capital and Sustainable Development. *Conservation Biology* 6:37–46.—Hawken, P. 1993. *The ecology of commerce: A declaration of sustainability*. New York: Harper Business. —Passell, 1992.

—Repetto, R., R. C. Dower, R. Jenkins, and J. Geoghegan (1992), *Green Fees: How a Tax Shift Can Work for the Environment and Economy*. Washington, DC: World Resources Institute. —von Weizsäcker, E. U., and J. Jesinghaus. 1992. *Ecological Tax Reform: a Policy Proposal*.

50. Page, T. (1977), *Conservation and Economic Efficiency*. Baltimore, MD: Johns Hopkins University Press.

51. Daly, H.E. (1977), *Steady State Economics*. San Francisco: W. H. Freeman.

52. Cumberland, John H. (1994), Ecology, Economic Incentives, and Public Policy in the Design of a Transdisciplinary Pollution Control Instrument. In J. C. J. M. van den Bergh and J. van der

Straaten (eds.), *Toward Sustainable Development: Concepts, Methods and Policy*. Washington, DC: Island Press.

53. Tietenberg, Tom (1988), *Environmental and Natural Resource Economics* (2nd ed.). Glenville, IL: Scott Foresman and Company.

54. Kopp, Raymond J., and V. Kerry Smith. (eds.) (1993), *Valuing Natural Assets, the Economics of Natural Resource Damage Assessment*. Washington, DC: Resources for the Future.

55. Anderson, Robert C., Lisa A. Hofmann, and Michael Rusin (1991), *The Use of Economic Incentive Mechanisms in Environmental Management*. Research Paper #051. Washington, DC: American Petroleum Institute Research.

56. Although the terms regional economic development or local economic development are often used to refer to economic growth projects, such projects do not necessarily satisfy the criterion for economic development as defined in this book, which is improving net social welfare while avoiding increased throughput.

57. van Dyne, Larry (1995), The Gang that Beat Disney. *Washingtonian* 30(4):58–63, 114–127.

58. Cumberland, John H. (1990b), Public Choice and the Management of Regional Resource Systems: The Case of the Chesapeake Bay. In Manas Chatterji and Robert E. Kuenne (eds.), *Dynamics and conflict in regional structural change, essays in honour of Walter Isard, Vol. 2*, pp. 227–242. London: Macmillan.

59. Herzog, Henry W. Jr., and Alan M. Schlottman (1991), *Industry location and Public Policy*. Knoxville, TN: University of Tennessee Press.

60. Cumberland, John H., and F. van Beek (1967), Regional Economic Development Objectives and Subsidizaton of Local Industry. *Land Economics* 4:253–264.

61. Sarokin, David, and Jay Schulkin (1991), Environmentalism and the Right to Know: Expanding the Practice of Democracy. *Ecological Economics* 4(3):175–189.

62. Young, John E. (1994), Using Computers for the Environment. In Lester R. Brown (ed.), *State of the World*, pp. 99–116. New York: World Watch Institute.

63. Rice, Faye (1993), Who Serves Best on Environment? *Fortune* June 26:114–122.

64. U.S. Environmental Protection Agency (1994), *The Toxic Release Inventory*. Washington, DC: Author.

65. Cumberland, John H. (1974), Establishment of International Environmental Standards – Some Economic and Related Aspects. In *Problems in Transfrontier Pollution*, pp. 213–229. Paris: OECD.

66. Brown, L.R. (1997a), *State of the World*. Washington, DC: Worldwatch Institute (annual).

67. Cumberland, John H. (1974), Establishment of International Environmental Standards – Some Economic and Related Aspects. In *Problems in Transfrontier Pollution*, pp. 213–229. Paris: OECD.

68. Cumberland, John H., James R. Hibbs, and Irving Hoch (eds.). (1982), *The Economics of Managing Chlorofluorocarbons, Stratospheric Ozone and Climate Issues*. Washington, DC: Resources for the Future, Inc.

69. Schuler, Richard E. (1994), January 4. *International Mechanisms to Achieve Voluntary Reductions in Atmospheric Concentrations of Greenhouse Gases*. Paper presented at the meetings of the Allied Social Science Association, Peace Science Session, Boston.

70. Schuler, Richard E. (1994), January 4. *International Mechanisms to Achieve Voluntary Reductions in Atmospheric Concentrations of Greenhouse Gases*. Paper presented at the meetings of the Allied Social Science Association, Peace Science Session, Boston.

Further Reading

- Barbier, Edward B., Joanne C. Burgess, and Carl Folke (1994), *Paradise Lost? The Ecological Economics of Biodiversity*. London: Earthscan.
- Bhayani, S.J. (2009), Environmental Social Responsibility: A Comparative Analysis of Perceptions of Indian Managers, Journal of Accounting and Finance, vol. 23. No. 2 April- September, pp15-33.
- Boulding, Kenneth (1985), *The World as a Total System*. Sage Publications.
- Cairncross, Frances (1991), *Costing the Earth: The Challenge for Governments, the Opportunities for Business*. Boston: Harvard Business School Press.
- Costanza, Robert (ed.). (1991), *Ecological Economics: The Science and Management of Sustainability*. New York: Columbia University Press.

- Costanza, Robert, Bryan G. Norton, and Benjamin D. Haskell (eds.) (1992), *Ecosystem Health: New Goals for Environmental Management*. Washington, DC: Island Press.
- Costanza, Robert, Charles Perrings, and Cutler J. Cleveland (1997), *The Development of Ecological Economics*. Cheltenham, U.K.: Edward Elgar.
- Costanza, Robert, Olman Segura, and Juan Martinez-Alier (eds.) (1996), *Getting Down to Earth: Practical Applications of Ecological Economics*. Washington, DC: Island Press.
- Culbertson, John Mathew. *Economic Development: An Ecological Approach*. Knopf.
- Daily, Gretchen C. (1997), *Nature's Services: Societal Dependence on Natural Ecosystems*. Washington, DC: Island Press.
- Daly, Herman E. (1978), *Steady State Economics: The Economics of Biophysical Equilibrium and Moral Growth*. W. H. Freeman & Co.
- Daly, Herman E. (1996), *Beyond Growth: The Economics of Sustainable Development*. Beacon Press.
- Daly, Herman E., and John B. Cobb, Jr. (19940, *For the Common Good: Redirecting the Economy Toward Community, the Environment, and a Sustainable Future*. Beacon Press.
- Denton, T. (1998), "Sustainable Development at the Next Level", Chemical Market Reporter, Vol.253, No.7, pp.3-5.
- Faber, Malte, Reiner Manstetten, and John Proops (1996), *Ecological Economics Concepts and Methods*. Cheltenham, U.K.: Edward Elgar.
- Faucheux, Sylvie, David Pearce, and John Proops (1996), *Models of Sustainable Development*. Cheltenham, U.K.: Edward Elgar.
- Folke, Carl, and Kåberger, Tomas (eds.). (1991), *Linking the Natural Environment and the Economy: Essays from the Eco-Eco Group*. Dordrecht: Kluwer Academic Publishers.
- Gowdy, John (1994), *Coevolutionary Economics: The Economy, Society and the Environment*. Boston: Kluwer Academic Publishers.
- Guide, V.D.R., Srivastava, R., and Spencer, M.S. (1996), "Are Production System Ready for Green Revolution?" Production & Inventory Management Journal, Vol.37, No.4, pp.34-51.
- Gunderson, Lance H., C.S. Holling, and Stephen S. Light (eds.). (1995), *Barriers & Bridges to the Renewal of Ecosystems and Institutions*. New York: Columbia University Press.

- Hart, Stuart L., (1995), "A Natural-resource based View of the Firm," Academy of Management Review, Vol.20, No.4, pp.986-1014.
- Hayes, R.H., and Wheelwright (1979), "The Dynamic of Product-process Life-cycles," Harvard Business Review, Vol.57, No.2, pp.127-136.
- Hickle, G.T., and Stitzhal, D. (2003), "Apportioning the Responsibilities for Product Stewardship: A Case for a New Federal Role," Environmental Quality Management, Vol.12, No.2, pp.1-16.
- Hoffman, A. (2001), From Heresy to Dogma, Stanford Business Books, C.A.
- Jackson, Tim (ed.). *Clean Production Strategies: Developing Preventive Environmental Management in the Industrial Economy.* London: Lewis Publishers.
- Jansson, AnnMari, Monica Hammer, Carl Folke, and Robert Costanza (eds.). *Investing in Natural Capital.* Washington, DC: Island Press.
- Kitazawa, S. and Sarkis, J. (1998), "The Relationship between ISO 14001 and Continuous Source Reduction Programs," Working Paper, Clark University, Worcester, M.A.
- Klassen, R. (2000), "Just-in-time Manufacturing & Pollution Prevention Generate Mutual Benefits in Furniture Industry." Interfaces 30(3), 95.
- Knight, Richard L., and Sarah F. Bates (eds.). (1995), *A New Century for Natural Resources Management.* Washington, DC: Island Press.
- McDonough, W., and Braungart, M. (1998), "The Next Industrial Revolution." The Atlantic Monthly, Vol.282, No.4, p.82.
- Meadows, Donella H., Dennis L. Meadows, and Jorgen Randers (1993), *Beyond the Limits: Confronting Global Collapse, Envisioning a Sustainable Future.* Chelsea Green Publishing Co.
- Myers, Norman (1993), *Ultimate Security: The Environmental Basis of Political Stability.* New York: W. W. Norton & Co.
- Ottman, J., and Terry, V. (1998), "Strategic Marketing of Greener products", The Journal of Sustainable Product Design, Vol.5, (http://www.greenmarketing.com/Articles_and_Speeches.html).

- Pojasek, R.B. (2000), "Quality Toolbox: Striving for Environmental Excellence with the Baldrige Model." Environmental Quality Management. 9(3), 91-99.
- Porter, M.E. and Vander Linde, C., (1995), "Green and competitive: Ending the Stalemate," Harvard Business Review, Vol.73, No.5, pp.120-134.
- Prugh, Thomas, Robert Costanza, John H. Cumberland, Herman Daly, Robert Goodland, and Richard B. Norgaard. 1995. *Natural capital and human economic survival*. Solomons, MD: ISEE Press.
- Sarkis, J., (1998), "Evaluating environmentally conscious business practices," European Journal of Operation Research, Vol.107, pp.159-174.
- Sarkis, J., Liffers, M., and Mallete, S., (1998), "Purchasing operations at Digital's computer assets recovery facility," Greener Purchasing: Opportunities and Innovations, ed. Russel,T,, Greenleaf Publishing, Sheffierd, England, pp.270-281.
- Schmidheiny, S., (1992), Changing Course, MIT Press, Cambridge, MA.
- Schmidheiny, Stephan. 1992. *Changing course: A global business perspective on development and the environment*. Cambridge, MA: MIT Press.
- Schulze, Peter C. 1996. *Engineering within ecological constraints*. Washington, DC: National Academy Press.
- Shrivastava, P., (1995), "Ecocentric management for a risk society," Academy of Management Review, Vol.20, no.1, pp.118-137.
- Starik, M., (1995), "Should trees have managerial standing?: Towards stakeholder status for non-human nature," Journal of Business Ethics, Vol.15, pp.207-208.
- van den Bergh, Jeroen C. J. M., and Jan van der Straaten (eds.). 1994. *Toward sustainable development: Concepts, methods, and policy*. Washington, DC: Island Press.
- Van Der Laan, E., Dekker, R., and Salmon, M., (1996), "Product remanufacturing and disposal. A numerical comparison of alternative control strategies," International Journal of Production Economics, Vol.45, No.1-3, pp.489-498.
- Walley, N. and Whitehead, B., (1994), "It's not easy being green," Harvard Business Review, Vol.72, No.3, pp.46-52.

Index